As fate would have it, Peter Jewell, my mentor since 1966, died in Cambridge on the very day that I was putting the finishing touches on the preface. I dedicate this book to his memory and hope that he would have approved of its final form.

Myth and Reality in the Rain Forest

How Conservation Strategies
Are Failing in West Africa

JOHN F. OATES

UNIVERSITY OF CALIFORNIA PRESS
Berkeley   Los Angeles   London

University of California Press
Berkeley and Los Angeles, California

University of California Press, Ltd.
London, England

© 1999 by the Regents of the University of California

All photographs by author unless otherwise credited.

Library of Congress Cataloging-in-Publication Data

Oates, John F.
   Myth and reality in the rain forest : how conservation strategies
are failing in West Africa / John F. Oates.
      p.   cm.
   Includes bibliographical references.
   ISBN 0-520-21782-9 (alk. paper)—ISBN 0-520-22252-0 (alk. paper)
   1. Wildlife conservation—Africa, West.   2. Sustainable
development—Africa, West.   3. Rain forest animals—Africa, West.
I. Title.
   QL84.6.A358O28   1999
   333.95′416′0966—dc21   99-20220
                                                               CIP

Manufactured in the United States of America

08   07   06   05   04   03   02   01   00   99
10   9   8   7   6   5   4   3   2   1

The paper used for the text in this publication is both acid-free and
totally chlorine-free (TCF). It meets the minimum requirements of
ANSI/NISO Z39.48-1992 (R 1997) (*Permanence of Paper*).

Contents

Illustrations

Preface

In their book *The Myth of Wild Africa*, published in 1992, Jonathan Adams and Thomas McShane argue that "classic" conservation methods used to protect African wildlife, such as the establishment of national parks, have been inspired by a romantic European myth of Africa as a primeval wilderness filled with animals, a wilderness that needs to be protected against the ravages of human beings and particularly against African hunters.[1] Adams and McShane suggest that this myth ignores the reality that African societies coexisted with wildlife for generations before the coming of Europeans, and they contend that these societies can continue to do so. The authors argue that the best way to conserve African wildlife is to give rural people ("communities") greater control over the management of the animal populations living around them. *The Myth of Wild Africa* also endorses the idea that economic development is not necessarily an enemy of wildlife conservation, and it presents conservation and development as two parts of a single process.

I think it is no coincidence that the views expressed by Adams and McShane correspond closely with the official policy of the World Wide

Fund for Nature (WWF), known in the United States and Canada by its original name, the World Wildlife Fund. Adams once worked for WWF and McShane still does, and in their book the authors acknowledge that influential individuals in that organization have encouraged their writing. WWF's policy is laid out in the *World Conservation Strategy*, a document published in 1980 jointly by WWF, the International Union for the Conservation of Nature and Natural Resources (IUCN, now known as the World Conservation Union), and the United Nations Environment Programme (UNEP).[2] In this document conservation is described as a utilitarian process involving the management of natural resources as part of a process of sustainable development. Such sustainable utilization of nature is emphasized in *Caring for the Earth*, a 1991 revision of this strategy.[3] In particular, *Caring for the Earth* stresses the importance of giving local communities a prominent role in the design and management of integrated conservation and development activities.

In this book I argue that such policies are as, or more, myth-based than the older "preservationist" policies debunked in *The Myth of Wild Africa*. Although Adams and McShane do give passing acknowledgment to the fact that rural Africans, like all people, tend to exploit natural resources to the maximum for short-term gain, without regard for the future, the central thesis they and organizations such as WWF and IUCN promote is that economic development is not inherently antithetical to the conservation of nature and that rural people will tend to be more protective of wildlife if they are given greater control over it. Such rural people are generally presumed to live in harmonious cooperative communities with long-term ties to the land on which they are located—an alternative romantic myth that has become even more pervasive than the myth of Africa as a primeval wilderness.

My own experiences in Africa, over a span of more than thirty years, suggest to me that, when it comes to conserving wildlife, there are great dangers in pursuing the policies advocated in publications like *Caring for the Earth* and *The Myth of Wild Africa*. When put into practice in the real world, these policies have tended to have effects opposite to those articulated by their proponents. For instance, the emphasis on the close relationship between economic development and conservation has led to a view of wildlife conservation as predominantly an exercise in materialism, at local, national, and international levels; meanwhile, the ethical and aesthetic principles of conservation that strongly guided the founders of the World Wildlife Fund have been reduced to secondary considerations. And the emphasis on "communities" as functional units has led to a neglect of abundant evidence that human societies in rural Africa, like those elsewhere, typically have a hierarchical structure dominated by a few powerful individuals, who may wish to advance their own personal interests.

Perhaps most dangerously, the proponents of community-level action usually ignore the mobility that modern Africans, like other people, show when faced with political unrest and economic challenges. In the face of these challenges, people have tended to move to frontier areas of low population density, the very areas where nature reserves are often located. Offering the benefits of "development" to migrants who lack long-term ties to the area to which they have moved can accelerate rather than slow immigration to the frontier, and it will therefore tend to increase the destructive pressures on wildlife and its habitats.

These thoughts, and the final plan for this book, crystallized in my mind at the beginning of 1996 while I was camped by the Suhien River on the edge of Ghana's Nini-Suhien National Park. I was searching for populations of several kinds of monkey known only from this part of Ghana and from adjacent areas of Côte d'Ivoire to the west. Although Nini-Suhien was supposed to be a protected area, I found that it was completely open to hunters and to collectors of other forest produce; the park guards who accompanied me were unable to lead me to the edge of the park and had no knowledge of its interior. In the park I could not find any surviving members of a local form of red colobus monkey, and I began to think that it might be extinct. Further surveys by my colleagues and me over the next two years only confirmed this depressing conclusion and supported the view that Thomas Struhsaker and I had arrived at some years previously, that Ghana's forest wildlife was facing a crisis.[4]

This crisis is not unique to Ghana; many of its underlying causes can be found operating elsewhere in Africa and to varying degrees in other parts of the tropical world. Ghana's red colobus monkey has been driven to extinction by hunters using ordinary shotguns to supply the market for "bushmeat" in West Africa. Much of this meat is sold in towns and cities where customers will pay high prices for it. Many of the hunters and other people exploiting the forest are relatively recent migrants to the area who grew up in distant parts of the country and have no feeling of traditional ownership of the resources they are exploiting; their families are probably paying some form of fee to a local chief for the right to farm near the forest, on land to which the chief controls access. Loggers may have preceded the farmers, opening up roads and also making payments to local rulers.

As I will describe in chapter 7, these pressures on the wildlife of Ghana's forests have been obvious for decades and, in the 1970s, they led the government to establish two rain forest national parks, one of which was Nini-Suhien. But the Ghanaian economy was severely stressed, and little funding was allocated to management of the parks. In addition, few people within or outside Ghana showed much concern for the parks' wildlife. Not until 1990 did foreign conservationists begin to take interest in these rain forest parks, which obviously lacked the spectacular herds of large mammals typical of many East African savanna parks. In the spirit of the new international conservation policy, planning began in that year for a project that would be supported by money from the European Development Fund and would attempt to integrate a greater effort at park management with human development activities. Seven years later, after considerable sums of money had been paid to foreign consultants to formulate the plans, and after delays had been caused by European Union bureaucrats demanding that the plans devote more resources to "community development," the park management project began. During this time, no extra resources—such as personnel, vehicles, and other equipment—were allocated for protection of forest wildlife, and little attention was given to the implications of the fact that most people living around the parks were migrant farmers rather than traditional landholders. By the time the management project got under way, few large mammals remained in either park and the red colobus monkey—reported as present in both parks at the time of their establishment—was extinct, not only in the parks but also in the rest of its range. The forest vegetation of the parks survived, however. The parks had earlier been government-managed forest reserves. Farmers have generally respected the boundaries of these "classic" protected areas, established in colonial times for the safeguarding of watersheds and timber supplies. Although Ghanaian forest reserves have often been heavily logged and their vegetation damaged by fire, in most cases they still contain a substantial tree cover.

Satellite imagery clearly shows the straight boundaries that separate the remaining forest in many of southern Ghana's reserves from the deforested land outside the reserves managed by local communities. But little or no effort has been made to regulate hunting within the reserves. In the absence of any serious constraints, local hunters have behaved like most human hunters elsewhere, including those who fish in the seas around Europe and North America: their hunting has intensified as wildlife populations have declined, and when some species have become locally extinct or rare the hunters have switched their attention to other species. Economic development in Ghana has not slowed this process; indeed, hunting has probably increased as demand has risen for bushmeat in the growing towns and cities.

The main argument I set forth in this book, therefore, is that there are serious flaws in the theory that wildlife can best be conserved through promoting human economic development. It is a powerful myth that has made all those involved in its formulation feel good. When first formulated it seemed to provide the best of several worlds: both wildlife and people would benefit, and because the improvement of human well-being was stated as a fundamental policy goal, conservationists themselves would not feel uncomfortable about incorporating their own search for a materially better life into their conservation plans. In reality, though, the approach has had disastrous consequences for many wildlife populations. Most important, it has led all concerned to assign low priority to basic protection efforts that, because they must involve some element of law enforcement, are considered to be "antipeople" and therefore opposed to human development efforts. Yet the conservation and development approach has done little for human development in most places where it has been applied. The material benefits that have trickled to ordinary rural people from integrated conservation and development projects have often been slight relative to those that have flowed to political leaders and bureaucrats in the countries where the projects have been put into practice, and to the consultant experts and conservation administrators (based mostly in North America and Europe) who have planned the projects.

Second, I argue that community-based conservation is much easier to achieve in theory than in practice. Not only do most real communities not conform to the harmonious ideal implicit in international conservation policy, but these communities inevitably operate within the context of nation-states which, however imperfect they may be, strongly influence local events. Power struggles within and between these states inevitably have strong influences on conservation efforts and can overwhelm these efforts when they erupt into war.

I put forward the case that substantial parts of wild nature (*biodiversity* in current parlance) will be lost if those involved in conservation planning do not rethink their approach and return to the principles on which many conservation organizations were founded: that nature is worthy of protection for its intrinsic value and for the aesthetic pleasure it can bring to many people. The continued existence of wild animals, plants, and places can provide many satisfactions to present and future human generations in all countries. And a major role of national government is to orchestrate policies that are in the best long-term interest of the nation's people as a whole. Therefore, while not ignoring the concerns of local communities, conservation organizations should make greater efforts to help national governments preserve nature. By so doing they will, in the long run, benefit rather than harm the interests of a majority of citizens.

I present this argument within a framework that describes my personal history of research and conservation activities in the forests of Africa and India. By taking this subjective and somewhat anecdotal approach, I hope that my argument may be more accessible to a wider audience than might be reached with a more formal academic account. Although I work in a university, I know that most real-world conservation is not done by academics, and that academics have only a partial influence on the framing of conservation policies.

In chapter 1, I describe the growth of my own interest in West Africa and of my feelings about the intrinsic value of wildlife. In chapter 2, I recount some of my early exposure to conservation efforts in Africa and India, experiences that brought home to me the pressures facing tropical nature, but that also showed me that "classic" (or "conventional") conservation can work in developing countries. In chapter 3, I review some of the origins of the international conservation movement and consider how its position came to shift from one that espoused the protection of nature for its own sake to one that regards conservation as a component in a process of economic development. I suggest that this shift occurred in part out of political and financial expediency, and particularly out of the desire to tap into the large sums of money becoming available from international development-aid organizations. Here I also consider how, having persuaded themselves that conservation was part of a process of human development, many conservationists adopted from development planners the notion that the community rather than the nation was the most appropriate level at which to intervene to modify human behavior.

Chapters 4 to 7 give detailed descriptions of conservation projects in which I have participated in the West African countries of Sierra Leone, Nigeria, and Ghana (see map 1). These chapters provide the evidence to support my argument that the development approach to conservation has been a failure in the forest zone of West Africa. I hope that readers will be patient with the details I present in these chapters. The detail is there for two important reasons: first, to provide evidence to strengthen my case, and, second, to provide a permanent record of the history of some projects and nature reserves that in many cases are well known locally but, despite their importance, have received little attention in the outside world.

Having looked at the crisis facing conservation in West Africa, I consider in chapter 8 another well-established conservation myth, that although many species may be doomed in the wild, they can be saved by captive breeding in zoos and similar holding facilities, places from which

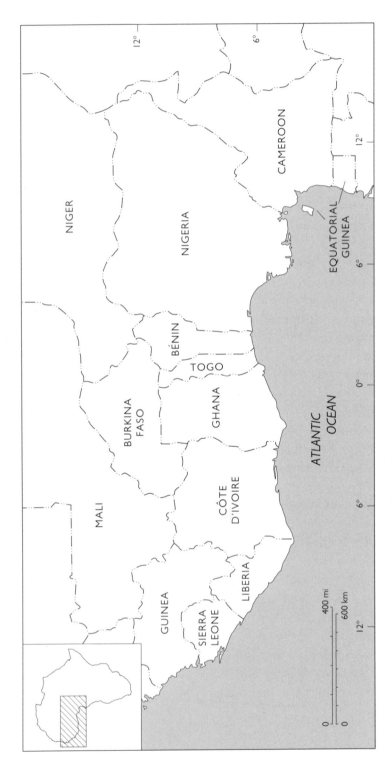

Map 1. The countries of the coastal region of West Africa.

they may one day be reintroduced to the wild. I am certainly not the first person to look at captive breeding with a critical eye; I include a review of this approach to conservation because some readers might consider it to be an obvious remedy to the crisis I describe. I suggest that it is not a cost-effective remedy and can divert attention and resources from efforts to protect wild populations that still have a chance of survival. I propose that zoos can best assist conservation through their ability to interest the public in wildlife and its predicament rather than through attempting to save endangered species by keeping them in captivity. In this chapter I consider the powerful influence of the naturalist and writer Gerald Durrell who, as I describe in chapter 1, played a major role in stimulating my own early fascination with the forests of West Africa.

In a concluding chapter I summarize my views on the corrupting influence of the utilitarian, materialistic approach to conservation. Suggesting that more traditional approaches can work, I cite India as an example of how conservation policies that emphasize protecting forests and wildlife from human exploitation can succeed even where there are dense human populations and widespread poverty. I also discuss how conservation efforts can be financially supported in poor countries if these efforts are no longer tied to development assistance. I suggest that the money from rich countries that is currently channeled into conservation through development agencies would be better utilized if put into trust funds set up to support national conservation efforts or individual protected areas.

I realize that some of the individuals and organizations I refer to in this book will feel that their intentions or actions have not been properly represented. Although I know that there are many thoughtful and well-intentioned people in the conservation world, I have come to disagree with some key elements of the strategies that they are pursuing. I recognize that in explaining my disagreements, I have accentuated problems arising from the pursuit of what I regard as misguided approaches, and that in so doing I may not have adequately acknowledged some conservation successes. For any offense this may cause, I apologize in advance.

Because I did not want to interrupt my account in order to frequently cite the names of authors whose work I have used—the traditional style of the scientific academy—I have instead listed my sources in a set of endnotes. In another effort to reduce clutter in the text, I have referred to most people by their first and last names when they are first mentioned, and often subsequently by their last name alone; titles such as Sir, Professor, Dr., and the Honorable are omitted. This usage not only simplifies the account but also helps to avoid confusion in the cases where an individual's title changed between events I describe. I hope that those concerned will understand that no disrespect is intended by this omission.

In a fast-changing world, events will inevitably render parts of my account outdated by the time it appears in print. I must hope that some of my pessimism about current trends proves unfounded, and that the future will bring improvements in the prospects for West Africa's wildlife.

Acknowledgments

In the decades encompassed by this book, a very large number of people have assisted me in my tropical field research or have in other ways contributed to shaping my world view and my thinking about conservation; I thank them collectively, for they are far too numerous to acknowledge individually. A few individuals do, however, deserve special thanks. My parents provided an environment in which my interest in other living things could flourish: my late father, Arthur, by quietly tolerating the strange collection of animals with which he had to share his house and his vacations, and my mother, Kathleen, by actively encouraging my interest through her own love of animals. The books and documentary films of the naturalists David Attenborough and Gerald Durrell had a profound influence on the direction in which my interests developed, as I describe in the first chapter of this book. At University College School I was lucky to have in Geoffrey Creber a biology teacher who excelled in part because he was a research scientist himself. When I moved on to University College London I found myself in a wonderfully free-thinking environment, where I was taught by some of the world's leading biologists and where I shared my experiences with an exceptionally congenial cohort of students. As my career in tropical field research developed, I was fortunate to work with a series of wise mentors, who all became my close friends: Peter Jewell, Thomas Struhsaker, and Steven Green. In the course of my fieldwork, Rauf Ali, Pius Anadu, and George Whitesides have been especially good colleagues. The difficulties of doing research in Africa have been eased by Willow and Lance Tickell, Martha and Peter White, Rachel and Nigel Wakeham, Frances and Philip Hall, and Liza Gadsby and Peter Jenkins, all of whom generously made their homes available during visits to town or campus and provided many other practical services.

Since 1978, the Anthropology Department at Hunter College of the City University of New York (CUNY) has been very supportive of my frequent field trips. My research has been sponsored by many organizations, to all of whom I am most grateful; special thanks are due to the U.S. National Science Foundation, the Research Foundation of CUNY, and the Wildlife Conservation Society (formerly the New York Zoological Society).

This particular book project was encouraged from its inception by Tom Struhsaker, who in the course of discussions and research collaborations over many years has had a major influence on the development of my thinking about conservation issues. In researching documentary evidence for my account I was helped by staff at the World Conservation Monitoring Centre (Cambridge) and in the library of the Zoological Society of London, and by Eric Sargis (CUNY) in New York. Other helpful information was provided by Rauf Ali, Cynthia Booth, Julian Caldecott, Francis Conant, Arikpo Ettah, Gerald Creed, Keith Eltringham, Stephen Gartlan, Philip Hall, the late Theo Jones, Devra Kleiman, and Richard Lowe.

Tom Struhsaker patiently read draft versions of most of the book's chapters and provided many thoughtful comments. In a further effort to improve the book's accuracy I solicited additional reviews from some key participants in the projects I describe: namely, Graham Dunn (chapter 1); Peter Jewell and Steven Green (chapter 2); George Whitesides (chapters 4 and 7); Pius Anadu (chapter 5); Liza Gadsby (chapter 6);

Michael Abedi-Lartey (chapter 7); and Ardith Eudey and Fred Koontz (chapter 8). I am most grateful to all these reviewers, even though I have not always followed their advice on matters of interpretation, opinion, or style.

For donating the use of photographs to illustrate this account, I thank David Attenborough, Lee Durrell, Fred Koontz, Lysa Leland, Noel Rowe, the U.S. National Zoological Park, the Wildfowl and Wetlands Trust, and the World Wide Fund for Nature.

Last but not least, I thank Doris Kretschmer of the University of California Press for her enthusiastic support of this project and for her many constructive suggestions during the final preparation of the manuscript.

Abbreviations and Acronyms

The world of international conservation and development planning is replete with acronyms. These, and some common abbreviations, appear frequently in this book.

ADMADE   Administrative Management Design for Game Management Areas. Zambian project designed to devolve a large measure of responsibility for the management of wildlife (and revenues accruing from management) to local residents.

AT & P   African Timber and Plywood Company. Logging and timber-processing corporation, with operations in Nigeria, Ghana, and other tropical-forest countries. A subsidiary of the London-based United Africa Company.

BBC   British Broadcasting Corporation.

BBTC   Bombay Burmah Trading Corporation. Corporation based in Bombay, involved in plantation management, especially tea plantations.

CAMP   Conservation Assessment and Management Plan.
                Term used by the CBSG to describe a conservation
                planning document for a species or group of species.

CAMPFIRE   Communal Areas Management Programme for In-
                digenous Resources. Program in Zimbabwe through
                which district councils take major responsibility for
                the management of wildlife and other resources on
                their land. Similar to ADMADE in Zambia.

CARE   Cooperative for Assistance and Relief Everywhere.
                Charitable organization concerned particularly with
                emergency relief and rural development. Founded
                at the end of World War II as Cooperative for Ameri-
                can Remittances to Europe (hence CARE packages).
                CARE USA is now part of CARE International,
                whose headquarters are in Brussels.

CBSG   Conservation Breeding Specialist Group of IUCN's
                Species Survival Commission. Formerly known as the
                Captive Breeding Specialist Group.

CI   Conservation International. Nonprofit organization
                based in Washington, D.C.

CRNP   Cross River National Park, Nigeria.

CUNY   City University of New York; Hunter College is a con-
                stituent senior college of CUNY.

EC   European Commission, short form of Commission of
                the European Communities. The administrative and
                technical-assistance organization for the European
                Union, based in Brussels.

ECU   European Currency Unit. Based on the value of a
                "basket" of European currencies, this unit is used in
                the budgets of EU-funded projects.

EDF   European Development Fund. Administered by the
                European Commission on behalf of the EU.

EU   European Union. An association of European countries,
                founded in 1993 and designed to promote closer Euro-
                pean integration. Formerly the European Community.

FAO   Food and Agriculture Organization of the United Na-
                tions, concerned with promoting the development of
                agriculture, forestry, and fisheries, and with nutrition
                and food security. Based in Rome.

GEF Global Environment Facility. Organization or "facility" designed to broker support from development agencies and development banks to conservation and environmental-management projects that contribute to development. Established as a joint venture of the World Bank and the UNDP in 1990 and housed at World Bank headquarters in Washington, D.C.

GPS Global Positioning System. Satellite-based navigation system, allowing geographical coordinates at any point on the earth's surface to be established using a portable receiver.

GTZ Deutsche Gesellschaft für Technische Zusammenarbeit, the German technical assistance agency.

IUCN International Union for the Conservation of Nature and Natural Resources, now known as the World Conservation Union. Based in Gland, Switzerland.

IUPN International Union for the Protection of Nature. Became IUCN in 1956.

JWPT Jersey Wildlife Preservation Trust. An outgrowth of the Jersey Zoo, founded by Gerald Durrell.

KfW Kreditanstalt für Wiederaufbau. Development credit agency of the German government.

NCF Nigerian Conservation Foundation. Nongovernmental organization based in Lagos.

NPFL National Patriotic Front of Liberia. Quasi-political movement led by Charles Taylor. Entered Liberia as an armed force from Côte d'Ivoire in 1989 and eventually took control of large areas of Liberia, before breaking into splinter groups. Taylor won election as President of Liberia in 1997.

ODA Overseas Development Administration of the British government, once known as the Ministry of Overseas Development. Renamed Department for International Development in 1997. ODA is also used as an acronym for Official Development Assistance.

PHVA Population and Habitat Viability Assessment. Assessment of a species' status and chances of survival for a specified period of time; typically involves the mathematical modeling of population trajectories.

PSG   Primate Specialist Group of IUCN's Special Survival Commission. Conservation advisory group chaired by Russell Mittermeier, President of CI.

RUF   Revolutionary United Front. Quasi-political assemblage of insurgent groups in Sierra Leone, led by Foday Sankoh. Collaborated with dissident soldiers to unseat the elected government in May 1997.

UCL   University College London, a constituent college of the University of London.

UK   United Kingdom of Great Britain and Northern Island, usually shortened to United Kingdom, or Britain.

UNDP   United Nations Development Programme. Based in New York.

UNEP   United Nations Environment Programme. Based in Nairobi.

UNESCO   United Nations Educational, Scientific and Cultural Organization. Based in Paris.

USAID   United States Agency for International Development.

WCI   Wildlife Conservation International. A former division of the New York Zoological Society, now the international programs of WCS.

WCS   Wildlife Conservation Society. Formerly the New York Zoological Society, based in the Bronx, New York.

WEMPCO   Western Metal Products Company. Manufacturing company based in Lagos, Nigeria, involved in logging and timber processing in Cross River State.

WWF   World Wide Fund for Nature, still known in the United States and Canada by its original name, the World Wildlife Fund. International headquarters in Gland, Switzerland. Many countries have semiautonomous national organizations, such as WWF-US (based in Washington, D.C.) and WWF-UK (based in Godalming, Surrey).

ONE

A Pilgrimage to Eshobi

I have reached the end of a journey, a journey that has taken me more than forty years. It is March 1996, and below me are the tin roofs of the village of Eshobi, nestled among the forested hills of southwest Cameroon. Our vehicle continues down the new logging road, a red-dirt scar through the trees, and stops at the house of the chief so that we can explain the purpose of our visit. I am not confident that we will find him at home. It is midmorning, and based on my experience of many other African villages, I think there's a very good chance that the chief will be out, perhaps at his farm. But as I get down from the pickup truck with my companions, a confident old man comes out of the house to greet us. Ushering us inside, he introduces himself as Elias Abang, chief of Eshobi. I feel an immediate thrill, for it is a man called Elias, and another called Andraia, I am seeking.

GERALD DURRELL'S MAGICAL WORLD

Elias and Andraia were the two Eshobi hunters who played leading roles in Gerald Durrell's first book, *The Overloaded Ark*, published in July 1953.[1] Sometime in the year following its publication, when I was about nine years old, I read this enchanting tale of a six-month animal-collecting trip in 1947–48 to what was then the British Cameroons. I had long been fascinated by animals. Like the young Gerald Durrell, I filled my parents' house in northwest London with pets, some of which were captured on excursions to ponds in the outer reaches of the London suburbs. I also made frequent visits to the London Zoo.

Durrell's book painted a picture of a magical world, where the fascinating monkeys, hornbills, and reptiles that I knew only as zoo and museum exhibits actually lived wild in exotic forests in a land populated by people who seemed considerably more interesting than the middle-class residents of postwar Hampstead Garden Suburb. Books read in our childhood, Graham Greene has said, are books of divination, influencing the future, whereas books read in later life tend only to modify or confirm views we already hold.[2] At an impressionable age, *The Overloaded Ark* fired my imagination and laid the foundations of a longing to see the forests and animals of West Africa for myself and to visit the magical world of Eshobi. I'm sure I was not alone in being profoundly influenced by this book; in a 1984 issue of the Bombay Natural History Society's newsletter, the Indian ornithologist and wildlife photographer Rishad Naoroji wrote that "when I was about 12 years old I read Durrell's THE OVERLOADED ARK in one sitting staying up till the early hours and I was hooked."[3] After this, Naoroji too longed to see the wildlife of Africa.

The Overloaded Ark is not as well known as two more celebrated Durrell books, *The Bafut Beagles* (1954) and *My Family and Other Animals* (1956), but it has a freshness about it and a sense of wonder in the tropics that I don't think are fully matched by any of Durrell's later writings. *The Overloaded Ark* set the pattern for more than thirty subsequent books that weave together descriptions of exotic locales with carefully observed animal and human behavior. Yet only the more comical and innocent elements of human behavior appear in Durrell's books; we rarely meet the darker characters who populate Graham Greene's accounts of similar tropical backwaters.[4] It is escapist literature: one of the appealing features of Durrell's world is that its people do not die or do anything very unpleasant to each other; they are free from many ordinary weaknesses and lusts. Therefore, although the literature is "nonfiction," it does not portray a strictly true world.[5]

But the writings of Gerald Durrell have functioned not only as escapist entertainment; his books, and those of writers in a similar genre, have been inspirational to a generation of conservationists. Yet while these books have inspired others, their romantic style may have contributed to the development of an approach to tropical conservation problems that often takes an idealized view of human behavior and avoids confronting some unpleasant realities. This chapter will look at some of the realities of Eshobi today, where human population growth, the spread of commercial agriculture, and the arrival of foreign logging companies are causing the rapid erosion of the remaining forest; the wildlife that the young Durrell pursued is now hard to find. This chapter will also describe the growth of my own fascination with the forests of the tropics and especially of West Africa, how I came to make my first adventures in the West African forest, and how these adventures led me to an even stronger conviction that wild nature has great intrinsic value.

ESHOBI TODAY

Gerald Durrell died of liver disease in January 1995, a little more than a year before my journey to Eshobi (see map 2); he was only twenty-two when he first arrived in the village (see plate 1), and from his descriptions in *The Overloaded Ark*, the hunters Elias and Andraia were some years older than he. Therefore, although I hoped I would meet someone who remembered Durrell's first visit, and who knew about Elias and Andraia, I did not dare to expect that I would meet both of these men myself. Cameroon (the former British Cameroons merged with French Cameroun to form a new, independent state in 1961) is well known for a

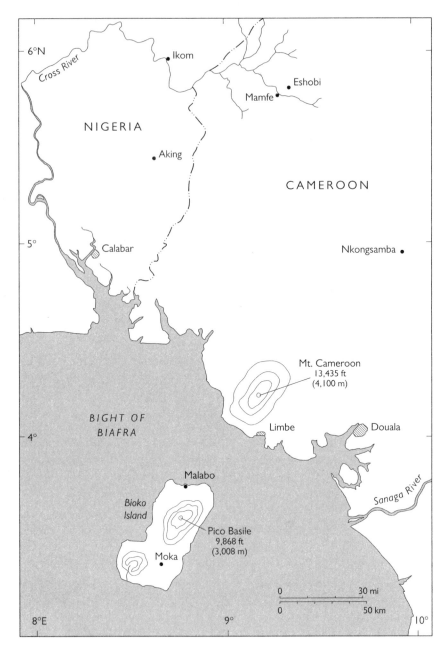

Map 2. Southwestern Cameroon, southeastern Nigeria, and Bioko Island, showing the location of Eshobi on the headwaters of the Cross River and Moka in the southern mountains of Bioko.

high prevalence of a great range of tropical diseases, and even today life expectancy at birth is only fifty-six.[6]

Yet as soon as I began talking to Chief Elias Abang (mostly in pidgin English, helped by my companion Philip Hium from the Wildlife Conservation Society project at Nguti), it became clear that he was indeed one of the hunters who appear in the early pages of *The Overloaded Ark*. So I asked him who the other hunter was who worked with Durrell, and he said, "Andrea." "Is Andrea still in the village?" I asked. "Yes," I was told, and the chief sent for him. Before long an even older man appeared, walking with the aid of a stick. This was Andreas Ebai Ncha; his friends pronounced his first name "Andrea" and Durrell had transcribed this as "Andraia." Andreas Ncha said he was born in 1914, and Elias Abang, according to his identity card, was born around 1919, meaning that they were probably in their thirties when they first met Durrell, and certainly at the height of their powers. Durrell praises them as very good hunters indeed and says that within a twenty-mile radius of Eshobi "they knew every path, every little stream and waterfall, almost every bush. They would melt through the thickest tangle of undergrowth with ease, and not a sound betrayed their presence, while I, hot and flat-footed, stumbled behind with a noise like a bulldozer in action."[7]

Yet although Durrell admired the courage of Elias and the quick-wittedness of Andreas, and relied on them totally as his guides in the forest and chief animal collectors, he presents them as rather simple village men, very much under the control of their "master," the young Gerald Durrell. This portrait is hardly surprising, given that Durrell had spent his earliest years in imperial India and was writing in the 1940s about a country under a colonial mandate. Indeed, given the time and place in which he was writing, Durrell's early works are remarkably free of racist tone.[8]

Even so, Elias Abang and Andreas Ncha were more impressive characters than I had expected (see plate 2). They were not grotesque in their physiques as I had expected from Durrell's account,[9] and they were wise and serious old men, not in any way simpletons. Abang, as traditional chief, was greatly respected in Eshobi; I was told, for instance, that he had introduced tobacco farming to this region (the Mamfe District) in colonial days, bringing the plants from French Cameroun. He had large cocoa farms, six wives, and thirty-two living children (twenty-four, he said, had died). Ncha had two wives and eight surviving children.

Abang and Ncha are not unusual in Africa in having wives who have each produced four or five surviving children; in the early 1990s the average number of children that a woman in Cameroon was expected to have was 5.7, compared to 6.3 in the early 1970s and 5.8 for Africa as a whole; the 1993 under-five mortality rate in Cameroon was estimated at 113 per 1,000 births, down from 264 in 1960.[10] Therefore, one of the most striking changes to have occurred in Eshobi and the rest of Cameroon in recent decades is in the size of its population. In 1950 Cameroon is estimated to have had 4.47 million people; in 1995 it had 13.23 million, an increase of nearly 200 percent.[11] Although it is likely that parts of tropical Africa had much higher human populations in the past than they had in the early years of this century,[12] it is undeniable that there have been very great population increases since World War II, probably in part because of lowered mortality rates associated with the spread of vaccination and antibiotics, but also because of a general improvement in rural prosperity. With growing population and growing wealth, farms and plantations have spread in rural Africa.

The Eshobi of my 1996 visit is a good example of the real rain forest world of today. Many changes have come to the village in the fifty years since Durrell first went there, changes similar to those that have occurred over much of western and central Africa, and that have brought us to the conservation crisis that is the topic of this book. In the 1940s Eshobi village was in two small clusters. Now, the two settlements have consolidated on one site as a large village of at least six hundred people. Cash crops such as cocoa and coffee have been introduced, and forest on cultivatable land has been cleared for several miles from the village.

On his first day in the forest with Elias and Andreas, Durrell encountered a group of putty-nosed guenons about three miles from the village. Now, I was told, you have to walk considerably farther to find much wildlife. Even so, some forest survives on steep hills very close to Eshobi; I spent one morning with hunters in this forest, but the largest animal I saw was a squirrel. In 1996 I could drive into the center of Eshobi, but Durrell had to walk there. He traversed the gorge of the Cross River on the north side of Mamfe town using a narrow suspension bridge erected during the period of German rule before World War I, and then he trekked more than five miles through the forest on a rocky path.[13] Now, the German suspension bridge is derelict, and you cross the river downstream on a large concrete bridge completed in 1991. The new bridge was constructed as part of a project, funded by foreign aid, to build a road north through the forest to the town of Akwaya, more than 40 miles away. This project collapsed after the completion of the bridge, but the bridge has allowed mechanized logging in the forests north of the Cross for the first time. A Lebanese timber company has obtained a concession to a large area of forest north of the bridge, and by the time of my visit many miles of road had been cleared for the company's trucks (see plate 3).

In his prelude to *The Overloaded Ark,* Durrell describes Eshobi as situated on the edge of a forest area "that stretches unbroken and almost uninhabited hundreds of miles northwards until it reaches the desolate mountains where the gorilla has its stronghold."[14] Some artistic license is at work here, for the area still inhabited by a small number of gorillas is the Takamanda Forest Reserve, only twenty miles north of Eshobi, in an area that has long supported villages. This country, the Mamfe Overside, was indeed largely forested until the arrival of the loggers. Logging was occurring at a rapid rate in early 1996 because at the end of that year a new law was to come into effect in Cameroon, requiring that 70 percent of all logs harvested be processed within the country. Such local processing would lower the loggers' profits, so they were cutting and shipping as many logs as they could before the new processing regulations came into effect. In West Africa, and throughout the tropics, increased hunting and farming typically follow in the wake of logging.[15]

Other aspects of "development" were also evident on my visit to Eshobi. In addition to Elias Abang, the traditional village chief, I met Gregory Ojong Abang, a Nigerian-educated government-appointed chief who represented Eshobi in local administrative councils. Chief Gregory asked if I could help bring a development project to Eshobi. I said that I doubted I could, and I asked about the apparently rich cocoa farms around the village; could not the farmers contribute to a community development project? Chief Gregory replied that these men tried to keep their money for themselves and their families. This is a good example of one of the more pernicious effects of development aid in Africa. It has cultivated a local attitude that foreigners do not expect Africans to do things for themselves and are ready to hand out money and material resources with few strings attached; all too often, such "development projects" have been paternalistic and have fostered dependency.

That Eshobi was quite capable of organizing some of its own development was clear from the fact that, before the new logging road reached their village, the people had themselves cut a motorable track from the new Cross River bridge to Eshobi; some villagers had bought secondhand cars and started running them on this road as taxis. They now talked of installing an electricity line from Mamfe. Eshobi surely was never quite as remote and untouched a tropical paradise as it seemed to a young reader of *The Overloaded Ark* in gray suburban England in the early 1950s, and four decades later the outside world certainly had the village firmly in its embrace.

LONDON ZOO'S INFLUENCE

Gerald Durrell was not the only early influence that brought me almost inevitably to the forests of West Africa. From a very young age I often visited the London Zoo in Regent's Park with my parents. In 1955, soon after I had read *The Overloaded Ark* and its sequel, *The Bafut Beagles,* my mother became a member of the Zoological Society of London, which ran the zoo. In those days, the Regent's Park Zoo had special Sunday-morning admission restricted to members and their families and friends (this privilege was discontinued in 1957). If they established good relations with keepers, members could go behind the scenes in some of the animal houses and feed and handle animals. My own favorite was the monkey house, which usually had many West African monkeys and apes on display.

West African animals were a major feature of the Regent's Park collection in the 1950s. The Curator of Reptiles, John Withers ("Jack")

Lester, had worked in a bank in the small British West African colony of Sierra Leone before the war and had subsequently returned there on several collecting trips. In 1948 George Cansdale became Assistant Superintendent of the zoo, and from 1951 to 1953 he was Superintendent, until his post was abolished in 1953. Cansdale had been a forest officer in the colonial Gold Coast (now Ghana) and brought many animals with him from West Africa. Cansdale took over as Superintendent from Cecil Webb. Webb had been an official curator-collector for the Zoological Society in the years immediately after World War II, and played a major role in restocking depleted collections at London Zoo and its country partner, Whipsnade Park. Among other places, Webb collected in the British Cameroons, where he met Durrell in 1948; Durrell handed over to him a tame chimpanzee, Cholmondeley, who features both in a chapter of *The Overloaded Ark* and Webb's own account of his collecting expeditions.[16] Animals obtained by Cansdale, Durrell, and Webb were on display at London Zoo during my early visits and must have influenced the direction in which my interests developed.

Although the literature from that time indicates little concern for the depletion of tropical rain forest and its fauna and seldom suggests that zoos should be playing an active role in conservation, the role of zoos in education and in inculcating a love of animals in young people was widely and reasonably acknowledged.[17] The London Zoo certainly played that role in my life, and I have found that other zoos have had the same effect on many of my students.

DAVID ATTENBOROUGH:
TROPICAL NATURE ON TELEVISION

Like many people in Britain, our family got its first television set shortly before the coronation of Queen Elizabeth II in June 1953, and we watched the ceremonies on a small black-and-white screen. At that time George Cansdale, in addition to his job at London Zoo, also hosted some popular television programs in which he displayed zoo animals on live television from the BBC studios in Alexandra Palace, not far from where we lived in north London. And in 1954 a series of half-hour films about East African wildlife made by the Antwerp-born filmmaker Armand Denis and his wife, Michaela, also began to appear on BBC Television. The films were initially presented under the title *Filming Wild Animals;* the Denises' famous series *On Safari* was to come later.

Influenced by these programs, David Attenborough, a young BBC television producer with a degree in zoology, came up with an imaginative plan to combine Cansdale's studio demonstrations of zoo animals with film footage of them being collected in their natural habitats. Thus were launched the immensely popular *Zoo Quest* expeditions, and Attenborough's career. The first *Zoo Quest* destination was Sierra Leone, decided on as a result of Attenborough's acquaintance with Jack Lester at the Regent's Park Zoo. According to Attenborough's later account,[18] he had met Lester while arranging to borrow some zoo animals for use in a televised lecture series by the zoologist Julian Huxley. Attenborough learned that Lester was eager to return to Sierra Leone, where he had many contacts.

A joint London Zoo–BBC expedition, led by Jack Lester, set off in September 1954, and the first *Zoo Quest* appeared on television on December 21. This first program was introduced by Lester, but he became ill soon after and the rest of the series was introduced by Attenborough himself. The series was a great success and was followed by several more expeditions and accompanying books. Attenborough's engaging personality and infectious enthusiasm for zoology had an inevitably strong influence on susceptible young viewers like me.[19]

I was further captivated by an edited version of the Sierra Leone *Zoo Quest* at a meeting for members' children at London Zoo in January 1956. I little thought, though, that I would eventually find myself operating from the very same base in Sierra Leone, the Njala agricultural research station (later a university college), from which Lester and Attenborough had gone in search of a rare bird, the bare-headed rock-fowl (*Picathartes gymnocephalus*), and other exotic African forest creatures (see plate 4).[20]

So at a very impressionable age, I had not only been infected by what Gerald Durrell has described as "zoomania,"[21] I had also been given a double dose of West African natural history by two very persuasive young men. In retrospect, it is not surprising that I was strongly influ-

enced. I had become determined not only to see the tropics, and especially West Africa, but to collect animals myself. After all, the main purpose of Durrell's and Attenborough's trips had been to collect animals
and bring them back to England. Although hardly anyone then suggested that there could be any ethical problem with such activity, I soon
realized that my schoolmasters did not consider the study of West
African natural history an appropriate career to develop out of their
careful instruction in Latin, Greek, and English literature. I learned to
keep quiet about my ambitions. Given my age, there was in any case little I could do to realize my dream. Instead, for several years I avidly
read each new Gerald Durrell book and eagerly awaited each new *Zoo
Quest* on television. And I acquired ever more exotic fish and reptiles
from local pet shops.

Of course, I still had no very realistic view of West Africa. Attenborough's films and writings, like Durrell's books, did not aim to portray
the more sordid aspects of life in the colonial tropics, and Jack Lester's
serious illness (of which he died in 1956) was mentioned only briefly in
the *Zoo Quest* series.[22] To me, it seemed that these intrepid collectors
visited countries where innocent natives lived in harmony with colorful
nature in warm climates, and where white men could do just about anything they wished. One of the few major disadvantages of the animal-
collecting life in West Africa seemed to be uncomfortable lorry journeys
along potholed roads, but at a distance this sounded like another appealing element of adventure. Both Durrell and Attenborough acknowledged in their writings that you had to look very hard in the forest to see
anything but insects, but their accounts inevitably focused on the high
points of their expeditions, their encounters with the rarest and most interesting mammals and birds. In other words, I was captivated as much,
or more, by the myth of the rain forest as by its reality.

FIRST FOOTSTEPS IN WEST AFRICA

At school, I was bored by most formal class work, but I read avidly in
the school library. Not dissuaded by the advice that a career in natural
history was not sensible, I specialized in biology and found myself in a

class where most of my fellow pupils were planning to be medical doctors. I applied to several universities to read for a zoology degree and was lucky to be accepted at University College London (UCL). On my application I noted the important influences of Gerald Durrell and David Attenborough on the development of my interests, and found myself at a subsequent interview being asked about their famous brothers. Fortunately I knew of the novelist Lawrence Durrell and the film actor (only later director) Richard Attenborough, and so in the autumn of 1963 I began a degree program at UCL. Here, I was privileged to have such teachers as the embryologist Michael Abercrombie, evolutionary biologist John Maynard-Smith, vertebrate paleontologists Kenneth Kermack and Keith Thomson, systematist Richard Freeman, and ecologists Roderick Fisher and Brian O'Connor.

Now I was in a learning program that stimulated my mind. Even more exciting than the formal course work was my discovery of university exploration societies. This particularly British phenomenon allowed students to get together in an organized, institutionally sponsored framework to plan summer trips to interesting overseas destinations, where they undertook research projects. I soon joined the UCL Exploration Society and began to think that perhaps my West African dreams could be realized at last. I found that the college, through the Exploration Society, provided small grants to approved expeditions, as well as advice about foundations and companies that gave financial or other material support to student expeditions. Even so, an expedition to West Africa would be expensive, and where would I go, to do what, and with whom?

Toward the end of January 1964 I bought a copy of the *Geographical Magazine* at a London news agent. Following articles about the Antarctic explorer John Biscoe, the history of the British fishing industry, and the Principality of Liechtenstein, was a short piece entitled "Fernando Po: Spain in Africa."[23] This was little more than a set of photographs by one Federico Patellani portraying Santa Isabel, the capital city of the Spanish-ruled island of Fernando Po in the Gulf of Guinea, about twenty miles off the coast of Cameroon. But the *Geographical Magazine* specialized in telling its readers how they could get to its featured localities, and surprisingly the January 1964 issue gave more information about getting to Fernando Po than to Liechtenstein. It noted that you could take a boat from Cadiz, in southern Spain, and that the voyage took about eight days. I was intrigued and made inquiries. It turned out that one could travel third class on the Trasmeditteranea company's mail and cargo boat from Cadiz to Santa Isabel for slightly less than the cost of the second-class rail fare from London to Cadiz (which was £16/10s, or about $46 at that time). Not only did this seem to be an affordable way of reaching tropical Africa, but the destination seemed particularly exciting: a little-known volcanic island (said by the *Geographical Magazine* to be "one of the most beautiful islands in the world") located in the very part of West Africa I had long wanted to visit. Within two weeks I had persuaded five others to join in: one of my former school classmates, John Reckless, who was now a medical student, and four UCL undergraduates: Michael Bovis, Graham Dunn, David Holberton, and Allan Rostron.

We decided to plan for an expedition to Fernando Po (today called Bioko) in the summer of 1964 and quickly put together a research program. Following in the footsteps of Durrell and Attenborough, and reflecting still-prevalent notions in the zoological community, our research projects were heavily biased toward collecting: reptiles and amphibians for the Natural History Museum in London, as well as mammals (especially primates), and rodent blood parasites. Our geographer, Mike Bovis, was to make a geomorphological transect of part of the rugged island. We were lucky to attract considerable support for our plans, both from our college and from outside organizations, including the Royal Geographical Society.

On July 26 we set off from Victoria Station with a strange collection of luggage. One item was a package of specially heat-treated milk, which the Express Dairy Company had asked us to test under tropical conditions. The tetrahedral cartons of this novel and secret product (the Express Dairy asked us not to tell the press anything about it) were already leaking by the time our train reached Paris, and it was not easy to convince the French Customs inspector that we should be carrying a large quantity of whole milk; as he pointed out, "We have milk in France." The milk never reached Bioko—it seemed to be fine, but its leaky packaging was not, and off the African coast we finally jettisoned several containers of what had by then become cheese.

Our ship, the *Domine*, left Cadiz on July 30 and sailed south for Africa, stopping first in the Canary Islands. The voyage itself was a zoological delight, although our bunks and food were very decidedly third class. Beyond the Canaries we plowed at night through fields of luminescent plankton and watched flying fish, sharks, and dolphins off the bow of our boat. At last I was living my long-nurtured dream, and so far the reality was as wonderful as the stories that had brought me here. On August 14 we steamed into the palm-fringed volcanic crater below the sleepy colonial town of Santa Isabel (now Malabo), the capital of Spanish Equatorial Guinea on the northern coast of Bioko.

With the advice and assistance of the local managers of the Ambas Bay Trading Company and Spanish officials (Equatorial Guinea was then one of the last remaining European colonies in Africa), we decided to base ourselves in Moka, in the island's southern mountains (see map 2). Here we spent a month collecting frogs, snakes, and small mammals in frequent rain—the far south of Bioko is one of the wettest places on earth, and the coastal settlement of Ureka has an annual rainfall of about 36 feet (see plate 5).

Ecologically, Bioko is interesting in more than just its wetness. Although the island is small (about 780 square miles) and many of its lowland forests have been cleared for cocoa plantations, the remaining forests resemble those of nearby Cameroon in containing one of the richest assemblages of plant and animal species in Africa. The main peak of Bioko reaches to almost 9,900 feet, and this altitudinal range adds to the diversity; on the upper slopes of the main peak and the southern highlands there is montane forest, and at the highest altitudes some heathland. Because it lies on Africa's continental shelf, with a sea channel only 200 feet deep separating it from Cameroon, Bioko must have been connected to the mainland during times of maximum glaciation in the Pleistocene epoch, including the last glacial episode that reached its peak eighteen thousand years ago. Since they became separated from mainland populations by the postglacial rise in sea level that began some ten thousand years ago, many of the island's animals have differentiated to become distinct subspecies. At the time of our visit, most of these sub-species were represented in museum collections by only a handful of specimens, and many of Bioko's species had probably never been docu-mented at all. Indeed, of the amphibians we collected around Moka, four were species that had not previously been reported from Bioko, al-though they were known from Cameroon. One of these, a small frog that we caught on our second day in Moka, was eventually identified as *Woltersdorffina parvipalmata*, a genus new to the collection of London's Natural History Museum. We also found a genus of shrew, *Myosorex*, that had previously been known only from Mount Cameroon and the mountains of East Africa.[24]

In Moka, we became especially fascinated by the nocturnal lemurlike galagos that we commonly saw in the beams of our lights in the patch-work of forest and cattle pastures around our base. We identified two species, Demidoff's dwarf bushbaby (*Galagoides demidoff*) and the larger Allen's bushbaby (*Galago alleni*). From the books we had brought with us, we realized that little was known about the natural history of the Allen's bushbaby, and so we concentrated our attention on this species and at-tempted to catch one alive. Two and a half weeks after arriving in Moka, we cornered a male in a small tree on the edge of a field and I managed to grab it by the tail as it tried to escape on a fence. With the help of the man-ager of the Ambas Bay Trading Company, we contacted London Zoo and soon received a cable back from Desmond Morris, Curator of Mammals, saying the zoo would be delighted to accept the animal and would pay airfreight charges. We took the bushbaby with us on our homeward voy-age, and during a stop in Lagos, Nigeria, we tried to get it on that day's British Overseas Airways Corporation (BOAC) flight to London. I had a foretaste of the world that I would increasingly have to grapple with, when paperwork resulted in a long delay at the Apapa docks in Lagos, and our bushbaby missed its flight. We left it with BOAC, and it eventu-ally reached London safely. Two months later a wrangle developed over who would pay the charges of the shipping agent who had helped arrange the transport of the bushbaby from our boat to the airport. Desmond Morris was reluctant to meet this expense (£55, at that time about $150), and it was eventually paid by the long-suffering managers of the Ambas Bay Trading Company, which was a unit of the much larger United Africa Company, based in London. It was United Africa Company managers who had helped Gerald Durrell with many of his logistical problems on his Cameroon expeditions. As long ago as 1893, Mary Kingsley found European traders in West Africa to be kind and hospitable, contrary to her expectations, and they helped her visit places she would otherwise never have been able to see.[25]

Despite the logistical headaches involved, the Bioko expedition had been such a stimulating experience that I was keen to get back to Africa as soon as I could. I had also become especially interested in the lorisids (the primate family to which the bushbabies belong). In the mid-1960s very little was known about the biology of the lorisid species found in the forests of equatorial Africa. Having become intrigued by the Bioko bushbabies, we were encouraged to learn more by two scientists who were themselves studying lorisids in the laboratory: E. C. B. Hall-Craggs of the Department of Anatomy at University College London and Gilbert Manley of the Wellcome Institute of Comparative Physiology at London Zoo. We decided to mount a second expedition to Equatorial Guinea and spend most of our time in the forests of mainland Rio Muni, from where five lorisids were reported: three species of bushbaby and the slower-moving, short-tailed potto and angwantibo. Two members of the first expedition, Graham Dunn and David Holberton, joined in, together with a new undergraduate, Brian Rosser.

Repeating our train and boat journey, we arrived back in Equatorial Guinea at the end of July 1965 and stayed there for eight weeks. On a brief stop in Bioko we managed to catch two more Allen's bushbabies at Moka, both females; these we sent to join the original animal at London Zoo. Then we went on to Rio Muni and spent many nights observing and collecting lorisids in the forests and plantations around Evinayong. Here we saw all three bushbaby species, as well as pottos, but no angwantibos. Most intriguing was the needle-clawed bushbaby (*Euoticus elegantulus*), an extremely poorly known species we had not seen on Bioko, but which turned out to be common around Evinayong. We were puzzled by a jellylike substance found along with insects in the stomachs of some needle-clawed bushbabies we shot, by their strange tongues and teeth, and by their ridged and pointed nails. Other zoologists had reported that Moholi bushbabies in the African savanna zone ate acacia gum, and in notes I made in Rio Muni I speculated that the *Euoticus* tongue might be used for licking the gum of the acacia-like trees in which we often saw the animals. Several years later, this was confirmed by the studies by Pierre Charles-Dominique in neighboring Gabon; Charles-Dominique reported that *Euoticus* feeds heavily on tree gums and uses its sharp nails to gain purchase on the bark when foraging head down on trunks.[26]

In September 1965 we returned to London not only with many lorisid specimens, and more frogs and reptiles for the Natural History Museum, but also with our heads full of new experiences. I was now twenty years old and absolutely determined to return to the forests of Africa. I little imagined that after another thirty years I would be literally following the road to Eshobi that I had once read about to meet Elias and Andreas in the flesh, or that by then I would so often feel disheartened to be in West Africa, walking through ever-diminishing forests almost devoid of large animals. And it was certainly unimaginable to me that, in the 1990s, international conservation organizations would be supporting projects in West Africa whose effects promoted human economic development at the expense of vanishing wildlife.

From Collecting to Conservation

Africa changed greatly between 1953 and 1954, when *The Overloaded Ark* and the first *Zoo Quest* appeared, and the time of our visit to Bioko ten years later. Most countries in tropical Africa gained their independence from colonial rule in this period, and independence initially brought an increased pace of economic development. The Spanish Equatorial Guinea we visited was a relic of a rapidly passing age; the country became independent in 1968.[1] Not only was the Equatorial Guinea of 1964–65 a relic, but our expeditions there—with animal collecting as the focus of our fieldwork—were also old-fashioned. It was commonplace in the colonial era for Europeans and Americans to collect exotic items from Africa and other parts of the tropics for their museums, galleries, zoos, and private homes; such behavior might be viewed as one facet of a larger pattern of exploitation. Even in 1964, my student companions and I, trained in the traditions of classical zoology, did not worry greatly about the ethics of animal collecting, which appeared to be a rather harmless activity; indeed, many zoologists still devote themselves largely to the collection and cataloging of specimens.[2]

But since the end of the 1950s, concern had been growing worldwide about conservation and environmental degradation. Painting a more somber picture than Gerald Durrell's *Overloaded Ark*, Alan Moorehead's *No Room in the Ark*, published in 1959, highlighted the damage being caused by poaching and encroachment in some of Africa's new national parks.[3] In the following year Durrell himself started to express his views on the need to interest people in conservation, and before long Rachel Carson's *Silent Spring* (1962) would raise huge public concern over the dangerous effects of pesticides.[4]

In 1960, as concern increased about the future of African wildlife in the face of population growth, economic development, and political independence, British naturalist Julian Huxley visited East Africa to investigate wildlife conservation issues on behalf of UNESCO, of which he had been the first Director General, from 1946 to 1948. His reports of alarming levels of habitat destruction and hunting led to a proposal for an international organization to raise funds on a large scale for conservation. Huxley recruited Max Nicholson, the Director General of the U.K. Nature Conservancy, to set up a working group to produce a plan for such a "World Wildlife Fund" (see plate 10). A prominent member of the working group was another British naturalist, Peter Scott, who became the first Chairman of the new organization, founded in 1961.[5]

Although concern about the impact of humans on wild nature in the tropics did not spread to a large number of people in western industrial societies until the 1960s, many individuals who lived in (or had visited) the tropics had become concerned much earlier. The first western organization formed specifically to address conservation problems in the tropics was the Society for the Preservation of the Wild Fauna of the Empire, founded in 1903. The British founders were predominantly big-game hunters, or former hunters, who were especially bothered about the destruction of game by what they regarded as indiscriminate hunting in Africa by Europeans; this gave these founders the nickname of "penitent butchers."[6] In 1950, the society changed its name to the Fauna Preservation Society,[7] and its journal became *Oryx;* the first issue of *Oryx* carried an article by E. Barton Worthington on the future of the African fauna, arguing that human population trends made it likely that most larger animals would be eradicated except in strictly protected areas.[8] By 1950, several important protected areas for wildlife already existed in Africa. In 1925, for instance, King Albert of the Belgians had created a gorilla sanctuary in the Belgian Congo that was later extended to become the Parc National Albert (now the Virunga National Park).[9] South Africa's Kruger National Park was declared in 1926, and Kenya's Nairobi National Park in 1946.[10] Many new parks were established in the 1950s.

The early 1960s saw not only spreading concern for conservation in the tropics, and especially in Africa, they also saw an upsurge of field studies on the ecology and behavior of African mammals. For instance, in 1959 George Schaller had arrived in the Virunga Volcanoes to undertake a pioneering study of mountain gorillas,[11] and in 1960 Jane Goodall began her famous studies of chimpanzees in the Gombe Stream Reserve in what was then Tanganyika.[12] These studies emphasized the long-term observation of animals in the wild with minimal interference by the scientists. The great-ape studies in particular attracted considerable public attention in America and Europe; charismatic animals were being studied by charismatic scientists, who worked on their own, unarmed, in the forests of tropical Africa, in popular imagination a very hazardous environment. The publicity given to this work, which initially emphasized the animals' peaceful nature, helped to make hunting and collecting much less fashionable than observation, photography, and protection.

Another significant development at this time was the opening, in 1961, of the Nuffield Unit of Tropical Animal Ecology at Mweya in Uganda's Queen Elizabeth National Park. This unit, later to become the Uganda Institute of Ecology, was established in part because the Trustees of the Uganda National Parks perceived a need for ecological research that could be applied to the active management of large mammal populations, which, under protection, appeared to be increasing beyond the capacity of the system to maintain them.[13] The Serengeti Research Project also began in 1961, studying the ecosystem of the Serengeti National Park and particularly the ecology and behavior of large predators and their herbivore prey; this project evolved into the Serengeti Research Institute, established in 1966.[14] In 1963, the *East African Wildlife Journal* (now the *African Journal of Ecology*) was launched, and it featured the results of this new wave of African field research.

NIGERIA: FIELDWORK AMID POLITICAL UPHEAVAL

I was not strongly exposed to academic thinking about wildlife conservation issues until the college year following our 1965 expedition to Equatorial Guinea. Taking a final-year undergraduate specialization in ecology, I found myself attending lectures given in University College London's master's degree course in conservation; this was the first such course in Britain, started in 1960 at the encouragement of Max Nicholson, whose role in the founding of WWF I have already mentioned. A series of guest lectures on mammalian ecology and conservation was given in this course by Peter Jewell from London Zoo's Wellcome Institute. Jewell had visited East and central Africa in 1962 to look at some of the new approaches to the study of African mammals in the wild, and he had witnessed the increasing restriction of large mammals to parks and reserves and the management problems this led to.[15]

Attending Peter Jewell's stimulating lectures only strengthened my wish to pursue postgraduate work on the ecology of African mammals, preferably nocturnal primates like the strange needle-clawed bushbaby that I had observed and collected in Equatorial Guinea. One option I considered was joining the staff of Makerere University in Uganda. Uganda intrigued me because reports suggested that a second, and completely unstudied, species of needle-clawed bushbaby occurred in its western forests.[16] But in the first part of 1966, Uganda was undergoing political upheavals. Prime Minister Milton Obote centralized power in his own hands, as Executive President; the ruling council of the Kingdom of Buganda rejected the new constitution, at which point troops under the army commander Idi Amin attacked the palace of the ruler (the Kabaka) and put him to flight.[17] Influenced by this prospect of civil unrest, I turned down the offer of a junior teaching position in the Zoology Department at Makerere and decided instead to accept a two-year appointment as research assistant to Peter Jewell, who had just been appointed as Director of a new Biological Sciences Division at the University of Nigeria, Nsukka, in the Eastern Region of Nigeria. Nsukka planned to develop its biological sciences program through academic collaboration with University College London, with funding support from the U.K. Ministry of Overseas Development (now the Department for International Development). While doing research in Nigeria with Jewell, I would be able to register for a Ph.D. at UCL. This seemed a very attractive option, because Peter Jewell was not only a leading mammalian ecologist, he also had strong commitment to conservation, a subject that increasingly interested me. In addition, Eastern Nigeria was immediately adjacent to Cameroon; it offered the possibility of further studies on a fauna very similar to the fascinating one I had met both in the pages of Durrell's books and in the flesh on Bioko.

The snag in this apparently perfect opportunity was again African politics. A military coup in January 1966 had led to the downfall of the civilian government that had ruled Nigeria since independence in 1960. The coup had brought to power J. T. U. Ironsi. Ironsi was an Igbo,[18] and therefore a member of the most numerous and powerful ethnic group in southeastern Nigeria, a group mistrusted by many other Nigerians. Ironsi himself was not part of the coup plot and had helped to foil a complete takeover of the government by the plotters. After four months in power, and in a parallel to events in Uganda, Ironsi announced a new constitution; this constitution abolished Nigeria's semiautonomous regions. Fearing political domination by southerners, and particularly Igbos, northern Nigerians launched a wave of pogroms in northern cities, where many Igbos were killed. In July, Ironsi was deposed in a northern-led coup. Although the new government, led by Yakubu Gowon, restored the regional system, it also put forward a proposal for a looser arrangement of smaller states. This plan was opposed by the Eastern Region, whose Igbo military governor, Chukwuemeka Odumegwu Ojukwu, had not been overthrown in the July coup.[19]

Despite the growing signs of instability, the British government told Peter Jewell that it believed major turmoil in Nigeria was unlikely, and so we continued planning for our project. But when I arrived in Nigeria on September 8, 1966, I found newly installed military checkpoints on the road between Enugu airport and Nsukka, and soon after my arrival a new and more terrible wave of massacres began in the north, in which tens of thousands of Igbos are thought to have died. More than a million Igbos began fleeing to the east, Ojukwu's position hardened, and there were increasing calls for the secession of the Eastern Region from the Nigerian Federation.

In the ten months I spent in Eastern Nigeria I visited many forest reserves, where I studied small rodents by day and continued learning about lorisid primates at night. Now, most of my work on the nocturnal primates was done by walking slowly along forest paths, using binoculars to observe animals that had been revealed in my headlamp's beam by the bright orange reflections from their eyes; I collected very few specimens. I recorded how the abundance of different lorisid species varied from one habitat to another, and I discovered that several species (including the needle-clawed bushbaby) that had been thought to be restricted to the southeasternmost corner of Nigeria actually extended through the forest zone right up to the Niger River (see map 3).[20] I also became much more acutely aware than I had been on my undergraduate expeditions of just how threatened some African rain forests and their wildlife were becoming. Eastern Nigeria has long been one of the most densely populated parts of Africa,[21] and in 1966 much of the area's original forest cover had already been reduced to small fragments, most of which were protected in government-managed forest reserves. The only relatively large areas of forest lay in the far east of the region, adjacent to the Cameroon border.

Even within many of the forest reserves of Eastern Nigeria, little natural forest remained. Large areas of natural forest had been converted by the so-called *taungya* system into monoculture plantations of exotic trees such as teak and *Gmelina*. The *taungya* system was introduced to Nigeria after World War II. It had first been used in colonial Burma for teak cultivation in the nineteenth century.[22] Under this system, an area of forest is first commercially logged, then allocated to farmers to be cleared and cultivated. In exchange for temporary farming rights, the farmers agree to plant among their crops seedlings of useful tree species

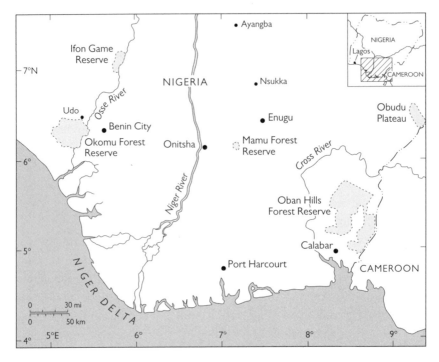

Map 3. Southeastern and midwestern Nigeria, showing major cities and the location of research and conservation sites mentioned in chapters 2, 5, and 6. The Oban Hills Forest Reserve became part of the Cross River National Park in 1991.

provided from forestry nurseries. As the planted trees grow up, the farmers are supposed to move on, after obtaining several harvests from their crops.

This *taungya* technique was an almost inevitable outgrowth of conservation practices that had become widespread in the European colonial empires. Forest management was nearly always seen as having a utilitarian purpose, with forest resources managed so as to bring long-term economic benefits to the colonial territories. Forests were protected not to preserve wilderness for its own sake and for aesthetic appreciation, but to ensure a supply of timber and safeguard water supplies. As such, they had a long history: the first tropical forest reserves seem to have been established by the British colonial administration on the West Indian island of Tobago in 1764 to protect water supplies.[23] Serious efforts by the colonial administration to manage Nigeria's forests began in 1897 with the establishment of the Office of Woods and Forests in the Lagos Colony and Protectorate. The first forest reserve was constituted in 1899, and reservation increased rapidly after the publication of a third Forestry Ordinance in 1916. These laws were formulated by the "father" of Nigerian forestry, H. N. Thompson, who had worked in Burma for the Indian Forest Service and was appointed as Nigeria's first Conservator of Forests in 1903. Although Thompson's new ordinance empowered government to constitute forest reserves and to manage the exploitation of forest products in these reserves, land title remained in the hands of the traditional owners.[24]

During my 1966–67 fieldwork I saw *taungya* farming accelerate in the forest reserves of Eastern Nigeria as the government made efforts to find farmland for the many Igbo refugees flooding in from the north. My main study site was the thirteen-square-mile Mamu River Forest Reserve (see plate 6), where in thirty-one days of fieldwork I recorded twenty-eight species of mammal and saw many nocturnal primates. Toward the end of my research, large areas of the remaining natural forest in Mamu had been given over to refugees for farming. Hunting of animals for food was also intense in Mamu and most of the other reserves I visited. This hunting was largely uncontrolled because management was directed toward tree crops rather than the ecosystem as a whole; indeed, forest officers themselves were often serious hunters.

Seeing these destructive trends, Jewell and I began making a case for the protection of the Eastern Nigerian forests and their neglected wildlife, arguing that there should be more emphasis on the conservation of the whole biological community than on the management of trees for commercial exploitation.[25] But we were voices literally crying in the wilderness, for political tensions had been increasing throughout our stay at Nsukka, and conservation was low on everyone else's agenda. The government of the Eastern Region orchestrated demands for secession, and students on the Nsukka campus were encouraged to attend political rallies, being told that going to the library instead of a rally was the sign of a traitor.

A crisis occurred when, on May 26, 1967, Gowon announced that Nigeria would be divided into twelve states (with the Eastern Region split into three). This precipitated the long-expected declaration by Ojukwu on May 30 that Eastern Nigeria was seceding from the federation as the independent nation of Biafra. In the tense atmosphere that followed, in which the Biafran people were constantly warned of the dangers from traitors and saboteurs, travel and fieldwork became very difficult.[26] Expatriates at the university began to hold meetings to discuss what they should do in the event of war; clear differences soon emerged between the professional, well-organized American plans and the amateurish plans of the British. In early June, most dependents of expatriates were evacuated, and on July 1, as BBC broadcasts predicted imminent war, Peter Jewell and most remaining expatriates left Nsukka. I followed two days later, taking a small boat across the Niger from Onitsha, with most of my research notes and a few personal belongings crammed into the single suitcase I was allowed to carry. On July 7, Nigerian federal forces invaded Biafra, with one of their first attacks directed against Nsukka. The gruesome war dragged on until January 1970, and I was not able to visit Nsukka again until 1972, after the completion of field studies on an entirely new Ph.D. project in Uganda. This was only the first of many times I was to be exposed to another reality: that human politics can have an overwhelming impact on biological research and conservation efforts in tropical countries.

UGANDA: KIBALE FOREST AND THE
CASE FOR RAIN FOREST CONSERVATION

It took me some time to settle firmly in a new course; the Biafran experience had been disquieting, and I had lost many belongings as well as a promising Ph.D. project. I tried to develop studies on the ecology of the small Chinese muntjac deer that were spreading through southern English woodlands after their escape from the Duke of Bedford's estate at Woburn. But my heart was not really in this project. The English woodlands were a cold and bleak contrast to the forests of West Africa; the muntjac themselves were nocturnal and secretive and harder to see than bushbabies; and landowners and their gamekeepers were often unhelpful and sometimes obstructive. I gave up this project after a year and spent a term as a temporary teacher in a grammar school. Then I helped edit an atlas of world wildlife for *Reader's Digest*,[27] and I began exploring ways to get back to Ph.D. studies in Africa.

During our stay in Nigeria, Jewell and I had learned of primate studies being made in nearby parts of Cameroon by Thomas Struhsaker, who worked for the Institute for Research in Animal Behavior, a joint operation of New York's Rockefeller University and the New York Zoological Society. In 1970 I heard from British primatologist Stephen Gartlan, who had joined Struhsaker in Cameroon, that Struhsaker was looking for a research assistant for a new study of colobus monkeys in western Uganda. Here was an opportunity not only to return to studies of African rain forest primates but to do it in an area that I had almost chosen four years previously, before opting for Nigeria. Through Gartlan I arranged to meet Struhsaker in London, and he subsequently offered me the position on his project.

On October 3, 1970, I flew into Uganda's Entebbe airport on the shores of Lake Victoria, and one week later I was at the Kanyawara Forest Station on the edge of the Kibale Forest Reserve (see map 4 and plate 7), where Struhsaker had established his base in a small house built by prospectors from a copper mining company. Struhsaker relished solitude and encouraged me to build my own house some distance away. This I did, erecting a wood-framed cabin clad with thatch and roofing sheets on the side of a small hill near the area of forest I had chosen for my research. While Struhsaker himself studied the behavior and ecology of Kibale red colobus monkeys, I made a comparative study of black-and-white colobus. My fieldwork extended until March 1972, and I made follow-up observations on visits in 1973 and 1974. These were the first prolonged studies of any of Kibale's primates, although zoologist Tim Clutton-Brock had spent two months looking at colobus in Kibale just before I arrived, following a sixteen-month study of red colobus at Jane Goodall's Gombe site in Tanzania.

Although our Kibale studies focused on the behavior of forest primates in relation to the availability of food in the forest, issues of conservation were never far from our minds. I traveled widely in Uganda and also visited Kenya and Tanzania, looking at other populations of colobus. In these travels I witnessed firsthand the management systems of many of East Africa's most famous national parks. But Ugandan

Map 4. Uganda, showing the location of Kibale in relation to some other major national parks in the western part of the country.

forest reserves, like those in Nigeria, were not strictly protected areas; most were managed by the government's Forest Department to supply timber, and some were also subject to *taungya* farming.[28]

Indeed, the Kibale Forest Reserve itself was being logged; when our studies began, many trees in the forest north of Kanyawara had already been harvested, and of those that remained many were being poisoned with arboricides in the hope that this would encourage the regrowth of relatively even-aged stands of commercially valuable trees. Struhsaker fought against this Forest Department management policy, not only on the grounds of the devastating effect that removal of most of the forest canopy was having on the forest wildlife (and especially its primates), but also because of the long-term dangers that arboricides posed to the system. To quantify these effects, Struhsaker organized a series of systematic primate censuses that he and I conducted in logged and unlogged forest. These indicated a clear decline in the abundance of most forest primates in heavily logged and poisoned forest compartments, although my own study species, the black-and-white colobus, was exceptional in that it tended to increase in numbers in logged forest.[29]

These observations and his previous experience in West Africa led Struhsaker to elaborate a case for rain forest conservation in tropical Africa as a whole. In an article he contributed in 1972 to the journal *Primates* at the request of the editors, Struhsaker pointed out that no part of Africa was still covered by endless tracts of undisturbed, primeval rain forest and that the conservation of those pieces of forest that did remain had been neglected.[30] He argued that examples of African rain forest should be conserved for several reasons: to provide reference standards against which changes in exploited forest could be measured; to act as reservoirs of plants and animals that could recolonize exploited areas, and that could one day be of economic value to humans; to permit basic scientific research on ecologically very complex systems; and to accommodate tourism. Struhsaker suggested that Western scientists in particular should be prepared to purchase examples of rain forest or arrange for long-term leases, if they wished to protect forest against commercial exploitation. And he recommended for special conservation attention four forests that he knew personally: the Taï Reserve in Côte d'Ivoire, the Douala-Edéa and Korup Reserves in Cameroon, and Kibale.[31]

In the light of future concern for the tropical rain forest, this was a far-sighted statement by Struhsaker, yet it also reflected long-held concerns of Western, and especially American, conservationists. Over a century before, in the 1850s, Henry David Thoreau had decried the destruction of the Maine woods by loggers and settlers and argued that the nation should formally preserve a "sample of wild nature," and that there should be "national preserves" in which bears and panthers could still exist "for inspiration and our own true recreation."[32] Growing American concern for the loss of wilderness, and particularly the urgings of John Muir, led eventually to the creation of Yosemite National Park in 1890 (the establishment of Yellowstone National Park in 1872 resulted more from a desire to safeguard its geysers and hot springs than from a desire to protect wilderness).[33] The protection of nature for its own sake, rather than for utilitarian reasons, was the essence of the American wilderness movement, and was a theme elaborated upon in Western countercultural critiques of materialism in the 1960s,[34] and which finds its voice today among "deep ecologists." Among other things, advocates of Deep Ecology argue that nature should be protected because of its intrinsic ("deep") value, and because of the psychological value to humans of integrating their lives more closely with those of other species.[35]

The contrast between the utilitarian approach to conservation common in Europe and the wilderness preservation approach, which continues to have many adherents in America, is probably in part a result of the different history of Western people's interaction with nature in the two continents. By the 1700s, there were few ecosystems in Europe that had not been heavily modified by cultivation, grazing, forest management, and urbanization; but in North America, Europeans met many systems that had been less intensively managed by a relatively low-density human population, and which therefore appeared more wild. Consider, for instance, François René de Chateaubriand's reaction to the wilderness of northern New York State after a visit in 1791–92: "In vain does the imagination try to roam at large midst [Europe's] cultivated plains . . . but in this deserted region the soul delights to bury and lose itself amidst boundless forests . . . to mix and confound . . . with the wild sublimities of Nature."[36]

When Struhsaker wrote his article for *Primates*, there were only a few strictly protected forests in the tropics; for instance, Malaysia's 1,677-square-mile Taman Negara park had been set up in the late 1930s (as the King George V National Park) to protect a rain forest ecosystem.[37] But no national park in Africa had been established with the protection of a rain forest ecosystem as its primary goal. African rain forests had not been completely ignored; European ecologists had expressed concern for the future of forests on Mount Nimba in Liberia, threatened by a mining operation, and IUCN had organized a mission to the Taï Forest, leading to its declaration as a national park in 1972.[38] But most African parks were almost entirely within the savanna zone and had been established primarily to protect populations of large game.

AFRICAN NATIONAL PARKS:
"CONVENTIONAL" CONSERVATION UNDER THREAT

The history of national parks in Africa was not unlike that in the United States. It is often said that colonial governments took land away from local people for parks, but this simplifies what actually happened. In fact, it was usually a small number of concerned individuals who developed the arguments for conservation of places they thought were very special; these people and their associates applied pressure on reluctant governments to take action. Kruger National Park came into being particularly as a result of the efforts of J. Stevenson-Hamilton, the warden of the Sabi Reserve that preceded the park.[39] In East Africa in the 1930s, Mervyn Cowie and others, concerned with growing pressures on wilderness areas, argued that there must be places where wild animals could exist without interference from human beings, but the governments of the British colonial territories opposed the establishment of national parks. Cowie finally stimulated action by writing to the editor of the *East African Standard* newspaper under the nom de plume of "Old Settler," advocating the destruction of all wild game in Kenya.[40] This produced an outcry, which eventually led to the establishment of a national parks board (with Cowie as Chairman) and to the gazetting of Nairobi National Park in 1946. Serengeti in Tanganyika followed in 1951, and the Queen Elizabeth and Murchison Falls National Parks in Uganda in 1952.

Seeing a range of East African parks for myself in the early 1970s strongly persuaded me of the efficacy of what is now sometimes called "conventional" or "exclusionary" conservation (the establishment of parks and strict reserves under the management of national government). The Ugandan national parks I visited were generally well run, and contained magnificent arrays of large mammals rarely seen in the countryside outside the parks. But I also recognized that in certain circumstances other kinds of conservation schemes could work. I had seen the Samburu-Isiolo Game Reserves in Kenya, where county councils managed the reserves and balanced local people's needs with wildlife conservation, and after John Mason and I visited the Ruwenzori Mountains (Mason had been a fellow graduate student at University College London and now worked for the U.K. Nature Conservancy Council), we had suggested that similar management could be applied to the Ruwenzoris, a major hunting ground of the Bakonjo people.[41]

It has become fashionable to claim that conventional conservation does not work in Africa because it excludes local communities from managing their own land. For a time, conventional conservation did indeed break down in Uganda, but this was not so much because it excluded local communities but because national government itself failed. While I was in the Queen Elizabeth National Park in January 1971, I learned of a coup d'état by the army against the widely disliked government of Milton Obote, who had become a dictator with sweeping powers. Obote had gone to a Commonwealth conference in Singapore, apparently leaving behind a plan that army commander Idi Amin would be arrested during his absence. Instead, Amin turned the tables on Obote. For more than a year after the coup, Uganda was relatively calm, but in August 1972 Amin announced a decree expelling Asians from the country. From this point, Amin's regime became increasingly brutal and repressive, while the economy deteriorated. Amin was finally deposed by a force of Tanzanian soldiers and Ugandan rebels in early 1979, an action precipitated by a Ugandan invasion of northern Tanzania in October 1978. Economic chaos continued, and after elections at the end of 1980 Obote came back to power, to be finally deposed by Yoweri Museveni in 1985, following five years of guerrilla war.[42]

It was during the near-anarchy following the Tanzanian invasion in 1979 that the wildlife of the national parks suffered most. Poaching in the parks had increased since 1973, and the poachers, often armed with automatic rifles, had included Amin's troops; after the 1979 invasion, it was the turn of Tanzanian soldiers to machine-gun large mammals.[43] In three and a half months, approximately 14,000 of the 46,500 large mammals in the Queen Elizabeth National Park were killed (at that time this park had become known as the Ruwenzori National Park). The elephant population of Uganda declined from an estimated thirty thousand in 1973 to two thousand in April 1980; rhinos became extinct. In 1980 Eric Edroma wrote in *Oryx* that Uganda's national parks "are littered with elephant carcasses, poachers' camps and meat-drying racks."[44] Through all these upheavals, Kibale survived relatively unscathed in large part because Struhsaker, despite all the dangers and difficulties he faced, maintained a field station and research program at Kanyawara and supported the efforts of government game guards. However, farmers encroached on the southern part of the reserve, and the elephant population was greatly reduced.[45] This is another example of the significant role that a dedicated individual can play in the creation and maintenance of a conservation area. Kanyawara has now grown into a major international research station, under the management of Makerere University, and in 1994 Kibale finally became a national park.

Given the effectiveness of national parks in many parts of Africa in the 1960s and early 1970s, what has led to the perception that conventional national parks do not work in Africa or in developing countries elsewhere? Jonathan Adams and Thomas McShane have argued that the Western national park concept cannot work in an African context.[46] I am not convinced by their argument, which I will return to in the next chapter. Yes, many African parks did become increasingly ineffective during the 1970s and 1980s. But I believe that this was not so much because of their inherent flaws, but because of the economic, social, and political problems that developed in Africa through this period. The steep rises in the price of oil in 1973 and 1979 (resulting from the Arab-Israeli and Iran-Iraq wars and the actions of the OPEC cartel)[47] were accompanied by increases in the prices of manufactured goods and declines in the prices of some agricultural and mineral commodities. The difficulties presented to African economies by these trends were often compounded by corrupt government and by civil war or disorder. As a consequence, there was a general decline in the resources devoted by governments to conservation. Of course, spending on conservation was by no means the only area of government activity to suffer; severe cuts also occurred in such important sectors as health care and education (so that enrollment of children in primary schools slid from 77 percent in 1980 to 70 percent in 1990).[48] Meanwhile, the human population of Africa continued to grow at a rate of almost 3 percent per annum.[49] This population growth, and the poor employment opportunities provided by dislocated economies, led to more and more people seeking to support themselves by subsistence agriculture, creating extra pressure on wildlife habitats. At the same time, world prices for wildlife products such as ivory and rhino horn increased, leading to greater poaching pressure. Therefore, while government efforts to protect parks and reserves declined, destructive pressures on these areas intensified.

INDIA: CONFLICTS OVER THE WESTERN GHAT FORESTS

After my last visit to Kibale in 1974, I did not return to Africa until 1979. While at Kanyawara in 1971 I had met Steven Green of Rockefeller University, who had come to Uganda to help run a field course for Rockefeller graduate students in ecology and animal behavior. In 1973, Green went to India with his research assistant Karen Minkowski to study the behavior of the endangered lion-tailed macaque (see plate 8) in the monsoon rain forests of the Western Ghat mountains. Steve Green wrote to me from India, offering me a postdoctoral fellowship through which I would continue research at his site when he completed his two-year project. Specifically, I would study the behavioral ecology of the Nilgiri langurs that shared the lion-tailed macaque's forest habitat. Like Africa's colobus monkeys, the langurs of Asia are able to digest foods rich in cellulose, such as tree leaves, by using a fermentation chamber in the forepart of their stomachs.[50] Going to India seemed like an excellent opportunity to test some of the ideas I had developed during my research at Kibale about the basis of food selection in these monkeys, and to learn about the tropical forests of a different continent.

I traveled to India in March 1975, and as soon as I arrived I found myself embroiled in a conservation problem. Green and Minkowski lived in a small stone house at the settlement of Kakachi on a large tea estate high in the Ashambu Hills of Tamil Nadu State (see plate 9). The Ashambus (also known as the Tinnevelly Hills or Agastyamalai range) are the most southerly portion of the Western Ghats. These wet and rugged hills are one of the last places in South India to support an extensive area of evergreen *shola* forest, and they are home to what may be the largest surviving population of lion-tailed macaques (estimated by Green and Minkowski to number 195 in 1975).[51]

Green's study groups of macaques used not only the government-managed Kalakkadu Reserved Forest adjacent to the tea estate but also forests growing on the estate lands (see map 5). The company that ran the estate, the Bombay Burmah Trading Corporation (BBTC), had leased these lands from the original owner, the zamindar (local ruler) of Singampatti, in 1929. Over the years, BBTC had cleared much of the forest on their land to plant extensive areas of tea, eucalyptus, and coffee; in other areas the forest understory had been cleared and planted with cardamom. Forest was still being clear-cut when Green arrived in Singampatti, and some of the cleared areas were being planted with eucalyptus. The main advantage to the tea company of the continued felling was the income derived from selling timber. But the forest being removed was lion-tailed macaque habitat, and it was especially important habitat because it provided a link between the protected forests that lay on either side of the estate. In 1962 the Papanasam Reserved Forest to the north of the tea estate, together with the remaining former zamindari forests of Singampatti, had been constituted as a wildlife sanctuary (the Mundanthurai Tiger Sanctuary), and at the urging of Green and Indian conservationists, the Kalakkadu Reserved Forest to the south was also being considered for sanctuary status. Breaking the forested link between these two areas would further fragment the already precariously small and scattered population of lion-tailed macaques remaining in the wild in South India.

It was evident to Green that the timber company that BBTC had contracted to clear some of the Singampatti forest was breaking forestry laws (for instance, by cutting too close to rivers), while men brought in by the loggers were poaching deer and Nilgiri langurs. Green informed

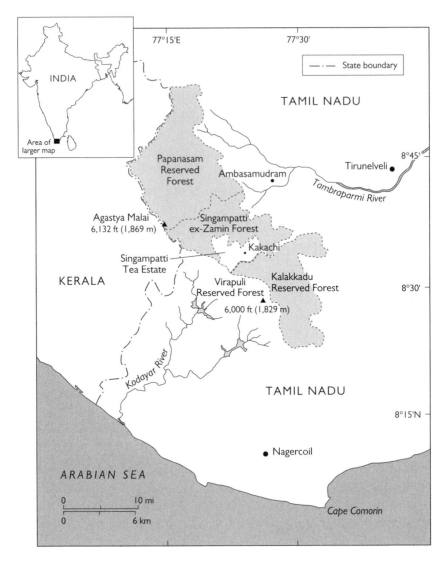

Map 5. The southern tip of India, showing the location of the Singampatti tea estate in relation to protected forests mentioned in the text.

BBTC managers about this, and he also stressed the conservation significance of the forests that were being cut. He began discussions with company officials and the Tamil Nadu Forest Department to try to stop illegal acts by the timber contractor, as well as to secure an agreement that a
significant forest corridor would be preserved through the tea plantations. But the pace of logging accelerated, and although the tea company
managers expressed their concern for wildlife conservation, they also
noted the importance of the logging to the company's profitability.
Meanwhile, Green and Minkowski were accused by the police—probably at the instigation of the logging contractor—of being spies, and
heard rumors of threats to their lives. Their walkie-talkie radios, with
which they communicated in the forest, had to be surrendered to the police, and although they were able to continue their work they kept out of
sight of the timber operations.[52] By the time Green left Kakachi in April
1975, no formal agreement had been reached with the tea company to
halt the logging.

At this point, I took over management of the primate research project,
as well as Green's efforts to save the forest corridor through the tea plantations. I was fortunate to find a strong ally in Dilnavaz Variava of the
Indian branch of the World Wildlife Fund; I monitored the situation on
the ground and reported to Variava, who applied pressure on central
and state governments and on the BBTC. This, though, put me in a difficult position; I was living on the BBTC estate as a guest of the estate
managers, while opposing the company's felling policy.

Soon, political developments at the highest level brought significant relief to the forests of the Ashambu Hills and the lion-tailed macaques.
While in India, Steven Green had been introduced by the respected ornithologist Salim Ali to the Director of the Prime Minister's Secretariat,
Salman Haidar.[53] The Prime Minister was Indira Gandhi, who had been in
office since 1966. On June 25, 1975, Indira Gandhi declared a state of emergency, designed to counter mounting opposition to her regime and a peti-
tion to bar her from office; she arrested many of her opponents and became a virtual dictator.[54] A few months later, Haidar saw a copy of
Green's final report, with its conservation recommendations, and brought
it to the attention of the Prime Minister. Like her father, Jawaharlal Nehru,

Indira Gandhi had a strong interest in wildlife conservation,[55] and she expressed her personal concern that immediate action be taken to protect lion-tailed macaques. This concern was translated into concrete action early in the following year. On January 31, 1976, the Prime Minister and her cabinet dissolved the elected Tamil Nadu Assembly, dominated by the opposition Dravida Munnetra Kazhagam (DMK) party, citing "maladministration, corruption and misuse of power for partisan ends."[56] Tamil Nadu was placed under President's Rule, bringing the state under the direct control of Delhi and therefore giving Indira Gandhi great authority over the running of the state. In February 1976 the Tamil Nadu Forest Department ordered a halt to clear-cutting on the BBTC estate, and in March the state government declared the Kalakkadu Reserved Forest a Wildlife Sanctuary.

The role played by the Prime Minister in the establishment of the Kalakkadu Sanctuary was reported by the widely read newspaper the *Hindu* on May 16, 1976. On May 29, the general manager of the BBTC Singampatti estates called me to a meeting and informed me of his company's view that Steve Green and I, through our efforts to stop the felling of forest on their plantation, had adversely affected the economics of their business and had abused their hospitality; we were no longer welcome on the estate, but we would not be physically evicted as this would leave the company open to further attack. So I was able to stay on at Kakachi, albeit in an uncomfortable social atmosphere; my house, for instance, overlooked the estate's small golf course, at which the managers frequently met for recreation. In November 1976, soon before I finally left Singampatti, I learned that the BBTC had made a formal agreement with the Tamil Nadu Forest Department to preserve a forested corridor through the tea plantation.

As my knowledge of the Ashambu Hills and their conservation problems had grown, I had begun to develop a proposal for the management of the hill range as a single ecological unit. Even the Kalakkadu and Mundanthurai sanctuaries included only a part of the range's rain forest and its lion-tailed macaque population. Another important link between the existing sanctuaries, the Virapuli Reserved Forest, had no strict protection; I had seen that it had been badly damaged by the construction of a large hydroelectric dam in the hills at Kodayar, and that it was being logged. I argued that all these forests, as well as adjacent areas in neighboring Kerala State, should come under integrated management as a Biosphere Reserve or national park.

When my studies of langur ecology came to an end in December 1976, I handed over the research project to an Indian graduate student, Rauf Ali. Ali was studying for a Ph.D. at the University of Bristol in England; he was supported by Green's grant and supervised by the ethologist John Crook, who had once been a research associate of Rauf's uncle, Salim Ali. While I analyzed my field data in the United States and in England, I also continued to make plans for an extensive survey of the Ashambu Hills, a survey that could produce the information needed to establish and manage the conservation area I had in mind.

I went back to India in July 1978 to finalize these plans, visiting central government offices in New Delhi and many people and sites in the south of the country, including the Mundanthurai and Kalakkadu sanctuaries. I arranged for the survey to be conducted by a joint team from the University of Madurai and University College London, with Rauf Ali and me as advisers. Over the next two years I helped with efforts to raise funds for the survey, finalize the plans for fieldwork, and obtain the crucial approval of the Indian central government. However, funds proved hard to come by, and Indian government approval was never forthcoming, perhaps in part because of the close involvement of foreigners in the project. Although the reasons for a lack of approval were never made clear, I finally learned in November 1980 that the project would not be sanctioned.[57]

Meanwhile, Rauf Ali continued his work in the area. Because of the tea company's hostile attitude, he was forced to make his base at the foot of the hills in the Mundanthurai sanctuary, where he studied the social behavior of bonnet macaques. But he continued monitoring the conservation situation in the Ashambu Hills and helped to stop new dam- and road-building projects in the sanctuaries. Now based in Pondicherry, Ali has maintained his involvement in the area to the present day. I was able to visit Mundanthurai and Kalakkadu with him in November 1995, and found that the two sanctuaries were now managed as one unit (the

Kalakkad-Mundanthurai Tiger Reserve), a unit vigorously protected by Promode Kant of the national conservation effort Project Tiger. The connecting forests of the upper elevations of Virapuli had not only escaped serious damage but had now been added to the Tiger Reserve, not because they were important for tigers, but because of their role in biodiversity conservation generally. The forest where we had studied lion-tailed macaques and Nilgiri langurs twenty years earlier was still intact and was being used for research on forest ecology by students from the University of Pondicherry (see plates 30 and 31).

LESSONS AND THOUGHTS FROM 1966 TO 1978

I learned many lessons in Africa and India in this period, although it has taken another twenty years for the full significance of some of these lessons to become clear. Especially in Nigeria and India I witnessed the growing pressures on small surviving areas of rain forest, and I gained a better appreciation of the large-scale demographic, economic, and political forces that were responsible for many of these pressures. But I also saw that the effects of these forces could be successfully countered, and that "conventional" protection of tropical ecosystems could work; that even in densely populated countries like Uganda and India, fine examples of natural ecosystems could be conserved by strong efforts to combat logging, cultivation, and hunting. The chances of success in conserving an area seemed to be greatly improved if individuals who had a special concern for it were prepared to fight a long battle for its protection (as witnessed by the efforts of Mervyn Cowie on behalf of the Nairobi National Park, Tom Struhsaker on behalf of Kibale Forest Reserve, and Rauf Ali on behalf of Kalakkad-Mundanthurai Tiger Reserve). It was apparent that scientists studying rain forests could play an important role in stimulating conservation efforts, and that conservation was most effective where a long-term research program existed, with resident scientists. Long-lasting conservation success was often best assured if these scientists included citizens of the country concerned.

My early fieldwork in Africa and India only reinforced my feelings about the intrinsic value of nature, feelings that had grown out of my childhood fascination with animals. I understood better what Thoreau and Muir had argued in the nineteenth century, that to observe wild nature can be a profoundly inspiring aesthetic experience that can satisfy deep human needs; therefore, nature conservation is not *against* humanity, but in the long run is something that can greatly enrich people's lives. From my fieldwork I was well aware of the immediate pressures on wild nature in the tropics from peasant farmers and hunters, and from larger-scale commercial activities. I realized that these pressures could not be ignored, but I was also strongly persuaded that ultimately the lives of all people—in both developing and developed countries—would be diminished if most of the remaining tropical rain forest and its wildlife were allowed to disappear. I found myself much in agreement with an argument that I had read in 1962 by Peter Scott, the first Chairman of the World Wildlife Fund. After visiting Africa in the early 1960s, Scott had written:

> For conserving wildlife and wilderness there are three categories of reasons: ethical, aesthetic, and economic, with the last one (at belly level) lagging far behind the other two. The first argument arises from questions like this: "Does man have the right to wipe out an animal species just because it is of no practical use to him, or is a nuisance to him?" . . . The aesthetic case is a simple one: "people enjoy animals; they find them beautiful and interesting, and often experience a re-creation of the spirit when they see them. To wipe them out . . . deprives present and future people of a basic enjoyment." . . . To the large numbers of people in the world who are protein hungry, the economic arguments will inevitably be the strongest, even though they may be the least enlightened. But let those who are not hungry be quite clear in their minds that if conservation succeeds mainly on the economic case, man will once more, as so often in his history, be doing the right thing for the wrong reasons. . . . The time may not be far distant when all men will recognize the value of wildlife and wilderness to mankind, and will be agreed that these natural treasures must be preserved in perpetuity just as certainly as the great art treasures of the world.[58]

Although such views have strongly influenced my thinking to the present time, they are no longer very fashionable views in the larger conservation movement. When my direct involvement in research and conservation efforts in South India ended in 1978, international conservation policy was on the threshold of a fundamental change. As I discuss in the next chapter, the new policy would attempt to find a compromise between the demands of the swelling populations of humans in developing countries and the concerns of conservationists to protect populations of nonhuman species threatened by these demands. The World Wildlife Fund, which in its early days under Peter Scott had emphasized the protection of nature for its own sake, was to play one of the key roles in the formulation of the new policy, which encouraged an unlikely marriage between conservation and development.

THREE

Conservation Falls in Love with Economic Development

In September 1970, just before I began my studies of colobus monkeys in Uganda, a meeting took place in Rome that signaled an important new trend in conservation. This meeting, which laid the groundwork for future coordinated international conservation planning, involved representatives of the International Union for the Conservation of Nature and Natural Resources (IUCN), the Food and Agriculture Organization of the United Nations (FAO), the World Bank, and the Conservation Foundation (of the United States). The Chairman of the meeting, held at FAO headquarters, was IUCN's Director General, Gerardo Budowski, who called for conservation to be "considered as an indispensable ingredient in development planning."[1]

This chapter will review the background to this Rome meeting and some of the major events that followed from it and resulted in a tight embrace of development agencies by conservation planners. The main thesis of this book is that this embrace has led to the design of inherently flawed conservation projects in West Africa and elsewhere, projects that can end up decreasing rather than increasing the chances for the long-term survival of wildlife populations. This chapter will also examine the origins of the current enthusiasm for "community-based" conservation efforts and discuss the dangers of this approach, which appears to be based in part on the myth that, left to their own devices, poor rural people in the tropics will inevitably act as good wildlife conservationists. The emphasis placed by international organizations on linking conservation with development has arisen not because it is clearly the only way to protect nature, but rather because of a particular series of historical events and because of the involvement of particular individuals in the planning of conservation strategies. Moreover, as we will see, political compromises and financial expediency have played major roles in the process of linking conservation with development.

MAX NICHOLSON AND THE UTILITARIAN
APPROACH TO WILDLIFE CONSERVATION

The 1970 Rome meeting was arranged by Max Nicholson (see plate 10), the man who had helped to establish both the World Wildlife Fund (WWF) and the conservation course I had attended at University College London; Nicholson was now head of the International Biological Programme's section on the Conservation of Terrestrial Communities and an influential voice in international conservation. Before joining the IBP, Nicholson had been Director General (from 1952 to 1966) of the U.K. Nature Conservancy, following ten years of work as a senior administrator in the British government. His civil servant's approach to conservation was to have a profound effect on international policy. His views about conservation at that time are summarized in his book *The Environmental Revolution*, published in 1970.[2] In this book, Nicholson argued that it was becoming impossible to make distinctions between ecology, conservation, and human affairs, and he talked of the need for professional, international planning for conservation that would permit "beneficial natural processes to operate to the fullest extent compatible with whatever justifiable human demands may need to be satisfied." It would be unfair to suggest that Nicholson did not have a strong and genuine interest in nature and its conservation. He had long been interested in birds, publishing *Birds in England* as a student at Oxford in 1926, and going on to become one of the major authors of a benchmark series, *The Birds of the Western Palearctic* (1977–94); he was also a prime mover in the establishment of the British Trust for Ornithology.[3] Yet it seems clear that Nicholson relished administration and politics, and he evidently believed strongly in the importance of integrating conservation into the planning of human economic development.

Nicholson's views were not unique, of course; they were shared by an increasing number of wildlife managers and other conservation professionals. In the two decades following World War II, international conservation efforts, especially in Africa, had concentrated on the establishment of protected areas such as national parks and on the management of wildlife populations in these protected areas. Like John Muir, Aldo Leopold, and members of the wilderness movement in the United States, individuals such as Mervyn Cowie in Kenya and Bernhard Grzimek in Tanganyika had perceived ever-mounting pressures on wild nature in Africa and argued that it should be strictly protected for its own sake, because of its *intrinsic value* and not because of the use to which it might be put by people.[4] But during the 1960s, voices in the international conservation community such as Nicholson's were increasingly heard arguing that wise use (including sustained-yield exploitation) rather than strict protection was the only management strategy likely to ensure the long-term survival of many wildlife populations.[5] This change of emphasis seems to have resulted both from the evolution of thinking among conservationists and from public concern about the growing pressures on nature arising from human population growth and economic development. Especially in rich northern countries, citizens were becoming more vocal in their protests about the pollution of the human environment from radioactive fallout, the indiscriminate use of pesticides, and the effects on people and nature of large dam and mining projects.[6]

It was against this background that the 1970 Rome meeting took place, a meeting at which it was clear that IUCN had become a strong supporter of the human-use-orientated view of conservation promoted by Nicholson. This was not always IUCN's position, however. The organization had begun life as the International Union for the Protection of Nature (IUPN), following a conference at Brunnen in Switzerland in 1947. This conference recommended that the new organization establish an international code for the protection of nature and work to establish a set of international reserves. The published proceedings of the conference suggest strongly that the participants' main concern was to protect nature because of its intrinsic value, and that they saw protection as an urgent need because the destruction of wild things and wild places had accelerated during and after World War II.[7] The IUPN became the International Union for the Conservation of Nature and Natural Resources in 1956. As the organization and its plans for international conservation projects had grown, so had its need for money. This need led to the founding of the World Wildlife Fund, to which I referred in chapter 2.[8]

The initial conception for WWF was that it would make national appeals; these appeals would raise funds that the international organization would direct toward conservation projects identified by IUCN as having high priority. The WWF came into being in September 1961 and began its work at IUCN's new headquarters at Morges in Switzerland, on the shore of Lake Geneva, just west of Lausanne. In the same year, the first national appeal began in the United Kingdom. As WWF grew, many of the national appeals argued for greater autonomy and the right to spend some of the money they raised on projects of their own selection. In 1986, WWF International renamed itself the World Wide Fund for Nature; most national branches followed suit, but the American and Canadian branches retained the name World Wildlife Fund. Although WWF now operates independently of IUCN, the international headquarters of the two are still in close proximity in Switzerland (since 1979 at Gland, a few miles down the shore of Lake Geneva from Morges), and their policies have evolved in synchrony, each moving progressively away from a position that nature should be protected for its own intrinsic value, toward the position that conservation should be integrated with efforts to satisfy basic human needs.

The collaboration between representatives of international conservation and development agencies that Max Nicholson had helped initiate in 1970 was taken an important step further by the United Nations Conference on the Human Environment, held in Stockholm in June 1972. The conference was apparently proposed by Sweden, which had become increasingly concerned about the effects on its territory of pollutants, such as pesticides, heavy metals, and acid rain, that were originating in other countries.[9] In an influential report prepared for this conference, published as *Only One Earth*, Barbara Ward and René Dubos focused on issues of pollution, population growth, and development; less than two pages of the report was devoted to wilderness preservation, and species other than *Homo sapiens* were hardly mentioned.[10] The report ended with a utopian call for more cooperative global planning for health, education, farming, city services, and pollution control, and the transfer of more resources from rich to poor countries. Max Nicholson was one of 152 international consultants who contributed ideas to this report, the tone of which echoes his earlier call for more international planning, while adding emphasis to the needs and problems of developing countries. This emphasis on bringing development planning into environmental management was reflected in the IUCN Director General's address to the United Nations conference, in which he talked of the need to plan for "conservation for development."[11]

The Stockholm conference led to the founding of the United Nations Environment Programme (UNEP). In 1974, UNEP was installed in new headquarters in Nairobi, and in 1975 Mostafa K. Tolba was appointed Executive Director of the organization. Tolba, an Egyptian microbiologist, had been an administrator and bureaucrat since the late 1950s. In the same year, UNEP made funds available to IUCN to help run the IUCN secretariat and employ consultants, and IUCN announced that it was formulating a World Conservation Strategy.[12]

The link between IUCN and UNEP was to grow even closer in the next few years. By the beginning of 1976, IUCN had run up a budget deficit of 700,000 Swiss francs (equivalent at that time to about $268,000). The new acting Director General, Duncan Poore, held meetings with WWF and UNEP and secured from them guarantees of increased support.[13] In the same year, Maurice Strong (who had been Secretary General of the

Stockholm conference), was elected Chairman of the IUCN's governing council; he announced that one of his immediate aims was to generate greater support for the organization from governments, aid agencies, and the world of business.[14] On July 1, 1977, David Munro was appointed as the new IUCN Director General. He had been a special adviser to Tolba at UNEP and before that had worked for many years with the Canadian government, holding senior positions in the Wildlife Service, the Department of Indian Affairs and Northern Development, and the Department of the Environment.[15]

CONSERVATION AS A MEANS TO SUSTAINABLE DEVELOPMENT:
FRAMING THE WORLD CONSERVATION STRATEGY

As IUCN, in collaboration with WWF, now embarked seriously on the production of the World Conservation Strategy under Munro's direction, it was acting very much at the behest of UNEP, which had commissioned the Strategy and largely financed its production, providing $1,625,000 for this purpose in 1979–80.[16] The senior writer of the Strategy was Robert Allen, a British specialist in ecology and anthropology who was already writing about the importance of sustainable development when he joined IUCN in 1975.[17] A few years earlier, Allen (later to become Robert Prescott-Allen) had spent three months living with a hunter-gardener society in Ethiopia, and in 1973 he published *Natural Man*, which focused on hunter-gatherer and hunter-gardener societies and noted that they appeared to live healthy lives in harmony with their environments.[18]

The stage was clearly set, therefore, for a major conservation document that would put humans first, and in the second draft of the World Conservation Strategy, circulated in July 1978, the emphasis on sustainable development and conservation for utilitarian purposes was very clear. The first paragraph opened with the statement "The chief impediment to sustainable development is lack of conservation," and went on to define conservation as "the management of human use of the biosphere, and of the ecosystems and species that compose it, so that they may yield the greatest sustainable benefit to present generations while maintaining their potential to meet the needs and aspirations of future generations."[19] In 1980, the Strategy was formally launched by IUCN, UNEP, and WWF;[20] Munro proclaimed it "a response to the need to make development sustainable."[21]

It is understandable that people's concerns about the effects of population growth, industrialization, and the fruits of technological advances would lead to pressures on governments to pay more attention to safeguarding the human environment. To that extent, the need to take a more conservation-orientated approach to development planning is obvious. The need to regard nature conservation as an aspect of development is less apparent; yet by 1980, Peter Scott, one of WWF's founders, was able to write about development as a means of achieving conservation.[22] This change in attitude was a result not only of a shift in thinking by professional conservationists but also of a perception that compromises had to be made that took into account financial needs and political pressures.

The political compromise involved in the World Conservation Strategy—which argued that conservation should be regarded as an integral part of economic development in poor countries—was a response to the opinion that conservation was an idea that only the rich could hold, and that the promotion of conservation policy by richer, developed nations was a device by which these nations could delay the development of poorer ones and maintain their hegemony. Poorer countries had been signaling their concern that global agreements on controlling pollution could hold back their own economic development, and Indira Gandhi had stated at the Stockholm conference in 1972 that poverty was the greatest polluter.[23] Evidence that IUCN was concerned to defuse allegations that it represented a rich elite is found in a glossy illustrated booklet published to promote the World Conservation Strategy; in this publication, IUCN argued that it was a misconception to think that "conservation is concerned only with wildlife and wilderness and is thus a pursuit of an elite minority unburdened by the pressing problems suffered by a majority of the world's people." Rather, it continued, "a lack of conservation is a main cause of such problems as inflation and unemployment, hunger and disease."[24]

So, as influential international conservation organizations moved away from the position that wilderness and wildlife should be protected for their own sake, the leading voices in conservation were increasingly those of professional public-policy planners and bureaucrats, rather than practicing naturalists and biologists. Conservation organizations began to employ more economists and sociologists and, enthusiastically embracing the idea that conservation and development should go hand in hand, more actively sought funds from bilateral and multilateral development organizations, or "donor agencies" (agencies that give or lend poorer countries money raised by taxing the citizens of richer countries).

As they grew larger and more bureaucratized, and as the planners they employed formulated more, and more grandiose, schemes, the conservation organizations' need for money also grew. From the outset, the liaison between conservation organizations and development agencies had to a significant extent been a relationship based on financial expediency, and this part of the relationship now inevitably deepened. Obvious sources of large quantities of money for conservation were the international development agencies such as UNEP, the World Bank, the Directorate-General for Development of the European Commission (the administrative arm of what is now the European Union), the U.S. Agency for International Development (USAID), the U.K. Overseas Development Administration (ODA, recently renamed the Department for International Development), and Deutsche Gesellschaft für Technische Zusammenarbeit (GTZ—the German technical assistance agency). To win the support of these agencies and of national governments in developing countries, conservation planners further de-emphasized the idea of protecting nature for its own sake.

But while many conservationists became eager to enfold themselves in the embrace of development agencies and their money, there has been less evidence that those concerned with promoting economic development have become ardent conservationists. For instance, in defining economic development, a recent textbook on the subject said nothing about conservation, and stated that economic development was best defined as the process whereby the real per capita income of a country increases over a long period of time, along with the number of features of "modernization" it exhibits, such as social equality. The poor economic performance of Africa was ascribed not to poor conservation policies but to such factors as an inflated public sector, underinvestment in rural infrastructure, political instability, and the breakdown of the rule of law.[25]

And what of the policies of the World Bank, the most important and certainly the richest international agency charged with promoting economic development? Has it truly embraced the linkage of conservation and development? As a consequence of the widespread criticism brought to bear on the bank during the 1980s, when the environmental devastation being caused by many of the projects it was supporting became known, the bank has tried to bring more consideration of conservation into its activities. In 1986, for instance, it adopted a policy requiring "wildlands" protection to be considered in economic planning.[26]

Recently, the bank has become more closely involved in conservation through its major role in the "Global Environment Facility" (GEF). The origin of the GEF has been traced to a 1987 report from the World Commission on Environment and Development (a commission chaired by Norwegian Prime Minister Gro Harlem Brundtland), which strongly endorsed the World Conservation Strategy's emphasis on sustainable development.[27] The Brundtland Report called attention to a lack of funding for conservation strategies that "improve the resource base for development," and this call eventually led to creation of a special fund that would be administered by the World Bank with the assistance of the United Nations Development Programme (UNDP) and UNEP.[28] The GEF, and the very large sums of money available to it (the initial fund was $1.5 billion), created high expectations, which have been only partly fulfilled. The World Bank itself has maintained tight control of the funds, which have been disbursed only slowly. In the first two years of the GEF, for instance, only $2.8 million was spent on actual biodiversity conservation projects, compared to $20 million spent on administration. As with other World Bank projects, the GEF has tended to support large government-sponsored and bureaucratized projects with a three-to-five-year time span, rather than small, long-term nongovernmental efforts.[29]

THE RISE OF COMMUNITY-BASED CONSERVATION

In its original form, the World Conservation Strategy was very much a call to governments to adopt policies that involved the careful, regulated use of resources. The Strategy was seen as an evolving plan that would be revised as new knowledge was gained and values changed. In the decade following the initial launch of the plan, the values of the institutions that had promulgated the strategy did indeed change. And so a second World Conservation Strategy Project was launched, again directed by David Munro, and again with Robert Allen as the senior writer. The result was *Caring for the Earth: A Strategy for Sustainable Living*, published by IUCN, UNEP, and WWF in 1991.[30]

Caring for the Earth was prepared in part for yet another United Nations conference, the Conference on Environment and Development (the "Earth Summit") held in Rio de Janeiro in June 1992. The revised strategy was even more strongly orientated toward improving human well-being than the first, and it laid particular emphasis on the concept of "sustainable living." *Caring for the Earth* espoused the idea of "cross-sectoral" planning by national governments (especially through the establishment of high-level units that would integrate conservation and development), but it also suggested levels of action additional to those of national governments. It argued the need for changes in personal attitudes and practices, and it argued that "communities and local groups" provided the easiest channel for people to take action to create "securely-based sustainable societies." "Communities" had featured only marginally in the first Strategy; now they were given a prominent role.

Increasingly, "conventional" conservation—the establishment of parks and similar protected areas by national governments—was being said to have failed in developing countries, particularly in Africa, and an obvious remedy to this failure was held to be an approach at a more local level. Three main factors seem to have influenced this thinking. First, as Clark Gibson and Stuart Marks have argued in an insightful review, economic conditions led to a weakening in the effectiveness of conventional conservation in parts of Africa in the 1970s and 1980s; budgets for government wildlife departments declined (making law enforcement less effective), rural poverty increased, and the value of game products such as meat and rhino horn increased (making hunting a more attractive occupation to rural residents).[31] Second, it had long been obvious that conservation efforts worked best if they had strong local support. And third, development planners had become increasingly involved in conservation, and for these planners "community development" was already an established practice.

In a critical review of the community approach to economic development, James Midgley has traced the concept to the 1944 British government report *Mass Education in the Colonies,* which advocated the promotion of agriculture, health, and other social services through local self-help, and which led to the establishment of community development programs in many African territories.[32] This, says Midgley, directly influenced the design of American and United Nations aid programs. It seems that the original enthusiasm for community development was as much the result of a shortage of government money as the result of ideology,[33] but the notion soon became quite deeply ideological, reflecting beliefs derived from social and political theories about how societies should be organized: "central to its rationale is a reaction against the centralization, bureaucratization, rigidity and remoteness of the state."[34]

The idea of the community as a basic unit of organization and cultural transmission in human society is, of course, even older than the notion of community development. After its initial introduction at the end of the nineteenth century, the community concept had a resurgence in the social sciences the 1950s.[35] Among social scientists and conservationists, the concept of "community" often seems to be rooted in the idea of a small, cohesive, egalitarian, and self-sufficient group, which may be fighting for justice against powerful external forces.[36] Yet, as Midgley has noted, the concept has remained poorly defined, although it is exemplified by two pervasive archetypal images: the traditional African village and the semifeudal Asian or Latin American peasant settlement.[37] In fact, there seems to be little hard evidence that real people in African villages are more likely than others to readily work together for the common good; like groups of people anywhere, individuals within a village often have very different interests, and it is usual for them to be differentiated in terms of status, income, and power.[38] After in-depth studies of cocoa farmers in Ghana, for instance, Polly Hill has observed that the egalitarian African village is a "Golden Age fallacy."[39] Indeed, there is a good deal of evidence that difficult times often promote division rather than cohesion in small communities: a classic case in Africa is provided by the Ik of northern Uganda, as described by Colin Turnbull.[40] In Europe, socialism led Romanian villages to become collections of autonomous, competitive households whose interests rarely overlapped with those of the village as a whole.[41]

Although the term "community" as it has come to be used by conservationists seems to be based on a mythic image of an African village, *Caring for the Earth* gives the concept a loose definition: "the people of a local administrative unit, such as a municipality; of a cultural or ethnic group, such as a band or tribe; or of a local urban or rural area, such as the people of a particular neighbourhood or valley" (in other words, a relatively small group of people). While stressing the importance of working with local communities, *Caring for the Earth* does acknowledge that communities vary greatly and may be divided by conflict; this acknowledgment is followed by the somewhat paternalistic advice that "a process of community-building may be necessary."[42] In other words, if a community of the right kind does not already exist for appropriate conservation action, it must be created by outsiders.

The World Conservation Strategy has therefore helped to foster the now widely held view that conservation, at least in poor countries in the tropics, should be viewed as but one component of a process of rural development that is most effectively addressed at a local level. This approach has strong paternalistic and political features. It is paternalistic in that the process is fostered and generally funded by outsiders from industrialized societies who wish to improve the lot of people they regard as less fortunate and enlightened than themselves, and political in that the "empowering" of local people is increasingly stressed.[43]

ANOTHER MYTH: THE SAVAGE AS CONSERVATIONIST

I consider this new conservation thinking to be potentially dangerous for populations of wild plants and animals, not only because it emphasizes the promotion of human economic development, a process that generally has had devastating consequences for nature, but also because it promotes a second myth, additional to the one that views rural people in tropical countries as typically living in cohesive, highly cooperative communities. This second myth is that people in these communities lived in harmony with nature until they came under the influence of western industrialized societies, and they would do so again if they were only given the chance (and a little outside help). For instance, the document *African Biodiversity: Foundation for the Future,* published in 1993 by the USAID-sponsored Biodiversity Support Program (in which WWF-US plays a major role), states, "In many traditional African societies, natural resource use tended to cause little damage to biodiversity, in part because of low population density. In addition, these societies fostered belief systems as well as social norms that encouraged or even enforced limits to exploitation."[44] Several chapters in the book *Voices from Africa: Local Perspectives on Conservation,* published in 1993 by WWF-US, claim that Africans lived in harmony with wildlife before the colonial era.[45]

In fact, there is little robust evidence that traditional African societies (or indeed "traditional" societies anywhere in the world) have been natural conservationists. On the contrary, wherever people have had the tools, techniques, and opportunities to exploit natural systems they have done so. This exploitation has typically been for maximum short-term yield without regard for sustainability; unless the numbers of people have been very low, or their harvesting techniques inefficient, such exploitation has usually led to marked resource depletion or species extinction.[46] There are instances where strict hunting controls have existed, but these have typically been in hierarchical societies where leaders have wished to control the access of others to resources, especially the rarest and most prized resources (such as the skins of large carnivores). Many areas of Africa did have large game populations at the beginning of the colonial era, but this was apparently more a consequence of low human population densities resulting from trypanosomiasis and slave-raiding than because game populations were intentionally harvested on a sustained-yield basis. Colonial rule, although it brought foreign control, also brought an end to most slave-raiding, it introduced a measure of political stability, and it led to improvements in public health. As human populations consequently expanded and settled new areas in the early decades of this century, large mammals were often eliminated by rural people, at least in areas where colonial game laws were not enforced or where effective protected areas were not established.[47]

There are many examples from all over the world of "traditional" peoples wiping out animal populations, especially when they have invaded previously unpopulated territories such as Madagascar and the islands of the South Pacific. Kent Redford, in an article focusing on traditional cultures in Amazonia, "The Ecologically Noble Savage," summarized recent evidence to the effect that before contact with Europeans, Amazonian people had had tremendous impacts on the forest and its wildlife and "behaved as humans do now: they did whatever they had to to feed themselves and their families."[48] Redford traces the myth of the noble savage to European Utopians and Romantics such as Thomas More and Jean Jacques Rousseau. Redford acknowledges that indigenous people have often had better and more sustainable ways of using tropical ecosystems than new settlers, but he argues that their techniques worked only because they had low population densities and limited involvement with market economies. Today, there are virtually no groups of people not involved to some extent with a global market economy, and the numbers of people in tropical countries continue to increase rapidly. Even if noble savages did once exist, their time is past and there is little point in conservationists trying to recreate them.

Kent Redford's colleague John Robinson, who is now head of international programs at the Wildlife Conservation Society, has argued cogently that *Caring for the Earth* presents a simplistic vision of the linkages between conservation and development, and that it "optimistically generalizes the concept of the noble savage to all of humanity."[49] He criticizes the manifesto for its emphasis on the improvement of human well-being rather than on the conservation of biodiversity as a whole. As he points out, sustainable use of part of the earth is not equivalent to conserving the biological diversity of that area; sustainably harvested maize fields can support many people at a higher material quality of life than can the same area of tropical rain forest. Therefore, programs aimed at producing sustainable development will not lead automatically to improvements in wildlife conservation; instead, they are very likely to lead to loss of wild habitats and species.

Nor will "empowering" local people necessarily lead to better conservation than is practiced under the aegis of higher levels of government. As Katrina Brandon and Michael Wells pointed out in a broad-ranging review of integrated conservation and development projects, local people, once fully empowered, might well decide to use resources in an unsustainable way, based on their present wants rather than possible future needs.[50] After all, most people in the world have always consumed rather than conserved resources, and Africa is no different from other areas in this respect. For example, after a careful study of local hunters in the Dzanga Forest of the Central African Republic, Andrew Noss concluded that these hunters were "opportunistic predators" rather than conservationists and would readily switch to other activities if their hunting drove prey populations to extinction.[51] In any case, foreign-funded development projects are probably a poor means of bringing more empowerment to local communities. As Mark Pires concluded from a study of community-based natural-resource management projects in Senegal, such projects do little to change deep-seated social and cultural practices, and by creating dependency on outside donors, they reduce people's inclination to solve their own problems.[52]

As I have argued here, the embracing of development by wildlife conservation organizations has not occurred because human economic development is clearly the most effective way to save threatened nature; it has occurred in large measure as a consequence of financial expediency and political compromises.[53] Yet the development approach is now widely accepted as the best, if not the only, way to effect conservation. Perhaps this is not just because of the money it has made available to conservationists but also because of the powerful effect that myths can exert on our actions.

PROSPECTIVE

The following four chapters will review my involvement with forest conservation projects in three West African countries: Sierra Leone,

Nigeria, and Ghana. These projects all began after the publication of the World Conservation Strategy in 1980. In Sierra Leone, the project involved establishment of a wildlife sanctuary at Tiwai Island. In describing the history of the Tiwai project, I will illustrate some of the problems that arose when we attempted to develop a conservation area in conjunction with local communities, and I will show how vulnerable such projects are to larger political and economic forces. Recounting my experiences in Nigeria and Ghana, I will give examples of some of the serious consequences that can ensue, in terms of the survival of forest wildlife, from attempts to put into practice the development and community-orientated approaches to conservation laid out in the strategies of IUCN, UNEP, and WWF. I will also try to show how the conservation projects I am most familiar with in these countries often seem to have been designed more to improve the career and financial prospects of consultants and administrators than to genuinely improve the survival prospects of forests and their wildlife. Such outcomes are surely an almost inevitable consequence of an approach to conservation that puts human material well-being ahead of protecting nature because of its intrinsic or aesthetic value.

FOUR

Tiwai

The Rise and Fall of a Community-Based Conservation Project

The southeastern corner of Sierra Leone, in West Africa, remained little influenced by the outside world until well into the twentieth century. The first settler colony of "Black Poor" from England was established in 1787 on the coast of Sierra Leone at what was to become Freetown, but the Sierra Leone Protectorate beyond Freetown was not established until 1896.[1] In the second half of the nineteenth century, internal warfare increased throughout the Liberian and Sierra Leonean area.[2] The dominant ethnic group in southeastern Sierra Leone is the Mende, and in their warfare the Mende captured many slaves. Among the Mende, as among other people in the area, the keeping of slaves was commonplace; it has been estimated that 50 percent of the people in Mendeland in the late nineteenth century were slaves.[3] Most slaves were put to work in agriculture and were settled in their own villages under the supervision of a headman. In the remoter parts of Mendeland, such as Pujehun District, over half the population were still slaves even in the 1920s.[4]

On the edge of Pujehun District, in the Moa River, lies the five-square-mile island of Tiwai (the name means "large island" in Mende). On the west bank of the Moa River, adjacent to Tiwai, is the small village of Kambama. According to an oral account given to me by Pa Luseni Koroma of Kambama (see plate 11), the chiefs of villages around Tiwai kept slaves on the island in the early decades of this century.[5] The slaves lived in small villages on the island, Pa Luseni said, and farmed it. Older people in Kambama still knew the names of nine settlements on Tiwai; each, according to Pa Luseni, had been the home of a group of slaves under one local "big man" who had farming rights.

After 1896, the British colonial administration of Sierra Leone made efforts to prevent warfare and stop traffic in slaves. Pa Luseni said that when he was a youth, he accompanied his father to meet a governor or other senior British official at "Bandajuma-Narroh"; according to Pa Luseni "the white man told the people not to be fighting, to make peace and unity among each other."[6] But the institution of slavery was not outlawed until 1928. It seems that around this time or soon afterward, the villages on Tiwai were abandoned and the island became less intensively cultivated than the mainland.

About fifty years after the slave-farming system at Tiwai ended, I had my first view of the island. It was August 6, 1979, and I had walked to Kambama from the nearest village of Baiama. The wet season was at its height in Sierra Leone, and it had been raining heavily since I had arrived in the country several weeks before. To reach Kambama I had to cross a flooded rice swamp[7] and climb a small hill into the village. After explaining the purpose of my visit to Pa Luseni and other senior men, I was escorted through a coffee plantation down to the bank of the Moa. The Moa is one of Sierra Leone's largest rivers, rising in the highlands on the Sierra Leone–Guinea border near the source of the river Niger. I was captivated by the appearance of the Moa at the Kambama waterside; here, it is an archetypal tropical river, broad and slow-flowing between tree-lined banks (see plate 12).[8] With several guides I clambered into a dugout canoe, and we paddled across the river to Tiwai. As a result of this journey, Tiwai was to become the site of a rain forest research and conservation project that closely involved people from local communities, and the island became Sierra Leone's first legally protected area for wildlife.

In this chapter I describe the history of the Tiwai project, including its eventual collapse in the face of a civil war whose roots lay in decades of inefficient and corrupt government. I explain how I came to choose this island for studies of primate behavior after finding that intensifying commercial hunting of monkeys and other mammals was making such studies impossible in many other parts of the West African forest zone. The pressures on wildlife that I saw led me to plan not only for research at Tiwai but also for a wildlife sanctuary there. From the outset, I conceived of a sanctuary whose management would closely involve local people. The evidence I saw persuaded me that this was the best course to follow: Sierra Leone's national government was not acting effectively in resource conservation, nor in many other areas. But as I try to show in this chapter, community-based conservation is an endeavor more easily undertaken in theory than in practice. At Tiwai, local antagonisms stalled efforts to establish a sanctuary management structure, and the impact that larger external forces made on our plans could not be avoided; such forces included powerful individuals in the national university and national government, as well as national nongovernmental organizations and foreign-based organizations. From 1982 to 1991 the presence of our primate research project and the funding associated with it acted as an anchor for conservation efforts as these forces jockeyed for influence over Tiwai, but the research project could not continue once law and order broke down completely.

THE OLIVE COLOBUS: A UNIQUE WEST AFRICAN MONKEY

I had come to Tiwai in 1979 in the course of searching for a site at which I could study olive colobus monkeys. A year before reaching Tiwai I had joined the faculty of the Department of Anthropology at Hunter College, at the City University of New York (CUNY). When I joined Hunter, I had hoped to continue with primate research and forest conservation efforts in South India, but foreign scientists were not welcome in India at that time, and as noted in chapter 2, the central government did not give its approval for the further work I planned. So I began to consider other options. West Africa still intrigued me, and so did one uniquely West African forest primate, the olive colobus monkey (see plate 13).

Tom Struhsaker and I had found a range of ecological and behavioral differences between black-and-white colobus and red colobus in Uganda's Kibale Forest, and we had speculated on the evolutionary origins of these differences.[9] I thought some of our ideas could be tested by a thorough study of the third kind of colobus monkey, the olive colobus, an interesting animal in its own right.[10] Another factor attracting me back to West Africa was that, although West African primates had featured in some early accounts of primate ecology, few long-term observational studies of primates in this part of the continent had been conducted since the beginning of the new wave of tropical field ethology in the late 1950s.

In the era before it was standard practice in field studies to habituate animals to the presence of a scientist and then to observe them over many months, the olive colobus had been the subject of one of the most detailed statements to be made on the natural history of a rain forest primate; this was a 1957 paper by the zoologist Angus Booth.[11] Booth had gone out from Britain in 1951 to take a teaching job at the University College of the Gold Coast (now the University of Ghana). He traveled widely in Ghana and the neighboring Côte d'Ivoire collecting mammals, birds, and reptiles. He developed a special interest in primates, and he made careful notes on the behavior of the animals he collected. Booth was prolific in publishing the findings of his collecting expeditions,[12] and his papers contributed significantly to the development of current thinking on the role of ice-age climate change in the evolution of the African mammal fauna.[13] Most of Booth's writings dealt with groups of species, but his olive colobus paper was an exception, dealing with only one; he said that he highlighted this species not only because so little had previously been reported about its natural history, but also because W. C. Osman Hill of the Zoological Society of London had recently published a detailed account of its anatomy (based particularly on specimens collected in Sierra Leone by the zoo's Jack Lester).[14] Booth's paper offered many intriguing insights on the biology of the olive colobus, such as the mother's habit of carrying her infant in her mouth, and the animal's proclivity for associating with groups of other monkey species, especially small *Cercopithecus* monkeys (or guenons). But given the nature of Booth's research, he had no quantitative long-term behavioral data that could be compared with data on colobus at other sites. He might well have gone on to collect such information, but he died suddenly in 1958.[15]

A WEST AFRICAN SURVEY FINDS
A GROWING TRADE IN MONKEY MEAT

So it was that in 1978 I started planning a survey to locate a suitable site for a long-term study of olive colobus ecology and behavior. I hoped to find a site where I could study other primate species too, and where CUNY students could work. In planning my survey, I contacted scientists who were working in the countries where I knew the olive colobus was found: Sierra Leone, Liberia, Côte d'Ivoire, and Ghana. I was told that the hunting of wildlife was so intense in Liberia that observing forest monkeys would be difficult and habituating them to close observation almost impossible.[16] Ghana, I learned, was undergoing such a serious economic and political crisis that essential items like food and fuel were hard to obtain, and organization of a field survey would be extremely difficult. For these reasons, I decided to focus my attention on Sierra Leone and Côte d'Ivoire.

My main contact in Sierra Leone was Peter White, a zoologist I had known at Makerere University in Uganda, who had been on the faculty of the Department of Biological Sciences at Sierra Leone's Njala University College since 1975. White, who became department head in 1979, was trying to encourage research in his department, and he described a very welcoming attitude to foreign scientists in the country. Monkeys, he reported, were relatively abundant and easy to observe in Sierra

Leone, because unlike people in other parts of West Africa, many who lived in the forest zone of the country were Muslims who did not eat monkey meat.

I arrived at Njala College in the middle of July 1979 and spent much of the next six weeks surveying forests in the southeast corner of Sierra Leone, the area from which the olive colobus had been reported. Njala had originally been established near the end of World War I as the head-quarters and research station of the Agriculture Department of the colonial government of Sierra Leone. One of its chief aims was to undertake research on crop rotation schemes that would improve the efficiency of the long-established bush-fallow system.[17] The long history of bush-fallow (or slash-and-burn) cultivation in Sierra Leone soon became evident to me as I traveled around the country.[18] I was disappointed to see how little forest remained, and I was also disturbed to find widespread signs of commercial monkey hunting. Most of this hunting was either conducted or organized by Liberians. Although monkey meat was not popular in Sierra Leone at that time, monkeys were a favored food item in Liberia. Liberians had greatly depleted the populations of larger mammals in the most accessible areas of their own country and had therefore turned their attention to neighboring countries. I learned that for at least ten years before my visit, Liberians had been coming into Sierra Leone with their own guns, usually during the dry season, and setting up camps in forest reserves or villages. From these bases the hunters scoured the bush, often killing hundreds of monkeys in a week (see plate 14). Back at camp, the monkey carcasses were jointed and then smoked. After several weeks, small trucks collected the smoked meat and carried it to Liberia. The hunters were generally welcomed by villagers, who perceived monkeys as pests but who rarely had guns of their own. Unfortunately, the Liberian hunters seemed to concentrate their attention on the largest and most conspicuous species (red colobus, black-and-white colobus, and Diana monkeys), which did little damage to crops but were relatively easy to hunt and provided the largest return on the cost of a shotgun cartridge.

Despite the mining industries that enriched a small segment of the population, I found rural Sierra Leone to be poorer than areas I was familiar with in Nigeria, Uganda, and India, and its infrastructure less developed than in those countries. The Sierra Leone government was functioning poorly, and although the colobus monkeys being killed by Liberians were protected by law, no attempt was being made to enforce the law; indeed, in the district headquarters town of Pujehun I met a policeman hunting red colobus. Expatriates in the country reported that hunting pressure was increasing, and that monkeys were becoming harder to find. In the majority of the villages I visited, people knew of Liberian hunters, and twice I met groups of these hunters.

The impression I got from my first few weeks in Sierra Leone was, therefore, that it would not be easy to find a suitable site for the long-term study of the olive colobus and other primates. The only relatively large areas of little-disturbed forest I saw were on hilly terrain in a small number of government forest reserves. In these reserves I did not see any olive colobus, but I saw much evidence of hunting. One of these reserves was Kambui Hills North, where I stayed at Bambawo, ten miles north of the town of Kenema. Bambawo was the site of a former chromite mine whose buildings had been converted into a forestry school and finally abandoned. Gerald Durrell used Bambawo as a base in 1965 during a trip on which he had collected black-and-white colobus monkeys for the Jersey Zoo.[19] On my first walk into the Kambui Hills I met six men coming out of the forest carrying bundles of smoked monkey meat on their heads. A forester told me that he had sent a request to the police to come and remove these hunters from the forest, but there was no sign of the police during my visit. I did see some *Cercopithecus* monkeys in the Kambui Hills, but no colobus.

A FIRST VISIT TO THE ISLAND OF SLAVES

The only sites at which I saw olive colobus were small forest patches near villages and narrow strips of forest fringing rivers; none of these looked like good sites for long-term ecological studies. But while scrutinizing survey maps based on aerial surveys made in 1959 and 1961, I noticed a large island in the Moa River, in the far southeast of the country

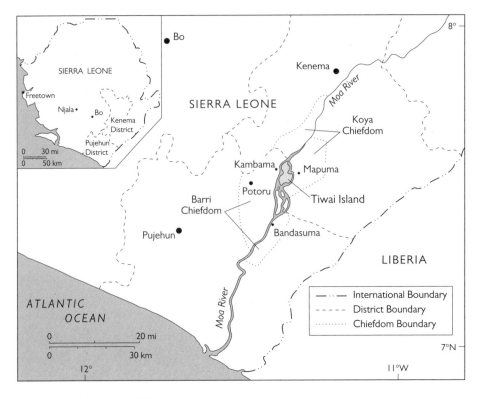

Map 6. The location of Tiwai Island in southeastern Sierra Leone in relation to chiefdom and district boundaries and to towns and villages mentioned in the text.

(see map 6). The island, labeled Tiwai, was shown as having no settlements and being largely covered with forest. No roads were shown reaching to the Moa. Tiwai, I thought, would be worth a visit; my readings and observations had suggested that the olive colobus was often found in riverine forest, and the relative inaccessibility of the island might have given it some protection from hunting.

I took public transport (operated by small trucks called *poda-podas;* see plate 15) to the town of Potoru in Pujehun District and there I arranged to charter a vehicle to take me another eight miles northeast from Potoru to the village of Baiama, which my survey map showed was the nearest village to Tiwai on a motorable track. In Potoru I found that the development-aid organization CARE was building new feeder roads in Pujehun District, and was upgrading the track to Baiama. It was therefore an easy drive to Baiama, and from there I set off with a guide to walk for about a mile and a half to the small village of Kambama, on the Moa River.

The people of Kambama were welcoming and cooperative, and they readily agreed to take me to Tiwai and show me around. Using the Mende names of primates I had learned, I questioned the villagers and found that they were familiar with all the forest monkeys of southern Sierra Leone as well as with chimpanzees. They said that all the monkey species occurred on the island and chimpanzees were abundant there.

On this first day I spent five hours on Tiwai. I found that the island did indeed have plenty of forest, and many of the trees in the forest were large and old. But the forest canopy was also quite broken in many places and the forest showed other signs of disturbance. On our walk we passed through a few farm clearings and several areas of "farmbush" (recently abandoned farmland). Presumably, when Tiwai was cultivated by slaves, farms covered a larger area of the island; but substantial areas must have lain fallow at any given time, and groves of trees were probably maintained near the now abandoned settlements. After the abolition of domestic slavery in Sierra Leone in 1928, the island's population declined and forest must have regrown. It appeared that farming was now increasing again.

Although I had been told that Liberian hunters did not cross to the island, I noticed a few old shotgun cartridges on forest paths. Even so, primates were abundant, and they seemed less afraid of people than at the other sites I had visited. I saw Diana monkeys, Campbell's monkeys, red colobus, and mangabeys; I heard black-and-white colobus; and I saw old chimp nests. I did not see any signs of olive colobus, but my guides assured me that the monkey occurred on the island and preferred areas of young bush near the river. Tiwai therefore seemed to offer some good possibilities as a study site, but it was completely lacking in facilities for a research base, and it was hard to reach. CARE engineers assured me, however, that their new road would reach Kambama by the end of the year. Unfortunately, while this would make Tiwai more accessible to researchers, it would also improve access for hunters.

Three weeks after my visit to the island, when I left Sierra Leone for Côte d'Ivoire to continue my search for a study site, I had not located a place more promising for long-term research than Tiwai.

DECIDING ON A RESEARCH SITE

Before traveling to West Africa I had been in touch with Gérard and Anh Galat, two French scientists who, I had learned, were studying primates in Côte d'Ivoire's famous Taï Forest, which was now a national park. The Galats invited me to visit their study area, and they met me at the airport in Abidjan when I arrived from Sierra Leone. A few days later we set off in their small pickup truck for Taï, in the far southwest of the country. On our journey I was struck both by the large numbers of timber trucks we passed and the devastated appearance of a landscape that must have been heavily forested only a few years previously.[20] Taï itself was very impressive; although it had suffered some selective logging, many big trees remained. In my three days in the forest I saw seven monkey species, including the olive colobus, as well as the tracks of elephant, pygmy hippopotamus, and leopard. But I also learned that Anh Galat was planning a study of olive colobus herself, and I was told that I would be unlikely to get permission for a primate study in the same area. I concluded that my best option was to try to set up a research program at a different site, from which any results could be usefully compared with the findings of the Galats' studies in Taï.[21]

During my next break from teaching at Hunter, in January 1980, I therefore hurried back to Sierra Leone to try and learn more about the olive colobus and further evaluate Tiwai Island as a study site. Now it was the dry season, and travel around Sierra Leone was considerably easier, especially since Peter White had loaned me his car. The CARE road had been completed to Kambama, and so I could drive right into the village. I greeted the old chief, Pa Luseni, and then I crossed back to Tiwai Island with two senior men, Laminah and Mustafa Koroma, sons of the chief. This time I spent seven hours on the island and visited new areas in the south. Because it was the dry season, new rice farms were being cleared in the bush, and I met several farmers and saw fresh cartridge cases. One farmer told me that Liberians had been on the island and had killed many monkeys. Even so, I encountered twelve monkey groups, although the animals seemed warier than those I had seen five months earlier. I had good views of all the monkey species I had observed before, and this time I also saw spot-nosed monkeys and black-and-white colobus. I still did not see or hear any olive colobus, but I was again assured that they were present, and I was shown trees whose leaves they were said to eat. I also saw the dung of pygmy hippopotamus, now a very rare animal in Sierra Leone and the neighboring parts of West Africa to which it is restricted.

I was impressed by the primates and other wildlife of Tiwai, but I was also concerned about the growing threat of hunting. I wrote a report to the Sierra Leone government in which I recommended not only controls on Liberian hunting, but also the creation of a primate reserve at Tiwai. I suggested that, as a first step, there should be consultations with the Paramount Chiefs of Barri and Koya on either side of the island, and I suggested that, if a reserve was established, any loss that local people might suffer from restrictions on their farming could be compensated for by providing them with employment in reserve management and by involving them in the management of any facilities that might be developed for tourists.[22]

When I submitted my report in April 1980, there were signs of a more promising future for wildlife conservation in Sierra Leone. In 1978 the British Council, at the request of the Sierra Leone government, had funded a University of Oxford ecology professor, John Phillipson, to prepare a report on wildlife conservation needs in the country.[23] Among his many suggestions, Phillipson had recommended the immediate gazetting of several areas that had long been proposed as game reserves or sanctuaries, and he argued the case for giving more resources and training opportunities to the Wildlife Conservation Branch of the Forestry Division. At the time of my second visit to Sierra Leone, Geza Teleki had begun a survey of chimpanzee populations in the country. Based on this survey, Teleki concluded that Outamba and Kilimi, two areas in the northwest of Sierra Leone that had been proposed as game reserves in 1965, held the most important chimpanzee populations and should be made into a national park. Teleki won WWF endorsement for a project to develop this national park, and he began a fund-raising and publicity campaign in the United States. Teleki and Peter White also began planning a new master's program in wildlife management at Njala College, which could serve to train the new staff that would be needed for expanded Sierra Leonean conservation efforts.[24]

It was against this background that I considered the feasibility of a research project at Tiwai. Even though I had not been able to see olive colobus there myself, I was convinced that the monkey was present. The island seemed to have potential as a wildlife conservation area and research site, but it also had disadvantages. Research facilities would have to be developed from scratch, and since the site was difficult to reach by public transport, one or more vehicles would have to be obtained. Experienced research personnel would have to be found, people who were prepared to live for extended periods at a remote location.

I was still trying to decide on a course of action when, in June 1980, I went to an American Society of Primatologists meeting at Winston-Salem in North Carolina to give a paper about my South Indian research. Here I met George Whitesides, a North Carolina native who was completing a thesis for his master's degree at Johns Hopkins University. For his thesis research he had studied multispecies primate associations in Cameroon's Douala-Edéa Reserve. He had also done fieldwork in South America, India, and Nepal. Whitesides was now planning to study for a Ph.D., and he hoped to conduct his dissertation research in Africa on primate community ecology. I told him about Tiwai, and he was very interested in its possibilities. We kept in touch, but before I made a final decision on developing a project at Tiwai, I decided to re-visit the Ayangba area of Nigeria, where I had learned that an isolated population of olive colobus existed.

DEVELOPMENT OF RESEARCH AT TIWAI

My January 1981 visit to Ayangba is described in chapter 5. I found that the area offered poor opportunities for long-term behavioral research, and so I decided to proceed with plans for a project at Tiwai Island. Peter White at Njala College was still keen to have such a project based in his department, and George Whitesides was still eager to participate in it. Whitesides was now in graduate school at the University of Miami, where his adviser was Steven Green, whom I had worked with in India. During 1981, Green, Whitesides, and I began framing proposals for funding agencies; a research project at Tiwai was going to require con-siderable resources, given the remoteness and lack of facilities at the site. We were fortunate to be awarded grants by the U.S. National Sci-ence Foundation and the Research Foundation of CUNY, and we pre-pared to begin research the following year. In March 1982, Whitesides traveled to Sierra Leone, arranged accommodation and formalities in Freetown and Njala, and visited Tiwai and nearby areas. He confirmed both that the olive colobus was present on Tiwai, and that the island was indeed the most suitable research site in that part of Sierra Leone. In June, I traveled from Nigeria to meet Whitesides, and over the next four weeks we obtained the endorsement of local chiefs for our research; we established a base camp on the western side of the island, downstream from Kambama; and we began cutting a grid of trails through the is-land's forest.

The Tiwai project developed considerably in the next few years. By the time the site had to be abandoned in April 1991 as rebels moved into the area, much research had been done on the island's primates, includ-ing long-term studies on the behavioral ecology of the olive colobus and three other species;[25] large vegetation plots had been established and were being monitored, and there had been studies of plant chemistry and soils;[26] there had also been research on mongooses, rodents, electric fish, and primate parasites, and on human use of forest resources.[27] Anglia Television had made a full-length documentary about the island, paying special attention to the chimpanzees. The chimpanzees of Tiwai, like those in nearby parts of West Africa, use stones to crack open hard-shelled nuts to extract oil-rich seeds, and the Anglia team was able to film this behavior from blinds in the forest.[28]

ESTABLISHING SIERRA LEONE'S FIRST PROTECTED AREA

Basic ecological research, though, was only one part of the Tiwai project. The surveys I had made in West Africa in 1979–81 had brought home to me just how great were the destructive forces acting on the forests and wildlife of the region, and especially how heavy was the hunting pressure on monkeys in areas that had previously been lightly touched backwaters. From this point onward, conservation efforts would be a large part of my work.

From the time of my first visit to Tiwai I had felt that the island deserved special conservation status. There was no other area in the Sierra Leone rain forest zone where all the country's forest primates could be seen so readily, and the island's small size and the natural barrier provided by the Moa River made it an area that could be protected relatively easily. There was little hunting on the island by the local villagers (most of their animal protein came from fish, which were abundant in the Moa River); the island was farmed, but this farming had been relatively light for several decades. However, in the years immediately following my first visit to Tiwai, the hunting threat from Liberians became acute, and farming pressures grew as Sierra Leone's rural population increased and its economy stagnated. I felt that conservation measures at Tiwai would have to be initiated urgently, before it went the way of most of southern Sierra Leone outside forest reserves and became largely farmbush with a low density and diversity of monkeys and other mammals. But how was this to be done? I had visited many forest reserves in the course of my initial survey, and I had seen that the Sierra Leone Forestry Division (which also administered game laws, through its Wildlife Conservation Branch) had few resources and was not exercising effective management of the existing reserves. The division had very few vehicles (and these were mostly in the capital, Freetown), and its staff were poorly paid and equipped. I thought that if Tiwai acquired, for instance, the legal status of a game reserve administered by the Forestry Division, this would most likely be a reserve only on paper, with little real protection. I therefore began discussions with people around Tiwai about a more locally based protection program.

Our base camp, and the adjacent forest that became our first research area, lay on land where people from Kambama made farms. To facilitate our research, we agreed with the senior men of Kambama that they would not farm or otherwise disturb the forest in our study area in return for a small annual payment and the employment of Kambama residents as field and camp assistants. At the same time, Paramount Chief V. K. Magona VI of Barri Chiefdom, within which Kambama was situated, agreed to place a ban on hunting on the island. And we initiated discussions with Chief Magona and with the leaders of Kambama about how a more permanent nature reserve and field station might be established on the island. One possibility we explored was a formal agreement with Njala College, under which the chiefdom would agree to a long-term lease of the island to Njala, which would manage the site. In August 1983, I discussed these ideas with Prince Palmer in the Forestry Division headquarters in Freetown. Palmer suggested that under the terms of the country's 1972 Wild Life Conservation Act, the local people could request that Tiwai be declared a game sanctuary. This status, Palmer explained, would leave the area in the hands of the local people, but would give it protection from hunting under national law. Game sanctuary status would also allow farming to continue. We thought that a small amount of farming would be compatible with conservation, as it would maintain habitat diversity.

Palmer's suggestion of a game sanctuary seemed worth pursuing, and its establishment would not be incompatible with our continuing to negotiate with Njala about the establishment of a permanent research station. I therefore discussed the sanctuary idea with Chief Magona, and he put the matter to the Jorgba section of the chiefdom, within which he said Tiwai fell; the section leaders agreed to the proposal, and it was endorsed by the chiefdom as a whole. On February 18, 1984, Chief Magona wrote to the Chief Conservator of Forests in Freetown with a formal request for a sanctuary. It took more than two years for this request to be acted upon; after receiving the request, the Forestry Division conducted its own investigation as to the suitability of the site, and then had to prepare paperwork for the cabinet. Finally, the sanctuary came into being on January 1, 1987—the first area in Sierra Leone to become specially protected for its wildlife.[29]

CONSERVATION EFFORTS EXPAND

George Whitesides's study of Diana monkeys was completed in 1984, and Georgina Dasilva and Glyn Davies took over as the resident Tiwai primatologists, studying the ecology of black-and-white colobus and red colobus monkeys. Land management issues had come to take up a growing amount of researchers' time, and our research camp was increasingly attracting casual visitors, mostly expatriates resident in Sierra Leone who had heard about the island and its wildlife. This convinced us that a distinct conservation program would need to be established, with its own personnel who could help in producing a sanctuary management plan and in developing a special campsite and nature trail for the use of visitors. By setting up a distinct program to cope with visitors, we could take pressure off researchers and lessen disturbance of their study groups of primates; in addition, a small-scale tourism program would bring income to local people and so encourage their continued support of conservation efforts. We began discussions in 1985 with the Forestry Division and the Peace Corps office in Freetown about recruiting a U.S. Peace Corps volunteer who could assist with sanctuary development. A volunteer who was already teaching in Sierra Leone was located; this was Anne Todd, who had a degree in behavioral biology and was keen to take the Tiwai assignment.

Todd began work at Tiwai in July 1986, supported by a grant from the Wildlife Conservation International (WCI) division of the New York Zoological Society (now the Wildlife Conservation Society). Concentrating initially on increasing public awareness of what was happening at Tiwai, Todd traveled to many towns and villages in the vicinity of the island, often hiking long distances on bush paths, and she spoke at public meetings and to school classes about conservation. In January 1987, a site for a visitor's camp on Tiwai was selected in consultation with people from Kambama, and the construction of thatched shelters soon began. A nature trail was laid out through one of the primate study areas; interesting features of natural history along the trail were labeled and described in a simple written guide. Todd trained local people to run the visitor's camp and act as guides, and she organized an artisans' cooperative to produce crafts for sale to visitors. The Tiwai Nature Centre opened officially in September 1987 and received 190 visitors in its first ten months; it soon became one of the most popular holiday destinations for expatriates in Sierra Leone, and it was used by groups of students from local schools.[30]

In addition to establishing education and visitor programs, Todd had to spend much of her time in the day-to-day management of the research camp at Tiwai, and in maintaining relations with chiefdom and government authorities. As research and conservation activities in and around Tiwai had expanded, so also had the need for additional management personnel. By now, the Peace Corps office in Freetown was developing a distinct park management and conservation program with the Forestry Division. We decided to request from this program a second Tiwai volunteer, preferably someone with experience in park planning who could help develop a sanctuary management plan. This resulted in the recruitment of Bill Eichenlaub, whose training was in environmental science and who had worked at the Haleakala National Park in Hawaii from 1983 to 1985. Like Todd, Eichenlaub was already in Sierra Leone and was based in Potoru, where he had been teaching science in the secondary school and helping establish fishponds. While in Potoru he had observed with concern the continuing trade in monkey meat in the area; this business was in the hands of a few powerful individuals who employed local hunters and arranged transportation of the smoked meat to the Liberian border, where it was sold. Eichenlaub took up his assignment at Tiwai in September 1987, with WCI providing support for his fieldwork.

Nineteen eighty-seven was therefore an active year at Tiwai, a year when we tried to move from a project concentrating on primate research to one that attempted to establish the management both of a permanent conservation area and of a Sierra Leonean research station that could be used for training and research by students and scientists from inside and outside the country. In June, a conference on the development of a Tiwai field station was held at Njala under the auspices of the new Research and Development Services Bureau of the University of Sierra Leone. Following this conference, the University of Miami and Hunter College agreed to make small annual contributions to cover basic operating costs at Tiwai, on condition that members of their institutions remained involved in work on the island and that the University of Sierra Leone made a similar commitment (for instance, by providing administrative support). The American universities also donated funds to allow a start to be made on construction of a permanent building at the Tiwai research camp. Work on this building, of compressed mud-cement blocks on a concrete foundation, began toward the end of 1987 and was completed the following year.

CONFLICTS BEGIN OVER TIWAI

The original handful of foreigners studying monkey behavior on Tiwai had not raised a great deal of concern among local leaders. This situation changed as the project developed. People realized that considerable outside influence and money might be coming into the area, and that formal proposals on long-term land management were being prepared. Early in the project the elders of Barri chiefdom had assured us that Tiwai lay entirely within Barri, and the villagers of Kambama told us that they were the people with farming rights on the island.[31] But it soon became clear that Koya Chiefdom, on the east bank of the Moa River adjacent to Tiwai, also laid strong claim to at least part of the island. Inquiries with the Ministry of Internal Affairs in Freetown and a study of old records in the District Office in Pujehun (records ravaged by the tropical climate and insects) did not resolve the question of where a chiefdom boundary lay. The most authoritative chiefdom map we could find seemed to place Tiwai in Barri, but the island was not portrayed accurately on the map. Apparently, the location of the chiefdom boundaries in the Tiwai area was an issue that had never come to the attention of government, and until 1965, when 1:50,000 maps were produced based on aerial photography, an accurate map of the island had never been available. We learned that one reason why ownership of the island was a sensitive matter was that alluvial diamonds were mined in the river channels around Tiwai Island and, to a more limited extent, along stream courses on the island itself.[32] As other sectors of the Sierra Leonean economy became dysfunctional, diamond mining was becoming an increasingly significant source of income; mining rights were therefore a very serious issue, and they could be compromised by a government notice stating that Tiwai lay in one chiefdom rather than another.

Land ownership in the area was complicated further by local history. When the first British colonial official, T. J. Alldridge, visited this area in 1890 to sign treaties with rulers, the senior person in Barri country was "Queen" Nyarroh.[33] Nyarroh had become the ruler of Barri after the death of her husband, who was the chief of Bandasuma, a town on the Moa River about twelve miles south of Tiwai.[34] Pa Luseni of Kambama told me that when Nyarroh's rule began, both banks of the Moa River on either side of Tiwai had belonged to Barri. But, explained Pa Luseni, Nyarroh fell in love with the chief of the Koya country, who lived at Bogboabu on the east bank of the Moa north of Tiwai; Nyarroh gave to the chief of Koya those parts of Barri that lay immediately east of Tiwai.[35] At the start of our project, the Koya villages of Mapuma and Segbwema near Tiwai on the east bank of the Moa still had close connections with Kambama on the west bank. One of the senior men in Kambama, for instance, who became town chief for a while, had wives and households in both Kambama and Mapuma. If Kambama and Mapuma were part of the same "community" from an administrative point of view, issues of ownership and management of Tiwai might have been resolved rather easily; but now they lay not only in different chiefdoms but in different administrative districts and regions of Sierra Leone (Barri was in Pujehun District in the Southern Province, and Koya in Kenema District in the Eastern Province).

Matters came to a head upon publication of the government notice constituting the Tiwai Island Game Sanctuary in October 1987. The request for a sanctuary had been submitted by Chief Magona and the chiefdom council of Barri in 1984, and the gazette notice referred to Tiwai as being located in Barri. On publication of this notice, Paramount Chief M. M. Kanneh of Koya informed us that, unless Koya's rights to Tiwai also were formally recognized, conservation and research activities on the island would have to cease. Threats began to circulate that our research camp would be destroyed and monkeys shot.

We therefore arranged a meeting of the Barri and Koya chiefs at Tiwai in early December 1987, and in the meeting we suggested that a board of trustees be established for the wildlife sanctuary. This board that would be headed by the two Paramount Chiefs and would include representatives of the University of Sierra Leone, the Forestry Division, and the recently formed Conservation Society of Sierra Leone.[36] We proposed that the board would manage the wildlife sanctuary and make an agreement with Njala College on the operation of a field station. At the meeting it was agreed that Bill Eichenlaub would act as liaison between the chiefdoms to help bring this administrative body into existence, although in his role as a planning adviser he would not be able to impose any particular arrangement.

As 1988 continued, Eichenlaub found it difficult to make progress in the establishment of an administrative body that satisfied both chiefdoms. This was frustrating, for Eichenlaub was on a two-year assignment and his management plan was due to be completed by the end of August 1989; it would be impossible for him to produce a realistic plan without an administrative structure for the Tiwai sanctuary agreed upon by the two chiefdoms and by the universities involved in research. Eichenlaub therefore began to seek help from people in Freetown in resolving the chiefdom dispute.

As Tiwai's profile rose in Sierra Leone, further conflicts arose. I learned that Abu Sesay, Peter White's successor as head of the Department of Biology at Njala College, felt that I still exercised too much control over Tiwai research and its funding; Sesay also feared that responsibility for research at Tiwai was being shifted from his department to the university's central administration in Freetown. Meanwhile, the Peace Corps office in Freetown had begun to view Tiwai as an increasingly important component of Peace Corps activities in Sierra Leone, no doubt in part because of the success of Anne Todd's work. This caused another set of difficulties, as Peace Corps administrators began to make plans for future volunteer assignments at Tiwai without informing the other people involved at the site. The Peace Corps was eager to see conflicts over the administration of activities at Tiwai resolved because they needed to know clearly to whom their volunteers were answerable.

THE TIWAI ISLAND ADMINISTRATIVE COMMITTEE

When I traveled to Sierra Leone in June 1988, I hoped to find some way to resolve these conflicts and clarify my own role in conservation and research activities at Tiwai. Soon after arriving in Freetown I talked to John Waugh, another Peace Corps volunteer who was helping develop the new Conservation Society, and Sama Banya, President of the Society. Banya said that he was arranging a meeting with K. Koso-Thomas, the Vice Chancellor of the University of Sierra Leone, a meeting he hoped would lead to a resolution of the problems. We agreed that the meeting would be held in July, after I had visited Tiwai.

The meeting took place in the Vice Chancellor's office on July 5. In addition to Banya, Waugh, and myself, Abu Sesay from Njala College and other representatives of the Conservation Society and the Peace Corps attended. At the meeting we concluded that the best way to move forward in establishing a field station and an effective conservation area at Tiwai was to create an advisory committee consisting of representatives of the University of Sierra Leone, the Conservation Society, the Ministry of Agriculture, the Peace Corps, the Paramount Chiefs of Barri and Koya, and the administrators of the Southern and Eastern Provinces. Sesay noted that the Tiwai Field Station would have its own separate management committee, chaired by himself, and that there would be a field station advisory committee, on which I would serve. The following week, just before I left Sierra Leone on July 12, a second meeting was held at the office of the Chief Conservator of Forests. This meeting went beyond recommending an advisory body and instead decided to formally establish a Tiwai Island Administrative Committee, chaired by the Chief Conservator of Forests, A. P. Koroma.

I was disheartened by the results of these meetings. I thought that the proposed committees would rarely meet and would therefore be ineffective in dealing with day-to-day management problems, and I was dismayed by what I considered the marginalization of the chiefdoms and the shift of control of activities at Tiwai to "big men" in Freetown and Njala.

The inaugural meeting of the Tiwai Island Administrative Committee took place at Njala College on October 12, 1988, at a time of year when neither Steven Green nor I could be in Sierra Leone. Although we could not be present, the Chairman did announce that our universities would each have one seat on the committee. Peace Corps volunteer Bill Eichenlaub was appointed General Manager of the wildlife sanctuary and asked to identify areas that could be zoned for farming.[37] Inevitably, some of the struggles for power over Tiwai surfaced at this meeting. Chief Kanneh of Koya refused to attend, and sent a letter of protest saying that Koya would not participate in the Administrative Committee until the ownership of the island was resolved to the chiefdom's satisfaction. And Sesay expressed his concern that his department at Njala College was not adequately represented on the committee. A second meeting was held on December 9, in Kenema, again without Hunter College or the University of Miami represented, and again boycotted by Chief Kanneh. Another key person missing from these early meetings was S. S. Magona, the Member of Parliament for the area that contained Barri Chiefdom and a relative of the Paramount Chief; he complained that the Chief Conservator of Forests should not be summoning him to discuss the management of land in his own chiefdom.

The Administrative Committee held another five meetings up to January 1992. It achieved little in terms of establishing an effective local management system that, in the absence of foreign scientists or Peace Corps volunteers, would protect the island and promote research in the long term. Apart from the small revenue that accrued from visitors, almost all Tiwai operating funds continued to come from the United States (from our universities, the New York Zoological Society, and the Peace Corps). At one point, a game guard (a forestry employee) was posted to the island, but he left after a few weeks. Abu Sesay at Njala requested a budget line from the University of Sierra Leone administration for the operation of a Tiwai field station, but such funds were never made available. Meanwhile, major decisions on the use of the island, especially by foreigners, began to be made by the Chief Conservator of Forests in Freetown.[38]

The committee did, however, provide a framework for those involved in different activities at Tiwai to meet and air their concerns, and gradually the elders of Koya Chiefdom became more cooperative. The Forestry Division began to schedule meetings at times when either Green or I would have a chance of attending, and in January 1991 we were both able to attend the first committee meeting to be held on Tiwai Island itself. By then, Koya was satisfied that its joint claim to the island was recognized, and so both Paramount Chiefs attended this meeting, along with Member of Parliament S. S. Magona. It was agreed that from then on the chairmanship of the Administrative Committee would be in the hands of the chiefs, who would hold the position on an annually rotating basis. But at the end of March 1991, before this new structure had started to function, rebels invaded southeastern Sierra Leone, and this led to the end of all research and conservation efforts at Tiwai.

PRELUDE TO COLLAPSE

The ineffectiveness of government in Sierra Leone, the rebel insurgency that began in 1991, and the collapse of the southeast of the country into the anarchy and brutality that followed is best understood in the context of the recent political and economic history of the country. Since its independence from Britain in 1961, Sierra Leone had been viewed as politically one of the most stable countries in Africa. From 1968 to 1985, Sierra Leone was ruled by the paternalistic and occasionally authoritarian Siaka Stevens ("Pa Siaki"). As D. F. Luke and S. P. Riley have explained, Stevens maintained his position by political artfulness and the careful dispensation of patronage.[39] He used this position to enrich himself and his close associates, who included powerful Lebanese businessmen. Little attention was given to development of the national economy or maintenance of public services such as health and education. No vigorous actions were therefore taken to address the damaging economic effects on Sierra Leone of the oil-price rises of the 1970s and the accompanying declines in the prices of export commodities. As the population increased (from 2.2 million in 1963 to an estimated 3.2 million in 1982), most people experienced an obvious fall in their standard of living.[40]

In failing health, Stevens handed over power in August 1985 to a carefully chosen successor, the military commander Joseph S. Momoh, whose presidency of the one-party state was endorsed two months later by a national election in which he was unopposed. Siaka Stevens died in quiet retirement in Freetown in 1988. From Stevens, J. S. Momoh inherited not only a stagnant economy but also growing debts; in 1985–86, two-thirds of Sierra Leone's export earnings were needed to service debt obligations.[41] Momoh attempted to reform the economy, but his moves were cautious and some analysts thought that he paid excessive heed to political advisors who would have been adversely affected by tough reforms. By 1990, Sierra Leone's "Index of Human Development" calculated by the United Nations Development Programme was the lowest of any country in the world. Gross national product per capita was three hundred dollars, life expectancy at birth was forty-two years, and the adult literacy rate was 13.3 percent.[42]

Given the deteriorating state of the country's economy during this period, the poor performance of the Forestry Division and the University of Sierra Leone, both funded by the government, is not surprising. As the economy collapsed, we experienced increasing difficulty obtaining fuel for Tiwai project vehicles and cooking stoves, as well as other essential supplies. The black market in hard currency flourished, and bribery and thievery became common. Such behavior was widely condoned because legitimate employment offering wages sufficient to support one person, let alone a family, had become extremely rare; a general atmosphere of dishonesty therefore began to pervade Sierra Leone.[43] It is not surprising that when the first rebels entered Sierra Leone from Liberia in 1991, they found many young men ready to join them.

COLLAPSE

In December 1989, civil war began in Sierra Leone's neighbor, Liberia, when Libyan-trained followers of Charles Taylor invaded from Côte d'Ivoire, intent on toppling the government of Samuel K. Doe, of which Taylor had once been a part. Liberia's economy was also near collapse from mismanagement, with the country owing $1.2 billion that it was thought unlikely to repay.[44] By July, Taylor's National Patriotic Front of Liberia (NPFL) controlled much of the country. The NPFL began to split into factions, one of which, led by Prince Johnson, captured and killed Doe. Meanwhile, a multinational West African force, led by Nigeria and assisted by Sierra Leone, had intervened to deny the rebels control of the capital city, Monrovia. Strangely, while Liberia degenerated into chaos, little fear was expressed in Sierra Leone that the war would spill over the border.

But in early April 1991 reports began to appear in the international press of plundering raids by NPFL men into southeastern Sierra Leone. These raids had begun at the end of March, and they were initially assumed to be motivated mainly by the desire of Taylor's men to obtain equipment and food. But by the beginning of April the border incursions seemed to involve an organized force, and there was speculation that Taylor was punishing the Sierra Leone government for its help with the Nigerian intervention in Liberia. On April 3, the insurgent force reached Zimmi, fourteen miles south of Tiwai. At this time the Anglia Television film team were at Tiwai with their producer Caroline Brett, and American graduate students Cheryl Fimbel of Rutgers University

and Annette Olson of the University of Miami. A Peace Corps administrator from Freetown brought word of the insurgency to the island and
advised an immediate evacuation of the foreigners. On April 5 the film
crew abandoned Tiwai, leaving Fimbel and Olson to make their way to
Bo in the project's battered pickup truck the following day. Three days
later the rebel force, apparently consisting of Liberians and Sierra
Leoneans, took over Potoru, the headquarters of Barri Chiefdom, cutting
off access to Tiwai. Over the next week the insurgency spread, and Nigeria and Guinea sent troops to bolster the Sierra Leone government
forces.[45]

Sporadic fighting continued in southeastern Sierra Leone for several
months, but by the end of 1991 government forces had regained control
of the area around Potoru. I went out to Sierra Leone at the end of December and set about arranging a visit to Tiwai. I was advised that I
could probably safely make a day trip to Tiwai if I took a military escort
from the army garrison in the southern regional capital of Bo. After obtaining permission and an escort from the army commander in Bo, I set
off for Tiwai in our Niva jeep early on January 6, 1992.

On our way to Potoru we passed through several army checkpoints
decorated with fresh human skulls, said to be those of rebels. In Potoru,
many of the houses had been destroyed and only a few people were
around; everywhere, domestic animals were scarce. After obtaining further military permissions we drove on to Kambama, finding ourselves
stopped before the village by another military barrier decorated by another skull—a very different arrival from that of my first friendly welcome thirteen years before. After some debate we were allowed to enter
the village, where a contingent of soldiers was posted. I was relieved to
find that many of my friends and several of our staff were safe and well
in Kambama, but I was told that our camp cook, Mohamed Kallon, had
been killed by rebels, and that several young women had been taken
away by the rebels when they left the area. The villagers said that Kambama had been deserted for several months, and that they had scattered
into the bush and scraped a living as best they could, sometimes relying
on wild yams and other gathered food. Even though people had now
come back to Kambama, life had not returned to normal; the villagers

complained to me that the soldiers stationed there were making people feed them and do other chores.

In the early afternoon I crossed to Tiwai. The research station building was intact, except for missing doors and insect screening, but almost all our equipment and supplies were missing (see plate 16). I was told that the rebels had got to Kambama about two weeks after Fimbel and Olson had left, and that before this our staff had hidden the most valuable pieces of equipment in the bush and in the village. People said that the rebels had forced them to hand over most of this equipment on pain of death. Little or no hunting had apparently taken place on the island, however; the rebels and the army had saved their scarce ammunition for killing each other. Advised not to spend the night in the area, I returned, chastened, to Bo.

In the next few months, more normal conditions returned to this part of Sierra Leone. Soon after my visit, Paramount Chief Magona returned to take up residence in Potoru, more transport began running on the roads, and economic activity revived; no rebel actions were reported. In April, a group of young soldiers overthrew the government of J. S. Momoh. Led by twenty-seven-year-old Captain Valentine Strasser, these soldiers expressed disillusionment with the government's support of the army in the fight against the rebels; they pledged to bring the insurgency to an end, eradicate corruption and economic decay, and return the country to multiparty democracy.[46] The new government, seeming to model itself on the regime of Ghana's Jerry Rawlings and calling itself the National Provisional Ruling Council, was welcomed by most people in Sierra Leone.

In July and August 1992, George Whitesides was able to visit Tiwai for almost three weeks and make formal censuses of the wildlife. He found that populations of primates and other animals were as high or higher than in 1984. On this basis, we began to make plans to rehabilitate the research and conservation programs.

Peace, though, did not endure for long. The rebel insurgency soon revived and spread, and the new government proved no more effective in combating the rebellion than its predecessors. Travel in the Tiwai area became very hazardous. In September 1993, one of the Tiwai Field Station staff from Kambama, Luseni Koroma, got a message through to the head of the Department of Biological Sciences at Njala College that two months previously the leader of a twelve-strong contingent of soldiers based in Kambama had crossed over to the island with another soldier from Potoru "and shot many monkeys"; this report was filed away and no action was taken. Koroma also reported many rebel attacks on villages in the area, attacks in which people had been killed. By the time of my last visit to Sierra Leone in October 1993, Chief Magona and his family had taken refuge in Bo and Chief Kanneh of Koya had been in the town of Kenema, far from his chiefdom, for many months. Koya chiefdom was said to be largely deserted. The chiefs told me that they had been given reports of government soldiers as well as rebels mining diamonds in their chiefdoms, and harvesting kola nuts, coffee, cocoa, and monkeys.

During 1994 and 1995 the situation in Sierra Leone deteriorated further. In March 1994, three European missionaries were killed by rebels in Kenema District. In January 1995 Njala College was attacked and University of Miami graduate student Mohamed Bakarr, who was living on the campus and had been hoping to conduct research at Tiwai, narrowly escaped death. In February rebels seized the giant titanium-ore mine near Gbangbama in southern Sierra Leone, which had earned $61 million in 1993, 57 percent of the country's official exports in value terms.[47] By April, rebel forces were launching attacks on the outskirts of Freetown. Now the only safe way to travel up-country to Bo and Kenema was by air.

When the insurgency began in 1991, the rebels had appeared to be an offshoot of Charles Taylor's Liberian NPFL; now it was clear that they were largely or entirely Sierra Leoneans, and they had coalesced into a shadowy organization called the Revolutionary United Front (RUF), led by a man called Foday Sankoh. Sankoh was a former army corporal who had been accused of involvement in a coup plot against Siaka Stevens in 1971 and sentenced to seven years in jail. He was released from prison after serving six years of his sentence, and became a photographer.[48] The RUF did not publish well-articulated political goals, although it talked of removing foreign influence from Sierra Leone and restoring multi-party democracy. But distinctions between rebels and government soldiers also became hard to make; many "rebels," it was said, wore army uniforms, and they may indeed have been soldiers, or "sobels." As in Liberia, the rebels often acted more as independent armed gangs than as a disciplined military force. They terrorized the general populace, attacking villagers with cutlasses (machetes), and cutting off the arms or legs of men, women, and children. This caused many villagers to flee to cities and refugee camps, thus allowing the rebels to exploit the diamonds and other resources of the countryside, on which they maintained and enriched themselves.[49]

In April 1995, Valentine Strasser's government in Freetown staved off looming defeat at the hands of the rebels by bringing in a South African company called Executive Outcomes. Using Russian-built helicopter gunships and instituting armed convoy systems on main roads, this "army for hire" helped to beat back the rebels from the outskirts of Sierra Leone's major towns and reopen some of its diamond mines. Although Executive Outcomes says it was paid in cash by the government, there have been reports that in lieu of its estimated fees of $3 million per month, it negotiated a deal under which an affiliated company, Branch Energy, would receive major diamond-mining concessions.[50]

As a semblance of peace returned to parts of Sierra Leone, the government announced plans for an election. When doubts began to arise that Strasser would honor this commitment, he was overthrown on January 16, 1996, by his deputy, the armed forces chief Julius Maada Bios. The first round of the election went ahead in February, although voting was impossible in many rebel-controlled rural areas; in the second round of voting, Ahmad Tejan Kabbah was elected President. Soon after his election, Kabbah initiated peace talks with RUF leader Foday Sankoh, who had taken up residence in a luxury hotel in Abidjan, Côte d'Ivoire, and a cease-fire was arranged in December 1996.[51]

With these developments, our hopes rose that conservation and research activities at Tiwai might be revived, if populations of primates and other animals on the island had not been too heavily hunted. Our former site manager Momoh Magona, a relative of Chief Magona, was able to reach Tiwai at the end of December 1996, and he sent us a report through the Conservation Society in Freetown. He found camps and trails overgrown, and many traps on the island; he came across a large area mined for diamonds, and saw many spent shotgun cartridges near the miners' camp. Magona reported that the few animals he encountered fled rapidly, but he also saw nuts recently cracked by chimpanzees. He had found people living again in Kambama, and said that the area around the island was calm.[52] With this report in hand, Steven Green and I began discussing a reconnaissance trip.

But our hopes for resuscitating Tiwai, and the hopes of ordinary Sierra Leoneans for peace and economic revival, were soon dashed. In May 1997 rebels launched new attacks on towns in the north of the country, and in Kenema fighting broke out between local militias, called "Kamajors," and government forces.[53] The Kamajors, who have their roots in traditional local hunters' associations, had become an important security force in up-country towns in 1994, when government forces proved unable or unwilling to provide adequate protection for civilians.

On May 25 1997, soldiers staged a coup against Tejan Kabbah's government and the president fled by helicopter to Guinea. The rebellious troops released hundreds of prisoners from Freetown's main jail, including soldiers who had been arrested for plotting against Kabbah. One of these freed men was Major Johnny Paul Koroma, who became leader of the new military junta. Among the first acts of the new rulers were the abolition of any official status for the Kamajors, and an invitation to the RUF to join the new government. Rebel forces entered Freetown, and days of killing, raping, and looting followed. Foreigners were quickly evacuated, and soon all foreign diplomatic missions were closed. Nigeria already had some small military contingents in the country that had been helping the government, and these troops soon came into conflict with the forces of the new regime; Nigeria sent reinforcements from its peacekeeping group in Liberia, and these occupied the international airport and blockaded the port. Sama Banya, President of the Conservation Society, was among several prominent citizens arrested for allegedly plotting a countercoup.[54]

The international community refused to recognize Koroma's regime, which was steadfastly opposed by the Nigerian government. As order returned to neighboring Liberia, where Charles Taylor finally won election as President in July 1997, Nigeria began to transfer its peacekeeping forces from Liberia to Sierra Leone. In February 1998, after Koroma backed away from an agreement to hand power back to Tejan Kabbah's civilian government, Nigerian forces attacked Freetown and, apparently aided by a British mercenary group, ousted Koroma's military junta.[55] In March, Kabbah was brought back to Freetown by the Nigerian forces and he set about rebuilding a government, appointing Sama Banya as his Foreign Minister. Rebel activity continued in the main diamond-mining areas of eastern Sierra Leone, however, and by the end of the year had spread to much of the north of the country. In January 1999 rebel forces reinvaded Freetown. As I checked the proofs of this book, the rebels had been beaten back to the outskirts of Freetown by a Nigerian-led West African force, but large areas of the capital had been devastated and thousands of people killed, including Prince Palmer, who had originally suggested Tiwai's game sanctuary status.

In this situation, the prospects for a revival of research and conservation activities at Tiwai are bleak. Even if better government takes root in Sierra Leone, if some of the destruction to the nation's infrastructure is repaired, and if a measure of peace and security returns to the countryside, the hunting that evidently has taken place at Tiwai will have made it much more difficult to study the behavior of any monkeys that remain on the island.[56] Many of the people who helped us establish our project have now left the country or been killed, and Njala College has been left abandoned and derelict; this will obviously hamper the restoration and maintenance of a field station and conservation program. Tourism, an important component of the Tiwai conservation program, will surely take a very long time to revive.

Much of what we had originally worked for at Tiwai assumed that there would be well-functioning local communities containing young people with at least moderate levels of education and minds open to ideas about conservation. But during the rebel insurgency, large areas of the countryside were largely abandoned, and a cohort of young people has grown up in Sierra Leone with little education; hundreds of children have been involved in appalling violence, and been encouraged to commit rape, torture, murder, and cannibalism.[57]

LESSONS FROM TIWAI

Our research and conservation programs at Tiwai were suspended in
1991, only nine years after they had begun. In this relatively short time,
should they be judged a success or a failure? In terms of the establishment of a research program in a remote part of tropical Africa, Tiwai
was a success. Starting from nothing, we organized and operated a functioning research station and study area and accomplished a considerable
amount of field biology. The greater part of the research was conducted
by American and British graduate students and scientists. If a larger part
of the research had been done by Sierra Leoneans, and if Njala College
had taken a more active role in the running of the field station, the project might have been regarded as a greater success. But the head of the
Department of Biology at Njala College in the latter days of our project,
Abu Sesay, told me himself that field biology and conservation work are
not of great interest to most Sierra Leoneans. Even so, two undergraduate ecology field courses from Njala were taught at Tiwai by expatriate
researchers, and several small research projects had been undertaken on
the island by Njala undergraduates. Mohamed Bakarr was one of the Njala
students who took a field course at Tiwai, and he went on to enroll for a
Ph.D. at the University of Miami. Bakarr was planning studies of plant
ecology on the island when the insurgency took hold and was forced to
complete his doctoral work in the laboratory in the United States.

In the short term, at least, Tiwai was also a conservation success. Very
little hunting occurred on the island between 1982 and 1991, and the
small amount of farming that did take place was done in such a way that
it had minimal harmful impact on the forest. The conservation effort was
greatly helped by the presence of a scientific research project. Long-term
research projects and field stations have proved to be effective and relatively inexpensive aids to conservation efforts in many other tropical
forests around the world, such as Kibale in Uganda.[58]

But Tiwai was only a partial success in terms of some of my original
hopes for the island. A conservation area secure for the indefinite future,
with local people strongly involved in its management, was not established. Up to the point when the island had to be abandoned, individu-

als in the chiefdoms, the university, and the government had often been very helpful in supporting conservation, research, and education initiatives, but most of these initiatives had come from foreign scientists and volunteers, and help for them usually had a price of some sort. The pervasive (though not universal) Sierra Leonean attitude to activities at Tiwai was that "within certain limits we will cooperate with you, help manage that which you have established, or refrain from doing that which you would rather we not do, so long as you provide us in return with money or some other material reward."

Given the social, political, and economic context of Sierra Leone at the time, and given the fact that the idea for conservation and research activities at Tiwai was one that originated almost entirely with outsiders, these attitudes are not surprising. They were disappointing only because we often expected the people we dealt with to share some of our enthusiasm for studying and conserving tropical rain forest.

Although I have described Tiwai as a community-based conservation effort, the work there grew out of the interests and actions of outsiders rather than local people, and so it would perhaps be more appropriate to describe it as a conservation program that had strong community participation. I attempted from the outset to establish local participation in management at Tiwai for several reasons. From the time of my first visit to Sierra Leone, I had seen that the Forestry Division and most other arms of national government did not work effectively outside the capital city, and that where government did operate, it did so more on behalf of its own members than on behalf of the people as a whole. I had seen government-managed wildlife conservation working relatively well in parts of East Africa and in India, but in Sierra Leone, where central government was so flawed, I decided it would be better to promote a more locally based management structure. I saw that in rural areas, Paramount Chiefs and chiefdom councils were generally respected and, unlike the national government, still had considerable authority. In any case, local people were already using the island, but not in a very destructive way. Although Liberian hunters were a threat to the island's primates, local people had some antipathy toward Liberians and were not opposed to some limitation of their activities.

At Tiwai we adopted an approach to conservation that strongly involved the local community not because this was the fashionable thing to do (the wave of international enthusiasm for community conservation was to come later), but because given the circumstances of time and place we felt that this approach was likely to be the most effective strategy to protect something important to us. But accepting, as we did, the premise that conservation in such areas is unlikely to work without the cooperation and involvement of local residents is not the same thing as saying that conservation projects must have as their main goal the improvement of human well-being, or that the only way to effectively manage an area is to put it fully in the hands of local people.

The resources protected at Tiwai—remnants of the disappearing Guinean forest and its wildlife—were certainly of more than local significance, and it was always outsiders, more than local people, who appreciated them for their intrinsic interest. Local people were prepared to work with us to protect Tiwai if they could see some tangible benefit coming to them: for instance, in employment opportunities, in direct payments made by tourists and other users, and in the status bestowed on villages and chiefdoms for their involvement in activities that attracted international interest. But in the absence of these potential benefits there is little likelihood that Tiwai's forests and wildlife would have survived for long without action by the national government or other outsiders. Almost all the conservation initiatives at Tiwai were suggested by outsiders, and their implementation always flagged in the absence of expatriate supervisors. A similar point has been made by Margaret Hardiman, describing the operation of a public-health program implemented by the mission-run Serabu Hospital in southern Sierra Leone and designed to increase the involvement of village people in improving their health.[59]

Serabu hospital staff worked through traditional birth attendants and special village health committees; nurses from the hospital met with these committees at least once each month and discussed simple hygiene and nutrition measures and gave immunizations. But the initiative for this program had come from outside, and Hardiman wondered whether it had produced permanent changes in behavior, and whether it would continue to be effective without the constant encouragement and support of the Serabu staff.

Tiwai taught us some other lessons about the drawbacks of community-based conservation. Even an area as small as Tiwai (five square miles) fell within the purview of several different communities that, because they had old antagonisms as well as old ties, would not automatically cooperate with one another. The communities were jealous of benefits they perceived that others obtained while they did not, and they proved no more willing to work together than people within a single community (a topic I discussed in the previous chapter). Indeed, I was told several times by rural Sierra Leoneans that cooperative farming schemes would not work in the country because of individual selfishness and social unreliability.

Furthermore, even in a country like Sierra Leone where national government works poorly, no major project, and especially not one involving foreigners, can function without some central government involvement. To be in Sierra Leone at all, we had to have some authorization from the national government, and the more that activities at Tiwai came to have national salience, the more it became inevitable that people and institutions who had power in the nation would wish to have some influence over what happened at Tiwai. In a country with little real democracy, no major conservation or research effort is likely to function without the blessing of some of the people who hold the reigns of power. This must be recognized in the planning of conservation projects.

I also learned from the Tiwai experience, as I was learning in other parts of Africa, that foreign planners, consciously or not, had a strong tendency to design conservation plans likely to provide significant future benefits to themselves or their own organizations—either job opportunities for themselves or a continuing role for their organization. A case in point at Tiwai is the very complicated structure of the management plan produced by a Peace Corps volunteer; in this plan, the Peace Corps was written in for an indefinite period to provide the training and assistance that would be needed for the plan to be fully implemented. Such dependence on outsiders is not necessarily in the best interests of an African research station or conservation area, but it does serve the interest of the individuals and organizations involved in international "development," despite the fact that their goals are widely understood to include helping developing countries achieve full autonomy.

Finally, the Tiwai experience highlights the fact that conservation plans based on Western attitudes are vulnerable to African political realities. Even though I had already been through several political upheavals in Africa and India, my colleagues and I made plans for Tiwai on the assumption that Sierra Leone would continue to function as a nation and would somehow solve its problems. Despite some of the inevitable disappointments I experienced from having unrealistic expectations about human behavior, I (and I think most other expatriates involved) always assumed that conservation could be made to work at Tiwai if the right approach were taken. It was only at the time of my last visit to Sierra Leone, in October 1993, that I came to feel powerless in the face of the chaos engulfing much of the country. People are rarely prepared to accept a very gloomy view of the future; even the gloomiest conservationists and environmental activists usually present dire prognostications mainly because they hope that these will cause changes in attitude or policy. But in retrospect, a realistic reading of the Sierra Leonean economic and political scene as it unfolded in the 1980s might have suggested that a breakdown of the state was a strong possibility, and that efforts devoted to conservation would to a significant extent be wasted. Because the future is never certain, a likely grim future has never prevented people from acting on the assumption that things may turn out all right. But the Tiwai experience suggests that in planning for conservation in developing countries it is foolish not to consider the possibility and potential impact of serious political instability in the future, and to take this into account while allocating scarce resources.

FIVE

Okomu

Conservation Policies Undermine Forest Protection

The boatman had cut the motor, and we were quietly paddling and drifting in our dugout canoe down the murky Osse River, scanning the vegetation on the banks for signs of monkeys. To our right was swamp forest at the edge of the Okomu Forest Reserve, and to our left secondary forest and farmland. Suddenly there was a loud crash from the undergrowth on our left, and I caught a glimpse of five small monkeys moving quickly, one with a distinct white throat. A few minutes later, a similar monkey sprang out of thick undergrowth on the right bank of the river and paused in the open for a few seconds to look at us. These were my first views of white-throated guenons in the wild. It was January 23, 1981, and I was back in Nigeria for the first time since visiting the country briefly on my way back to England from Uganda in 1972. Some zoologists thought that the species of monkey I had just seen might be extinct;[1] evidently it was not.

My journey on the Osse River led me in the following year to make a broader investigation of the status of the white-throated guenon. In the course of that survey I saw that the pressures on wildlife and forests in southern Nigeria had greatly intensified since my last visit to the country; monkeys, for instance, were even more heavily hunted here than in Sierra Leone (see plate 17). Although the white-throated guenon was not yet extinct, it seemed to me likely that it and other species would soon be lost unless conservation resources were concentrated on protecting forest wildlife in a few key areas. These observations led me to make recommendations that eventually resulted in the creation of a wildlife sanctuary and conservation project in Okomu. Within ten years, however, this project was placing its emphasis not so much on wildlife protection as on providing economic development assistance to migrant farmers; it was these farmers who were one of the greatest threats to the viability of the new sanctuary and its rare monkeys. This emphasis on development rather than protection was promoted not by the state Forestry Department, which had management responsibility for Okomu, but by outside conservation organizations. In this chapter I explain how these things happened, and I discuss the lessons I learned from my involvement with the Okomu project.

SEARCHING FOR DISAPPEARING
MONKEYS IN A CHANGED LAND

My chief aim in visiting Nigeria in 1981 was to find out if this country offered better opportunities for field research on olive colobus monkey biology than did Sierra Leone. I had found that Tiwai Island in Sierra Leone had much to offer as a study site, but I was concerned about the difficulties of establishing a research project in a place with no existing facilities of any kind and no protected status.

I had only become aware that the olive colobus occurred in Nigeria in July 1979, when I stopped at the Natural History Museum in London on my way to Sierra Leone. In the museum, primate specialist Douglas Brandon-Jones drew my attention to a single olive colobus skin collected in February 1967 near Ayangba, east of the river Niger near Idah, by an American missionary called Paul Gross.[2] I was surprised, because in 1967 I had been living only fifty miles south of Ayangba, at Nsukka, and I had met Gross just a few months before he had shot this specimen. Peter Jewell and I had visited him in October 1966 to pick up some pet duiker antelopes and a red-capped mangabey monkey that he had donated to the small zoo at the University of Nsukka. Gross had lived in the Ayangba area for many years and had a strong interest in hunting and natural history. But when I visited Ayangba in 1966 I heard nothing about olive colobus monkeys, and none of the literature I had read said anything about the species being found in Nigeria. As the political crisis in Nigeria intensified, travel from Nsukka to the Ayangba area (which was in the Northern Region) became increasingly difficult, and we lost touch with Gross.

When I learned in 1979 that there was a Nigerian population of olive colobus living close to an area I was familiar with, I became intrigued with the idea of revisiting Ayangba, trying to locate the Gross family, and investigating the possibilities of a field study. I was also interested in some other Nigerian primates. Besides the olive colobus, my surveys in Sierra Leone and Côte d'Ivoire had made me curious about the distribution patterns of West African forest monkeys and about the causes of these patterns. In following up the field surveys with further literature and museum searches, I had become especially intrigued by two Nigerian guenon monkeys (*Cercopithecus erythrogaster* and *C. sclateri*) that appeared to have very restricted geographical distributions and which no one seemed to have seen in the wild for many years. Each species was known only from a few zoo and museum specimens, and the only places where specimens of the white-throated or red-bellied guenon (*C. erythrogaster*) had been collected in the wild were forest reserves in the vicinity of Benin City in southwestern Nigeria. I decided that after visiting Ayangba to look for olive colobus monkeys I would try to stop in Benin to learn what I could about *C. erythrogaster*. A search for *C. sclateri* would have to wait until a later time.

So it was that on January 1, 1981, I returned to Nigeria. I found a country greatly changed since my last, brief visit in 1972. In 1972, the average world price of petroleum had been $4.80 per barrel;[3] but by the end of 1980, Nigeria was selling its high-quality light crude oil at around $40 a barrel and producing just over 2 million barrels each day. Oil revenues paid to the federal government had come to account for 90 percent of foreign currency earnings and had given Nigeria hard-currency reserves estimated at $7–$8 billion.[4] This newfound wealth was financing ambitious road-building and agricultural development schemes, but the money flooding into the economy had also escalated corruption. A democratically elected civilian government, headed by President Shehu Shagari, had been in power since October 1979, succeeding the series of military regimes that had ruled Nigeria since January 1966. Members of this government were being increasingly accused of financial improprieties, but the continuing gush of oil money had diluted the pain that such abuses could inflict on the Nigerian people, and the next military coup was not to occur until 1983.

The first stop on my 1981 visit was at the University of Nsukka, where I met some of my former colleagues, and from Nsukka I took a series of four communal taxis to Ayangba. Ayangba, I found, was hardly recognizable as the town I had visited more than fourteen years before. It was much larger and was now the headquarters of a big agricultural development project supported by the World Bank. Many expatriates worked on the project, which boasted a club with a swimming pool, as well as badminton, squash, and tennis courts. The Gross family were still living in Ayangba, but they were out of town when I arrived, and so I arranged accommodation at the guest house of the development project. The Grosses returned the next day, and I stayed with them for two weeks, exploring the Igala country in the angle of the Niger and Benue Rivers.

I found that the few small forest reserves in Igalaland were being heavily exploited by loggers, while the little forest that remained outside reserves was being rapidly converted to farmland. When I had begun research at Nsukka in 1966, forest management in Nigeria was the responsibility of the four regional governments; with the creation of states in 1967, the management of forest reserves had been devolved to the states and control of exploitation had generally become much looser. At the same time, the explosive growth of the economy had increased the demand for timber. Paul Gross told me that hunting pressure too had increased markedly, the result of both the increase in size and prosperity of the human population, and the greater availability of more efficient guns. Monkeys had also come under extra pressure as a result of non-Muslims moving into the area; the original inhabitants were predominantly Muslim and traditionally had not eaten monkey meat.

Gross said he had not seen an olive colobus for several years and thought they might now be extinct in the area. After eight days of searching most of the remaining forest patches near Ayangba, I finally managed to glimpse four olive colobus with a mixed group of mona and putty-nosed monkeys in gallery forest along the Okura River.[5] This turned out to be my only sighting of olive colobus in Nigeria, and all the monkeys I encountered around Ayangba were very shy, presumably as a result of being hunted. Although I was glad to have been able to return to the area and see the olive colobus, it was apparent that Igalaland offered poor opportunities for long-term behavioral research.

I stopped in Nsukka for a night on my way back from Ayangba, and the next day I set off for Benin City, across the Niger; this involved a series of nine taxi rides, most of them alarming, especially on the narrow highway from Onitsha to Benin. Benin had been the capital of the Midwest Region when I first lived in Nigeria, and the Midwest Region had since become Bendel State. I found my way to the University of Benin campus on the edge of the city and made for the Department of Biological Sciences. Here I met Pius Anadu, a zoology lecturer who had arrived in Nsukka from Ibadan in 1967, shortly before the Biafran secession. Anadu, an Igbo, had served in the Biafran Army until he was wounded in the battle for Umuahia in 1969. He had returned to the University of Ibadan after the war to finish his Ph.D. on the ecology of small mammals. In Anadu's office I was happily surprised to see some of the small-mammal skins I had collected in the 1960s, which Anadu had rescued from the Nsukka campus.

I learned that Anadu was interested in the possibilities of research in the Okomu Forest Reserve, whose boundary lay only fifteen miles west of Benin City, and which was one of three wild localities from which old museum specimens of *Cercopithecus erythrogaster* had come (the location of Okomu is shown on map 3 on page 24). Anadu's technician Thaddeus Agbozele assured me that he had seen these monkeys in the wild in Okomu, and so we began making plans to see the forest the next day.

Before heading to Okomu I visited the small zoo at Ogba on the outskirts of Benin City, where Anadu had told me there was a collection of local monkeys. In a few small cages I found twenty-three monkeys of eight species; most exciting to me were two female guenons with distinct white throats that were labeled as olive colobus monkeys, but were evidently *Cercopithecus erythrogaster* (an ironic mislabeling, given that the primary purpose of my visit to Nigeria was to find olive colobus). The name *"erythrogaster"* is derived from the rust color of the belly hair of the type specimen of this monkey species in the London Natural History Museum. Where this type specimen was collected, other than in West Africa, is not known. Specimens subsequently collected in the wild near Benin City have gray bellies, and so did the two females in the Ogba Zoo.[6] For these animals the name "white-throated guenon," used by D. R. Rosevear in his checklist of Nigerian mammals,[7] seemed much more appropriate than "red-bellied guenon." Now that I had seen these white-throated guenons in a zoo, I at least knew that the species was not extinct, and I looked forward even more to my excursion to Okomu.

A day after learning about Okomu and seeing the Ogba Zoo monkeys, Pius Anadu and I set off for the forest in his Volkswagen Beetle.

OKOMU FOREST RESERVE

Okomu is a large reserve with an area of more than 460 square miles. The original reserve was established by the British colonial government in 1912, and an extension was added in 1935, when ownership of the reserve as a whole was handed over to the Benin Native Authority, a branch of local government headed by the traditional ruler of Benin, the Oba. Management was overseen by the colonial forest service, but the local government was responsible for employing staff, while revenues derived from forest exploitation went to the local government and the communal landholders.[8] By 1966, ownership had been transferred to the Local Council that had succeeded the Native Authority, and management was the responsibility of the Forestry Department of the Midwestern Regional government. In 1970, Bendel State (the successor to the Midwestern Region) took control of all forest reserves, although much of the revenue was still supposed to accrue to Local Councils.[9]

By the time of our visit in 1981, the forest was in no way a pristine wilderness. Since early this century, Okomu had been exploited for its rich stands of mahogany, and after World War II systematic rotational logging had been practiced in the reserve (see plate 18). More recently, some areas of the reserve had been cleared by *taungya* farming (described in chapter 2).

After arriving at Okomu, Anadu and I made a short walk through an area of recently logged forest. The forest canopy was very broken and we saw no monkeys. That night Anadu had to return to Benin, but I wanted to continue searching for monkeys early in the morning, and so we arranged that I would stay overnight at the settlement of Nikrowa in a rest house belonging to Okomu's main timber concessionaire, the African Timber and Plywood company (AT & P, a division of the United Africa Company). That night, over some beers, the AT & P managers told me of their concerns about how the forest reserve was being managed. Their own logging followed long-established working plans that had been drawn up by the Forestry Department many years previously.[10] But, they complained, the Forestry Department had been allocating one-mile-square forest compartments to other contractors many years before these compartments were due to be felled under the working plans (which specified a fifty-year felling cycle). A good deal of logging was apparently being done with no permits at all. This excessive allocation of logging concessions almost certainly involved the exchange of money or other favors and was related to the increasing indiscipline in Nigeria's political and economic life.

I was due to fly back to New York from Lagos the following evening, so I had very little time left to try and see a white-throated guenon. I decided that my best chance lay in taking a boat early in the morning up one of the rivers bounding the forest reserve. I was up before dawn, but there was no sign of the vehicle I thought I had arranged to take me the two miles to the river. So I ended up walking most of the way, and then wasted more time haggling over the price for hiring a canoe with an outboard motor. Finally, just before 8 A.M., our boat chugged away from Nikrowa waterside up the Osse River, enveloped in a light morning mist. Around 10 A.M. we reached the settlement of Ikoru, without having seen any primates and having only once heard a sound that might have been monkeys moving near the river. We took a break, and then decided on a different search strategy for the return trip to Nikrowa. After motoring a few miles downstream from Ikoru, we cut the boat's engine and drifted and paddled along the little-inhabited middle reaches of the river; this strategy paid off and eventually we spotted white-throats, as I described at the beginning of this chapter.

Elated at seeing these rare monkeys, I returned to the rest house to find that senior AT & P managers had been visiting, and that they had arranged an accommodation bill for me equivalent to fifty dollars, reducing my total reserves to ten dollars. In the early 1980s the government tightly controlled an artificially high currency exchange rate, and this made Nigeria an expensive place to do fieldwork. However, the local forest production manager, Eugene Dogwoh, took pity on me and gave me a lift to the small Benin City airport. Next morning I was back in New York.

NIGERIA OR SIERRA LEONE?

Now I was in a quandary. I had gone to Nigeria mainly to evaluate whether there was a more promising olive colobus study site there than in Sierra Leone, but I had found no site as good for such a study as Tiwai. Yet I had also become aware that white-throated monkeys and their forest habitat in Nigeria were in a perilous position, and that a more extensive survey was urgently needed to produce a conservation plan. I had enjoyed being in Nigeria again and was keen to undertake this more extensive survey myself.

In New York, I received a letter from Peter White at Njala College in which he encouraged me to pursue a project at Tiwai, and I also heard from George Whitesides and Steven Green in Miami that they were eager to join in a collaborative research project in Sierra Leone. I therefore decided that I should try to develop projects in both southwest Nigeria and Sierra Leone, and over the coming months I worked on two proposals for funding agencies; one, written jointly with Whitesides and Green, was for a community ecology research project on the primates of Tiwai, and the other was for a survey of forests in southwest Nigeria.

I decided that to be able to implement this plan I would have to take a leave of absence from my teaching duties at Hunter College in the spring of 1982 and initially work in Nigeria. Meanwhile, Whitesides would go out to Sierra Leone to reconnoiter a Tiwai study area, and I would travel from Nigeria in June to join him and help get research started. I would then have to take another leave in spring 1983 to begin olive colobus research at Tiwai. This plan came to fruition when I was awarded grants from the National Science Foundation and the City University of New York for Sierra Leone research, and from the New York Zoological Society and WWF-US for a Nigerian survey.

SURVEY OF SOUTHWEST NIGERIA

In January 1982, I flew back to a Lagos blanketed in the haze of the dust-laden Harmattan wind that blows from the Sahara during the West African dry season. For five months, from a base in the Department of Biological Sciences at the University of Benin, and working closely with Pius Anadu, I surveyed many forest areas in Bendel State, as well as in the nearby states of Ondo, Ogun, and Rivers. For transport I had a well-worn Volkswagen Beetle, loaned to me by Reginald and Jayanthi Victor, Indian zoologists teaching in the same department.

This survey found that white-throated guenons occurred over a much larger area than that encompassed by the few museum specimens I had located, all of which had come from within a 40-mile radius of Benin City. We saw the monkeys as far west as the Omo Reserve in Ogun State, and hunters reported their presence in the Niger Delta, 190 miles east of Omo (though it was not until 1989 that I finally managed to see a wild white-throat in the delta).

Although we were surprised to find these supposedly very rare monkeys over a large area, wherever we went we saw signs of massive pressures on the remaining forests, from logging, farming, road building and oil extraction; there was also intense and uncontrolled hunting for wild game ("bushmeat"). Government departments and public services were inefficient, and bribery was a stronger influence than the law in many important areas of human activity. Soon after I arrived in Nigeria, the *Economist* published a survey of Nigeria, in which it observed, "How can so much money and such high hopes engender such chaos? Why won't the telephones, or the bureaucrats, work? Why can't you turn on a switch, or a tap, or turn up for a scheduled flight, with any confidence that light, or a wash, or a journey, will result? Why, at almost every level of public and private administration, do people expect bribes?"[11] Nicholas Harman, the author of these words, gave no direct answer but cited the cumulative effects of colonial rule, the economic distortions produced by oil wealth, and the deep allegiance of people to extended families rather than to the nation and society as a whole.[12]

Given these evident features of Nigerian economic and social life, I thought that broad-scale recommendations for action to ameliorate the huge pressures on Nigerian forests and wildlife were unlikely to meet with much success (there had been many such recommendations in the previous twenty years, and they had produced few positive outcomes). I decided that the best hope our survey had of producing a real improvement in the chances for survival of white-throated guenons and their habitat lay in formulating very specific recommendations for concrete action in a limited area where success seemed possible.

The area that Anadu and I concluded was most worthy of concentrated conservation action was Okomu. I saw white-throated guenons and three other species of forest monkey more frequently in Okomu than in any other reserve; Okomu was also rich in birds, and hunters reported the presence of a few chimpanzees and forest elephants. Of the forest reserves that Anadu and I had visited, Okomu was the largest and appeared to be the least disturbed. The reserve was bounded on three sides by two major rivers, the Osse and Siluko, which hindered access by loggers and hunters, and the forest had had relatively careful past management. We therefore recommended both the immediate establishment of a seventy-four-square-mile wildlife sanctuary in the center of Okomu, which would be protected from hunting, tree cutting, and other exploitation, and the reintroduction of selective logging on a long rotation in the rest of the reserve. We also argued for the better regulation of hunting in areas of the reserve outside the central sanctuary, and for restrictions on the expansion of the plantations and settlements that already existed within the reserve. Not only were there already many immigrant farmers in Okomu, but in 1977 the state government had also allowed sixty square miles in the west of the reserve to be allocated on a ninety-nine-year lease to a federal oil-palm plantation project that had European technical and financial assistance.

After I returned to New York in July 1982, Pius Anadu continued with our work, which now had support from the Nigerian Conservation Foundation (NCF) and the Federal Department of Forestry. The NCF is an indigenous nongovernmental organization that was launched in 1982 to raise public awareness about the destruction of Nigeria's natural environment, to encourage and conduct conservation projects, and to raise funds to carry out these efforts. Its founder and Chairman was a Lagos businessman, Chief S. L. Edu, who had been President of the Lagos Chamber of Commerce and Commissioner for Health and Social Services in Lagos State. Having been involved in efforts to promote trade between Nigeria and the Netherlands, Edu had met Prince Bernhard at a time when Bernhard was the International President of the World Wildlife Fund.[13] Chief Edu was persuaded by Bernhard to join WWF, and he served for eight years as a trustee. Edu created the Nigerian Conservation Foundation as a local version of WWF, and today the NCF is one of the few formal affiliates of WWF in Africa.

In early 1983, our recommendations were presented in a report to the Bendel State government, to the federal government, and to the NCF.[14] Our report made detailed recommendations not only for conservation in Okomu but also more general recommendations for Bendel State as a whole. When our report was submitted I was back in New York, but Anadu kept an eye on Okomu and lobbied the state government to take action on our recommendations. Efforts to get a wildlife sanctuary established were delayed, however, by economic and political developments.

MORE ECONOMIC AND POLITICAL UPHEAVALS

While I was in Nigeria in the early part of 1982, the price of crude petroleum slumped to $28 per barrel from its high of $40 in early 1981. High prices had produced an oversupply of oil on world markets, along with a recession in the industrialized oil-consuming countries. In an effort to maintain the oil price, OPEC (of which Nigeria is a member) agreed to cut production levels. By April 1982, Nigeria was producing only 650,000 barrels of oil each day (worth $28 a barrel), compared with more than 2 million barrels at $40 a barrel in early 1981. Monthly revenues to the Nigerian government of more than $1.35 billion at the beginning of 1982 had dropped to $500 million by April.[15] The effects on Nigeria were disastrous. There were immediate cutbacks in government spending, and, in the longer term, living standards declined while external debt rose steeply. Gross national product per capita fell from $860 in 1982 to $640 in 1986, and external debt rose from $8.9 billion in 1980 to $21.9 billion in 1986.[16] Consumer prices climbed, unemployment increased, and disillusionment spread, especially after an election in mid-1983 that was widely regarded as rigged. On December 31, 1983, the Shagari government was toppled in a coup led by Major General Mohammed Buhari, who pledged to save the country from economic collapse.

DECLARATION OF A SANCTUARY

These events inevitably distracted governments in Nigeria from wildlife conservation efforts, which now had an even lower priority than in earlier years. The 1983 elections brought Shagari's party into power in Bendel State, and a new commissioner was appointed to run the Ministry of Agriculture and Natural Resources, which was responsible for forestry and wildlife issues. Anadu was told that the new commissioner needed time to study the files on Okomu. Hoping to stimulate some action, Anadu turned to the NCF. The head of the NCF Scientific Committee, A. P. Leventis (a director of one of the largest companies in Nigeria), agreed to meet with the Bendel State governor and stress the importance of Okomu. But before the meeting could take place the Buhari coup brought a new military governor to Bendel, and a new agriculture commissioner was appointed who also wanted to familiarize himself with the activities of his ministry before he would make any major decisions.

By the middle of 1984 I decided that I would have to visit Nigeria to promote action on our sanctuary proposal. In July I met Leventis in Lagos, and encouraged him to discuss the conservation of Okomu with the new Bendel governor, and then I flew to Benin City, where Anadu and I were able to meet briefly with the agriculture commissioner, who expressed sympathy with our proposals but appeared to be preoccupied with other issues. It was clear that a decision to declare a protected site within an important timber area was going be made with reluctance and would require the assent of the state governor. Anadu did not think it proper to address a direct request to the governor until the agriculture commissioner had formulated his own views about conservation in Okomu. This attention to protocol meant that Anadu's letter to Military Governor J. T. Useni was not delivered until March 1985.

Soon after this, Anadu learned that the previous civilian state government had granted licenses to several timber contractors to log much of the area that we had recommended for strict protection. Feeling that time was running out, Anadu contacted Leventis again and sought his support for further pressure on the governor; on May 13 Leventis wrote to Governor Useni, and he followed this up with a personal visit. I contacted our sponsors in the United States, and in June the General Director of the New York Zoological Society, William Conway, also wrote to Useni. At last, on July 25, the state's Executive Council discussed and approved the proposal for a wildlife sanctuary at Okomu, to become effective on August 1, 1985. Later that month, the Nigerian federal government changed hands yet again, when Ibrahim Babangida seized power in a palace coup.

An official notice of the creation of the Okomu Wildlife Sanctuary was not published until December 1986,[17] and in this notice the sanctuary's area had been reduced from our original recommendation of seventy-four square miles to twenty-six square miles. And, although the sanctuary now existed in law, it still had no practical protection and the forest within it was still being logged.

THE OKOMU CONSERVATION PROJECT BEGINS

In 1984, Anadu had been appointed to head a new Department of Forestry and Wildlife at the University of Benin, but the department lacked funds and trained personnel. In an effort to stimulate research and conservation efforts at Okomu and bring in some outside funding and expertise to assist Anadu's new department, I contacted Roderick Fisher of the Ecology and Conservation Unit at University College London (UCL) and suggested that the unit collaborate with Anadu on an Okomu management study. Fisher had been my teacher in the UCL Conservation Course in the 1960s, and he and I had collaborated on the abortive plans for a survey of the Ashambu Hills in South India in the late 1970s. In July 1985, Fisher visited Nigeria with the support of the British Council, went to Okomu, and met Anadu and Leventis. This resulted in a proposal both for a joint management study of the forest reserve and for an academic exchange between the two institutions; but no funding could be found to realize the proposal. Fisher did not entirely forget about Okomu, however, and in 1987 he put one of his students in touch with Leventis in London. This was Lee White, who had just finished his undergraduate zoology degree and was looking for an African field project to work on before he began doctoral research in Gabon on the effects of logging on rain forest mammals. I had first met Lee when he was a young boy in Uganda in 1970; he was the son of Peter White, whom I had worked with in Sierra Leone, and he had participated in the Tiwai project, both as a research assistant in the year before he began his undergraduate course and later as a member of a student expedition from UCL.

Leventis met White in August 1987 and decided to appoint him as a consultant at Okomu, considering this the first phase of a joint UCL/University of Benin project. Meanwhile, the NCF had arranged for Prince Bernhard to visit some of their projects later that year. In October 1987, Bernhard officially launched NCF's "Okomu Forest Project," with White as the first project manager. I had just returned to Nigeria to commence surveys in search of the country's other rare forest monkey, Sclater's guenon, so I was able to attend the launching of the project and introduce White to Okomu.

For its first year the project was run on a shoestring, with an initial budget of about 1,000 naira per month (then equivalent to about $250). But White was enthusiastic and energetic, and using a field team made up of NCF, state, and federal forestry employees he managed to bring poaching under control within the sanctuary. Small-scale facilities were established for visitors, and research on the forest ecosystem was initiated; research got a boost from an expedition of UCL undergraduates, who worked in collaboration with students from the University of Benin, supervised by Reginald Victor. However, logging in the sanctuary did not finally end until June 1988.

After one year, Lee White left Okomu and soon afterward began his doctoral research in the Lopé Reserve in Gabon. Franklin Farrow, one of the students who had participated in the UCL expedition, took over for a year as a volunteer manager on the NCF project. Farrow continued to supervise the protection staff in the wildlife sanctuary, but also studied management problems in the large area of the Okomu Forest Reserve that lay beyond the boundaries of the sanctuary. Anadu and I believed that the sanctuary and its wildlife would be viable in the long term only if the reserve areas outside the sanctuary remained as forest, carefully exploited for timber on a sustained yield basis.

Farming, however, was increasing in the reserve. The 1950 Working Plan for Okomu had proposed that 35 acres (14 hectares) be converted by *taungya* farming annually, up to a maximum of 2,450 acres (991 hectares).[18] But by the 1960s the *taungya* system, widely applied in southern Nigerian forests, was already beginning to break down; it became a way in which politicians and government officials could provide farmland to a rapidly growing and land-hungry population at no cost to themselves, while often obtaining rewards from the people granted land. Very little effort was made to ensure that the farms were quickly replaced by tree plantations, the system's original intention (see plate 19). A particularly large increase in *taungya* farming apparently took place under the civilian government of 1979–83, when most Forestry Department plans were abandoned.[19]

Almost all the farmers who were allocated land for *taungya* in Okomu were not local people but immigrants from more densely populated parts of Nigeria; they included Urhobo, Itsekiri, and Igbo people from areas far to the south and east of Okomu. Some farms were granted as political favors to "weekend farmers" who lived in distant towns and visited their farms only occasionally, using hired labor to maintain them.[20] By 1987, around 500 hectares (1,235 acres) were being allocated annually for farming in Okomu.[21] The Director of the Bendel State Forestry Department became so alarmed at the breakdown of the *taungya* system throughout the state that he described it as having degenerated into "a peasant shifting cultivation system which could eventually liquidate the forest reserves"; in September 1988 he placed a ban on any new farming outside already farmed areas.[22] This produced an outcry from the migrant farmers, and the Forestry Department was put under political pressure to reverse its policy. Although the policy remained in effect, it was largely ignored because the department was given so few resources to enforce it.

I visited Okomu again in July 1989, accompanied by Reg Victor. We learned from Franklin Farrow about the continuing spread of farms in the reserve. Farrow also told us that hunting was becoming more commercialized, with little of the game killed being consumed locally. We concluded that given the scale of settlement and exploitation now entrenched at Okomu, there was little chance that the reserve as a whole could be managed for sustained-yield timber production, as Anadu and

I had proposed in 1982. It seemed that the only hope for a viable forest ecosystem remaining at Okomu was for the existing sanctuary to be expanded while there was still unfarmed forest adjacent to it, and for this fully protected area (that might best have the status of a national park) to be surrounded by a buffer zone in which there was no intensive farming. It also seemed important that NCF make a clearer long-term commitment to Okomu, particularly by appointing a professional manager. Before leaving Nigeria I discussed these points with the Bendel Director of Forestry and with the NCF, of which Pius Anadu had now become Executive Director. On returning to New York I wrote a report to the NCF about my observations at Okomu, including recommendations on the extension of the sanctuary and the appointment of a qualified project manager.

In March 1990, Anadu wrote again to the Bendel Commissioner for Agriculture, expressing concern about the spread of farming in Okomu and the increase in hunting. He described NCF's plan to develop a master plan for the entire forest reserve that would, among other things, stabilize land use in settlements surrounding the reserve and establish a conservation education program.[23] The NCF also appointed a full-time Okomu Project Manager, Sylvester Orhiere, a native of Bendel State who had been working at Kainji Lake, Nigeria's first national park. Orhiere took up his appointment in April and soon negotiated with the Bendel Director of Forestry for a one-mile-wide buffer zone to be established around the wildlife sanctuary, a zone in which *taungya* farming and logging would cease within one year. Soon after this, Anadu wrote to the Military Governor of the state, asking that a much larger buffer zone be considered, in which no farming would be allowed and where timber exploitation and hunting would be phased out over a ten-year period; he noted that a one-mile-wide buffer zone around the existing sanctuary would not provide a total area large enough to form an adequate long-term refuge for wildlife. Anadu also proposed that the remainder of the reserve be considered a "support zone" in which land use would be stabilized by a combination of improved farming methods and agroforestry. This zone, it was suggested, would be developed with assistance from the U.K. Overseas Development Administration (ODA).[24]

It was through a deepening involvement with WWF-UK and the ODA in the late 1980s that the Nigerian Conservation Foundation had begun to consider including support zones in several of its field projects. Since 1988, NCF had been collaborating with WWF-UK on plans to create a national park in Cross River State in southeastern Nigeria (see chapter 6). In a report on land use and agricultural development around part of the proposed Cross River park, a team from the ODA's Natural Resources Institute had in 1989 defined a support zone as "a narrow zone surrounding the Park wherein lie those villages at present dependent, to some degree, on the Park area for their livelihood. It was proposed that for the security of the Park, every effort would be made increasingly to associate and involve these communities with the Park activities so that eventually they will become dependent on the Park and have a vested interest in defending it."[25] In other words, protection of the forest ecosystem would be attempted through creation of a development program focused on people living next to the area being protected. Such a program was now being proposed for Okomu.

"SUSTAINABLE DEVELOPMENT" COMES TO OKOMU

In chapter 3, I discussed the close links that had developed during the 1980s between conservation and development organizations. It is not surprising that Britain's Overseas Development Administration, cooperating with WWF and NCF, became involved in the Okomu conservation project, or that attention became focused more on support zone development than on protecting the forest itself.

It appears that ODA staff were first contacted by the UCL Ecology and Conservation Unit in early 1987 and asked to support the management study that this unit hoped to conduct in collaboration with the University of Benin. ODA did not immediately respond to this proposal, but in October 1988 Clive Wicks at WWF-UK asked Lee White to prepare a report on forest management in Bendel State, with recommendations for its improvement, that could be submitted to ODA.[26] White and Wicks had come into contact after White made a survey trip to the Oban Hills, a trip that led to the initiation of WWF's Cross River National Park project.

Clive Wicks had spent the early part of his career with the British-American Tobacco Company in Nigeria and other African countries, working in agricultural extension and management positions. He was now employed as a conservation-and-development executive at WWF, with responsibility for formulating and managing conservation projects funded by development agencies. It was apparently through the efforts of Wicks that ODA sent a consultancy team to Bendel State in early 1990 to "prepare a project in support of conservation, forest management and rural development initiatives in and around the Okomu Wildlife Sanctuary."[27]

The ODA consultants concluded that Bendel State was not truly committed to halting the conversion of natural forest to farmland. They observed that more information would have to be gathered before a project could be properly designed.[28] Subsequently, ODA sponsored an aerial survey and production of a land use map, but they did not get directly involved in the management of Okomu. However, their idea of promoting conservation by encouraging development in a support zone had now become embedded in NCF's own thinking.

In 1991 the NCF took a further step down the conservation-and-development road when it arranged with WWF-UK to appoint a British expatriate, Rachel Okunlola, as a Project Development Officer at NCF's Lagos headquarters. Okunlola's training and experience was in agricultural development; her position was funded by WWF and her main brief was to develop funding proposals for NCF field projects. Not surprisingly, these proposals emphasized development activities rather than protection.

One of the first fruits of this effort was a grant from the Lagos office of the Ford Foundation for a pilot study and experimental work in the Okomu Support Zone. Unfortunately, this zone was not outside the forest reserve, as in the Cross River National Park plan; instead, it was designated as those parts of the forest that lay *within* the reserve near the wildlife sanctuary. From this point on, the idea became entrenched among the various conservation planners and managers involved with Okomu that most of the reserve was an area of legitimate human settlement and cultivation. There had indeed been a number of villages within the boundaries of the reserve when it was first established, and the people of these villages were permitted to remain and to exercise certain use rights within the reserve, such as farming in designated areas ("enclaves"), and hunting, fishing, and gathering forest products (such as palm nuts and fronds, canes, roofing leaves, and fruits). But the order establishing the reserve specifically stated that such rights could not be acquired by newcomers.[29] Now conservationists, by following the philosophy that conservation should be linked to development, were acknowledging the rights of recent immigrants to live and prosper indefinitely within the forest reserve. And it was just such migrant *taungya* farmers, whose activities the Bendel State Forestry Department itself had been trying to restrict, who were causing some of the greatest forest destruction in Okomu.

Part of the Ford Foundation grant to NCF for pilot work in the Okomu Support Zone was used to pay a University of Benin sociologist, Francesca Omorodion, to undertake a socioeconomic survey. Omorodion's survey was conducted between August and November 1991. It focused on four settlements. Only one of these, Iguowan, was a true descendant of an indigenous community, one that had been there before the forest reserve was created. The other three, Arakhuan, Mile 3, and Nikrowa, were all settlements that had been created or greatly expanded as a result of logging or forestry operations. Although Nikrowa had its roots in an indigenous settlement, most of its residents were relative newcomers, originally drawn by opportunities in the logging industry or by *taungya* farming.

Taking the now-fashionable "participatory" approach to development research, Omorodion asked the villagers for their recommendations on actions that could be taken to mitigate the impact of conservation measures on them. They suggested that they be provided with cassava- and maize-grinding machines, good drinking water, electricity, goat and pig husbandry projects, a gin still, and sources of credit for trading. In her report, Omorodion accepted these suggestions as reasonable and also proposed a tree-species nursery that could provide seedlings to "plant up" the forest, so as to restore soil fertility and make timber exploitation more sustainable. The general thrust of Omoro- dion's report was that Okomu should be regarded primarily as a farm managed with the well-being of the people as its priority. Rather than examining how to mitigate the impact of farming on forest conservation, the report argued that "it is important that development programmes be propagated, to help reduce the effects of the Reserve/Sanctuary restric- tions on farming/agricultural systems." And in a bizarre twist of the original purpose of the sanctuary that Anadu and I had proposed, the report also noted, "A number of villagers suggested that NCF should gather the wildlife in the Sanctuary and convey them somewhere else. In fact, the villagers said that they are willing and available to assist NCF in the gathering of its wildlife mammals. The situation may probably be amenable if the support of the villagers is obtained through participa- tory development and conservation education programme."[30]

I did not become aware of this report until I visited Okomu in July 1992. Far from Omorodion's approach being dismissed as nonsensical, I found that a Support Zone Officer was now employed by NCF, working in the four settlements surveyed by Omorodion. The officer was distrib- uting improved varieties of maize and cassava, demonstrating im- proved agricultural techniques, holding meetings to discuss the estab- lishment of credit schemes, and planning for a piggery and poultry farm. Some of these activities were actually occurring within the new one-mile sanctuary buffer zone. No analysis of the possible long-term impacts of this strategy had been conducted.

Other signs were more reassuring. Logging activity in the reserve had declined. In August 1991, Bendel State had been divided into two new states, Edo and Delta. Okomu lay in Edo, which in February 1992 had temporarily banned all logging. While the ban was in effect, the state government had appointed a task force to reorganize the timber indus- try in an attempt to counteract illegal logging. The Project Manager, Orhiere, told me that hunting had also fallen off in the sanctuary, though he thought this too was partly a consequence of external factors: in- creases both in the costs of guns and ammunition and in government li- cense fees for firearms. At Arakhuan, on the very edge of the Okomu wildlife sanctuary, a set of old Forestry Department buildings had been redeveloped with the assistance of the Leventis Foundation to serve as the headquarters of the NCF project. These buildings included a conservation education center, a residence and office for the project manager, and accommodation for visitors, including student groups. But apart from the support provided by Leventis, no outside funds had been secured to help protect the wildlife sanctuary.

Because I was concerned by the likely consequences of the support zone program I had observed, I wrote to A.P. Leventis, expressing my view that this program was likely, through its assistance to migrant farmers, to lead to the growth of the human population in the forest reserve and increased pressures on the forest and its wildlife. I stressed the continuing need for a general management plan for the Okomu Forest Reserve that would take a broad view of conservation needs in Edo State and Nigeria and examine ways to restrict farming to areas well away from the wildlife sanctuary (for instance, by providing new opportunities *outside* the reserve).

Subsequently, Leventis visited Okomu, and he discussed my comments at a meeting of NCF's Scientific Committee. As a result, NCF decided to hold off on any new activities at Okomu until a review was carried out. When the NCF review team visited Okomu in January 1993, they found evidence of the dangers of trying to conserve a forest ecosystem by supporting economic activities. Almost all of the ten farmers who had been given tree seedlings to plant (along with improved crop seeds and cuttings) had failed to plant the trees, and explained that they did not want to risk losing their farms. Of the business schemes put forward by farming groups for credit assistance, the only one that appeared economically viable came from an Igbo women's group that traded in bushmeat and farm produce; fortunately, NCF decided not to support this group. Because Okomu residents were unwilling to disclose their earnings from hunting in the sanctuary, the review group found it difficult to evaluate what level of new income-generating activities would need to be supported to offset any losses caused by lack of access to the wildlife sanctuary. After some debate, the team agreed that because demonstration farming activities in Arakhuan lay within the sanctuary one-mile buffer zone, these should be terminated. But the team also agreed that modest support should continue to be given to farmers in other parts of the reserve; this would include help to two demonstration farms, support of group credit schemes used to buy improved crop varieties, assistance to backyard poultry- and rabbit-raising projects, and a loan for the repair of a cassava mill. They recommended that farming in the buffer zone be phased out, but they suggested that this take place over a three-to-five-year period, even though the state government itself had decreed that this farming should end by April 18, 1991.[31] The basic principle of encouraging development as an aid to conservation remained in place.

PLANTATIONS EXPAND

Farming and hunting were not the only threats to the integrity of the Okomu ecosystem. Equally disturbing was the continued allocation of large segments of the forest reserve to plantation companies. I have already referred to the sixty square miles granted to the Okomu Oil Palm Company in 1977. Subsequently, the state government had leased a further eight square miles for rubber planting to a local timber and plantation concern, Iyayi Brothers; this area was immediately adjacent to the northeastern corner of the one-mile-wide buffer zone around the wildlife sanctuary. Such leases are an example of one of the greatest abuses that has resulted from the devolution of control over Nigerian forest reserves from regional government to state government. At the state level, members of government tend to have close links with wealthy individuals or companies; this encourages corruption, especially in the absence of true democracy.

The next blow to Okomu came soon after NCF's review of its support zone development program. In February 1993, bulldozers began to clear forest for a new rubber plantation on an additional eight square miles of reserve land north of the wildlife sanctuary (see plate 20). This was to be an extension of an existing rubber plantation, the Osse River Rubber Estate, which lay between the reserve and the Osse River. This estate was jointly owned by the Michelin (Nigeria) Plantation Group (who had a 51 percent stake) and the Edo State government (49 percent). Osse River

Rubber had originally discussed their plans with the civilian government in 1981, but had not applied formally for a concession until 1988, when the plan had been opposed by the Forestry Department.[32] Despite the objections of both Forestry and the NCF, a lease was granted in 1991; the terms of the lease were extremely favorable to the rubber company, which was said to have paid only twenty naira (about three dollars) per hectare (equivalent to about six hundred dollars for a square mile).

The Nigerian Conservation Foundation and local environmentalists sought to halt this new clearance. With funding from WWF-UK, NCF commissioned an economist to conduct a cost-benefit analysis of the financial implications of converting the forest to a rubber plantation rather than leaving it in its natural state and harvesting it sustainably. The completed analysis, submitted to the Governor of Edo State in June 1993, argued that greater long-term benefits would accrue from harvesting the natural forest. Unfortunately, the analysis relied heavily on many highly speculative or questionable assumptions about the financial benefits of maintaining high forest. These assumptions included estimates of the financial value of protecting water supplies and fisheries, of potential income from tourism (estimated at one million naira annually), and of the value of "international transfers" such as an ODA development project; guesses about the sustainable harvesting of forest products included wild exaggerations (for instance, that seventy-four hundred putty-nosed guenon monkeys and two hundred eagles could be taken annually from each square mile of the concession area).[33] In the absence of a strong argument about conserving nature for its own sake, it is perhaps not surprising that the Edo State government found the more tangible benefits of a rubber plantation more convincing than these dubious and unbelievable estimates and allowed forest clearance to proceed. This is a good example of the danger of using economic rather than ethical arguments to protect rain forest.

A MASTER PLAN FOR "STAKEHOLDERS"

By the middle of 1993, therefore, the future of Okomu was looking increasingly bleak. Responding to the growing pressures on the reserve,

NCF revived the idea of producing a general management plan for the reserve. This idea of a "master plan" for the management of the whole of Okomu Forest Reserve had been around for a long time and probably had its origin in proposals that Anadu and I had made in 1982, recommending that the forested areas of Okomu outside the wildlife sanctuary be managed on a sustained-yield basis and that the expansion of plantations and settlements be restricted. In the decade since our original surveys, the number of people living in and exploiting Okomu had greatly increased, and this was going to make it very difficult to formulate for the entire reserve a workable plan that would have sustainable forestry as a primary use.

At the NCF offices in Lagos, Rachel Okunlola had been succeeded as Project Development Officer by another expatriate, Peter Coats, who contracted the preparation of an Okomu master plan to a British archaeologist, Patrick Darling. Darling had come to be involved at Okomu through studies of the large ditch-and-bank earthworks surrounding the town of Udo on the northern edge of the forest reserve.[34] These ancient defensive structures are widespread in southwest Nigeria, and Darling has become the leading authority on their location and history. Money to pay for Darling's work on a master plan apparently came primarily from the ODA and WWF in the United Kingdom through a program called the Non-Governmental Organization Joint Funding Scheme, in which ODA matched funds contributed by WWF.[35]

With the growing acceptance of the view that conservation should be regarded as a component of development, it was no longer surprising that money from a development organization, channeled through an international conservation organization, should be helping to fund someone with little or no experience in ecology or wildlife management to produce a major plan for a conservation area. Nor, given this background, were the contents of Darling's end product very surprising. The final draft of the master plan, which I first saw during a visit to Nigeria in early 1996, contained a thorough review of the history of the forest, and it recommended that the status of national park and/or World Heritage Site be given to the entire reserve. Although it did argue that there should be no further forest clearance, it also recommended that small farmers be assisted with infrastructural development, and that the interests of all the users of the reserve ("stakeholders" was the fashionable term used) be catered to, with ways found to reconcile their conflicting interests.[36] In other words, the plan made forest conservation just one component of a complex use system, in which the rights of people exploiting the forest for long- and short-term gain, both legally and illegally, were now given formal recognition.

PLANNING RESEARCH AS EXPLOITATION ESCALATES

Meanwhile, my own ability to influence any aspect of the management of Okomu had declined with the resignation of my colleague Pius Anadu from his position as Executive Director of the Nigerian Conservation Foundation. Because I knew that active research programs had stimulated and supported conservation efforts at other tropical forest sites, I thought that I might best make some continuing contribution to Okomu's conservation by trying to promote ecological research in the forest. But Okomu is not a well-known site, its forest is not "pristine," and its fauna is not spectacular; it is therefore not an easy place for which to raise research money, especially at a time when the quest for such funds has become highly competitive. However, I eventually managed to find a small grant from the London-based People's Trust for Endangered Species for one of my students, Laura Robinson, to make primate censuses in the wildlife sanctuary. These censuses, in the last three months of 1993, indicated that the sanctuary still contained viable populations of all the forest monkeys, but they also revealed evidence of hunting in the sanctuary. In January 1994 I visited Robinson, witnessed the clearance for the new rubber plantation, and arranged to provide some grant funds to the Project Manager, Orhiere, to improve protection efforts.

Unfortunately, Robinson decided not to pursue further work at Okomu, and so I began correspondence with Lee White about collaborative research in the forest. White had been the first manager of the conservation project back in 1987 and had maintained an interest in the forest. We had both become interested in the long-term history of African forests, and this topic was becoming an increasingly important part of White's research program in Gabon. With each of us having many commitments elsewhere, our plans to meet in Nigeria moved slowly, but we were finally able to get together in Okomu in 1996. By this time, Sylvester Orhiere had been transferred to NCF headquarters in Lagos, and his place as Okomu Project Manager had been taken by Alade Adeleke.

I spent eight days in Okomu in late February and early March 1996. I was accompanied by American primatologist Mary Glenn and her husband, Keith Bensen, a wildlife biologist; Lee White joined us a couple of days after our arrival. We made several surveys of the wildlife sanctuary as well as visited some of the remaining areas of natural forest to the south and east of the sanctuary, areas that in 1989 I had suggested adding to the sanctuary.

Some of our findings were encouraging, but most were depressing. On the positive side, we saw or heard in the sanctuary all four of the monkey species known from Okomu, including white-throated guenons. We also saw the tracks and droppings of elephants and buffalo. Among a still impressive array of birds, large hornbills were common. On the other hand, we found abundant evidence of poaching throughout the wildlife sanctuary. Along every trail we walked, we saw empty shotgun cartridges (some of them very fresh) and piles of spent calcium carbide from hunters' acetylene headlamps. We heard four gunshots, all clearly coming from within the sanctuary or from the one-mile-wide buffer zone. The number of monkeys and other mammals we encountered was small, and all the monkeys we saw were very shy and quiet, almost certainly the result of increased hunting pressure. This increased hunting in the sanctuary appeared to be the inevitable consequence of both an increase in the number of people living in the forest reserve (in the farming settlements and the plantations) and a decline in protection efforts. State and federal forestry staff were no longer participating in the antipoaching program, which was now entirely in the hands of a few NCF staff. At any one time, there were no more than nine guards employed by NCF on duty, and these guards were not making extended journeys or overnight stays in the sanctuary.

By now, much of the original forest to the north and west of the sanctuary had been cleared and planted with oil palms, rubber trees, and farm crops. More than eighty square miles of natural forest still grew to the east and south of the sanctuary, but most of this forest had been badly degraded by intense and uncontrolled exploitation. Since the state government had no field staff in place, and NCF guards were restricted to the wildlife sanctuary, there were virtually no constraints on illegal logging and the collection of plant products in the rest of the reserve; logging crews that we met could not produce permits, nor could a man helping to gather an estimated 250 bundles of bark from *Enantia* trees (used for medicinal purposes). We were told that most logging trucks left the reserve at night when the NCF staff manning the only checkpoint on the main road out of the forest were not on duty.[37]

However, while the remaining forest outside the sanctuary had been devastated, it had not yet been cleared for cultivation, and we concluded that it would regenerate if given adequate protection for an extended time. But we could see that this protection, which we still thought would be best achieved by designating the sanctuary and adjacent natural forest areas a national park, would have to come soon. Once all the valuable timber had gone from the forest outside the sanctuary, pressures would grow to convert it to farms or plantations. If that happened, only the sanctuary and its buffer zone would remain as natural forest; with an area of only forty-six square miles, such a forest would almost certainly not support populations of large mammals such as forest elephants and buffalo and would probably lose many other species over time.

In addition to surveying the condition of the forest and its wildlife, Lee White and I had examined two soil pits in the wildlife sanctuary. Each had an obvious layer of charcoal and pottery fragments seven to eight inches below the surface. Above this layer there was hardly any charcoal in the soil profile, but below it were scattered charcoal fragments extending to a depth of at least two feet. This evidence suggests a long history of shifting cultivation at Okomu, culminating in dense human settlement, followed by a population crash and forest regrowth. White arranged for radiocarbon analysis of the charcoal, and the results of this analysis showed that the uppermost charcoal layer dates from

700–750 years ago.[38] Not only is this fascinating in itself, suggesting a very dynamic forest history, but it also demonstrates the ability of such forests to regenerate after major disturbance, so long as reservoirs of forest species remain in the area to colonize the regrowing forest.

Toward the end of our stay, NCF's new Director of Technical Programmes, Ako Amadi, visited Okomu. With Amadi, White and I discussed some of our thoughts about future research, including more systematic soil sampling and primate studies; we also talked about the conservation problems and argued the case for a national park. Amadi, however, was not very encouraging. He gave his view that research by foreigners should take place only if it clearly built Nigerian research capacity (for instance, by providing funds and equipment for Nigerian researchers), and he did not seem to be in favor of the national park idea. He suggested that we put our observations on paper, but in the form of a report rather than recommendations. This we did, but we received no response from the Nigerian Conservation Foundation. I concluded regretfully that my close involvement with Okomu was no longer especially welcomed by the organization most directly involved in its conservation.

A NATIONAL PARK AT OKOMU?

It was clear from our observations in 1996 that urgent action was needed if an area larger than the existing wildlife sanctuary was to survive as natural forest within the Okomu Forest Reserve. It was encouraging that a master plan had been drafted, but the plan was complex, and it required large numbers of people with different interests to be brought together to cooperate in a common management structure, even though many of these interests involved the commercial exploitation of Okomu. Earlier, simpler management structures for the forest reserve and wildlife sanctuary had not always worked well, and this new structure would be much more difficult and expensive to operate. Even if the plan could somehow be made to work, this would take considerable time, time in which further erosion of the remaining natural forest and its wildlife was very likely; and if the plan did not work, there was a danger that the forest and its wildlife would be lost completely.

In our report to NCF following our 1996 visit, Lee White and I expressed our views about the flaws in the master plan, and we argued the case for bringing full protection to the 68 square miles of logged forest adjacent to the sanctuary and its buffer zone. We urged that efforts be made to give national park status to this combined area of 114 square miles.[39]

I had first suggested establishing a national park within Okomu in 1989, and in 1993 I learned that the Nigerian federal government was considering the idea of an Osse River National Park that would combine Okomu in one management structure with the Ifon Game Reserve, fifty miles away in neighboring Ondo State. Both the federal proposal and Darling's master plan envisaged the entire area of Okomu Forest Reserve becoming a national park. Unless Nigeria changed its national park concept, this seemed to me an unworkable proposition, given the large numbers of people living in Okomu and the high levels of commercial exploitation occurring over much of the forest.

The smaller area that White and I proposed for a park contained no human habitation except for the tiny Arakhuan settlement; it included both upland and swamp forest, and the Osse and Okomu Rivers formed natural boundaries at its eastern and western margins. We suggested that if this area became strictly protected, an attempt could still be made to manage the remainder of the original forest reserve along the lines of Darling's plan; but we pointed out that if such management proved ineffective, at least the most important remaining forest area would have been preserved.

Before I left Nigeria in March 1996, I visited Lawan B. Marguba, the Director of Nigerian National Parks in the federal capital, Abuja, to discuss the park proposals. I expressed our concern about the cost and impracticality of managing all of Okomu as a national park and presented our alternative idea for a smaller but more homogeneous, fully protected area. Marguba informed me that his office had already approved the Osse River National Park proposal (including the whole of Okomu together with Ifon), but he explained that this proposal could not yet be implemented because of budgetary constraints.

Visiting Nigeria again in 1997, I received both good and bad news about Okomu's status. I heard that the Michelin-owned plantation company was attempting to expand its rubber estate beyond the seven square miles already cleared and planted, bringing it right to the edge of the wildlife sanctuary. Meanwhile, the AT & P logging company had finally pulled out of Nikrowa, leaving behind a large settlement of unemployed people who had few options for supporting themselves other than farming in the forest reserve. Logging by small operators was said to be continuing apace in the remaining forest outside the sanctuary.[40] On the other hand, however, I was told that protection of the sanctuary itself had improved, and that a project advisory committee had been established, on which powerful local organizations were represented. Lawan Marguba informed me that some federal government funding was likely to be available for conservation in Okomu in the near future. I also learned that the butterfly expert Torben Larsen had visited Okomu in November 1996 and had collected 264 species of butterfly in the wildlife sanctuary in just five days; Larsen estimated that about 670 species of butterfly were probably present, and perhaps 500,000 species of all kinds. Larsen had strongly endorsed the conservation significance of the site.[41]

WHAT WENT WRONG AT OKOMU?

Several factors that I discuss repeatedly in this book came together in the 1970s and 1980s to erode conservation-orientated management in Okomu.

For more than fifty years after Okomu first became a forest reserve, management appears to have worked fairly well, with central and local government cooperating to control commercial logging, and with some of the resultant income finding its way to local residents. The indigenous inhabitants of the area retained rights to gather certain plant products in the forest and to hunt, and although they may not have been entirely satisfied with these arrangements, they accepted them.

With the Nigerian civil war in the late 1960s and the devolution of power to newly created states, the influence of central and regional governments on forest management greatly declined. By the 1970s the country's population was growing rapidly and the oil boom was pumping huge amounts of money into the economy. Forest reserves came under pressure both as potential sources of farmland for migrants from the most densely populated areas and as sources of profit for business interests seeking to exploit forest products or use the land for plantations. Destructive forces were therefore growing at the same time that government control of forestry was weakening. When the inflated economy collapsed in the 1980s, state government resources were severely curtailed and most of their limited budgets went to maintain the large bureaucracies that had been established in better times; spending on infrastructure and maintenance fell drastically. And as salaries failed to keep pace with rises in living costs, officials at all levels of government became more susceptible to corruption.

With the effectiveness of government declining (not just in Nigeria but in many developing countries), foreign-aid donors began to channel increasing quantities of aid money through nongovernmental organizations. This only exacerbated the problems of governments such as that of Bendel State, which even in the best of times had given relatively low priority to forestry and wildlife management. By the early 1990s, for instance, the Forestry Department of Edo State (the successor to Bendel) had no functioning vehicles left to help manage 2,200 square miles of widely scattered forests.

Meanwhile, international conservation organizations were adopting the view that conservation was best achieved in countries such as Nigeria by not only working with local communities but also by encouraging their economic development. This policy was applied in a broad fashion that took little account of local realities. By 1990, a majority of the local residents of Okomu were probably members of families that had recently migrated to the reserve. Identifying these migrants as residents eligible for assistance was hardly likely to encourage them to leave the reserve, which they had begun to do under pressure from the government Forestry Department. Influenced by the trend in international conservation policy, the Nigerian Conservation Foundation gave assistance to people living in the Okomu Forest Reserve, while basic wildlife protection was de-emphasized. Another aspect of this trend was that consultants who were brought in by NCF and WWF to advise on the management of Okomu were more interested in human development issues than in wildlife, and they rarely spent any time inside the forest. For instance, the archaeologist Patrick Darling (who was contracted by NCF and WWF-UK to produce the Okomu master plan) made clear to me and some of my colleagues when we met him in Okomu in March 1996 that forest and wildlife conservation were not issues of great importance to him. Darling gave his opinion that Western countries were devoting too much attention and too many resources to tropical rain forest conservation and too few to development problems; he also said he felt Nigeria could support a higher human population density, and that current levels of population growth were not a problem (in the period 1990–95, Nigeria's annual population growth rate was estimated as 3 percent).[42]

The pressures on all of Nigeria's rain forests in the last twenty years have been immense, particularly in the relatively well-developed southwest of the country where Okomu is located. There are probably no simple, practical measures that could have protected the Okomu ecosystem from considerable damage. But I think that some of the actions of conservation organizations and development agencies that I have described in this chapter have accentuated rather than ameliorated the threats to survival of the forest and its wildlife. The state government's enthusiasm for and capacity to protect the forest have not been strengthened, while the rights of some of the exploiters of Okomu to use the ecosystem for their short-term personal gain have been validated.

But although I think mistakes have been made at Okomu, it would be wrong to suggest that nothing of value has been achieved. Through the efforts of Pius Anadu, A. P. Leventis, Lee White, Philip Hall, and others associated with the Nigerian Conservation Foundation, a wildlife sanctuary has come into being at Okomu, and it has survived to the present day against considerable odds. But the sanctuary alone is small and, if it is not rigorously protected and made part of a larger area in which the paramount consideration is nature conservation, the forest will almost certainly lose some of its larger animal species in the near future.

In the next chapter I will describe another, larger, Nigerian forest conservation effort in which the intervention of international organizations created an even more people-orientated project than at Okomu, with some similarly damaging consequences for nature.

SIX

People First

The Cross River National Park

Grabbing at branches and exposed roots to stop myself falling down the precipitous stony slope, I struggled to keep up with William Atumuga, my much younger and more agile guide. Soon, William stopped and pointed to six gorilla nests clustered below us among a tangle of tree roots and exposed rocks. The platforms of roots, saplings, and folded branches were at least a month old. It was January 17, 1990, and we were in the Boshi Extension Forest Reserve in Nigeria's Cross River State. With another field assistant, we had spent the previous night camped on a narrow mountain ridge in the north of the reserve after hiking across rugged grass-covered hills from Atumuga's village of Anape, which lies on the edge of the high plateau of Obudu, close to the Cameroon border. The nests were the first direct evidence I had seen of the continued survival of gorillas in Nigeria. Over the next four months I was to see many other gorilla nests in the mountains in the north of Cross River State, but I never saw the apes themselves. My experience was similar to that of F. S. Collier, who visited the same forests in the early 1930s and reported, "I have never seen a wild gorilla, and my efforts to do so have always reduced me to that state of exhaustion which is most aptly expressed by the grouse-shooting profiteer's, 'Well, I wouldn't go no farther, not if they was golden eagles.'"[1] Collier was the Chief Conservator of Forests for Nigeria, and he published his notes anonymously in 1934. He thought that this gorilla population on the Nigeria-Cameroon border was in danger of being hunted to extinction "in no very long period of years," given that their number appeared to be low and their rate of reproduction slow.

It is remarkable that, sixty years later, gorillas were still present in the same forests where Collier had seen their nests and feeding remains, but not surprising that I saw gorilla signs only in places most inaccessible to hunters. In 1990 I was in Cross River State working on a project with WWF-UK and the state government, making a survey of forests and primates that was to be used in the formulation of a management plan for the Okwangwo Division of the proposed Cross River National Park. One of the chief aims in establishing this section of the park was to bring full protection, at last, to a large part of the remaining gorilla population in Nigeria—the most northerly gorillas in Africa.

My 1990 survey was not my first visit to the Boshi Extension reserve and the Obudu Plateau. My earliest visit there was in 1966 when, as I described in chapter 2, I was based at the University of Nigeria, at Nsukka, studying for my Ph.D. While I was at Nsukka I helped develop a proposal to study the gorillas and other wildlife in the forests on and around the Obudu Plateau. That study, developed in collaboration with the government of the Eastern Region of Nigeria, was part of an already existing plan to establish a national park in the area. The plan for a national park at Obudu had its origins in a report by George Petrides published the year before my first visit to the plateau.[2]

Petrides was a wildlife specialist at Michigan State University, and had visited Nigeria in 1962 to review wildlife conservation problems. He traveled extensively around the country and produced a report that drew attention to the excessive hunting of wildlife for the bushmeat trade. At that time Nigeria had networks of forest reserves and game reserves, but no national parks. Petrides recommended a national park system for Nigeria. Among several locations he recommended for park status were the Obudu Plateau and the lowland forests of the Oban Hills.

The recommendations of Petrides and my own plans for gorilla studies near the Obudu Plateau were set aside when civil war came to Nigeria in 1967. The Obudu area was in the breakaway republic of Biafra, where peace was not restored until 1970. The war was accompanied by political reorganization and followed by great economic changes in Nigeria. As a result of these upheavals, little more was heard in the outside world about conservation in Obudu and the Oban Hills until 1981, when J. B. Hall published a proposal for a national park to cover the complete ecotone from the lowlands of Oban to the montane plateau of Obudu.[3]

In the reorganization accompanying the civil war, the Oban and Obudu areas became part of the new South-Eastern State, later renamed Cross River after the river that rises in the hills of western Cameroon and eastern Nigeria and flows into the Bight of Biafra near the old port of Calabar in the far southeastern corner of Nigeria.

In this chapter I describe some of the history of efforts to study and conserve the little-known forests that were to become the Cross River National Park (see map 7). Through the involvement of WWF, the early proposals for a traditionally managed national park were replaced by a plan to create a park whose management would depend significantly on the support of people living around it. WWF's plan involved assisting these people in the development of their economy, in return for which they would not exploit the park's forests and wildlife. I show here how this approach led to expectations of wealth that could not be fulfilled, while doing very little to increase the protection of wildlife from intense commercial hunting. Money rather than nature conservation came to be the focus for many of those involved in the planning and early management of the new park, and wrangles over money eventually led to the

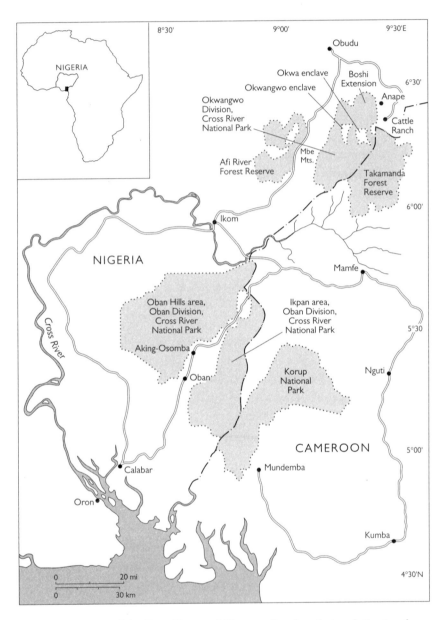

Map 7. The location of the Cross River and Korup national parks in relation to other places mentioned in the text. The boundaries shown for the southern, Oban, division of the Cross River National Park are those proposed in the park management plan; the current boundaries, based on the 1991 park decree, are those of the Oban Hills Forest Reserve shown in map 3 (p. 24).

withdrawal of a major part of the European support that had been expected to sustain the integrated conservation and development project.

THE NEGLECTED FORESTS OF OBAN

Lying to the south and east of the Cross River, the Oban Hills bear the largest area of unlogged lowland rain forest left in Nigeria. This forest is tenuously connected to another large forest area, Ikpan, that is contiguous with Cameroon's well-known Korup National Park. Korup first came to wide attention as a result of Phil Agland's documentary film, *Korup—an African Rainforest*. By contrast, the Oban forests have remained very poorly known.

The Oban Hills take their name from the small town of Oban on their southern edge. There are some notes about the area in the memoir of a colonial District Officer, P. Amaury Talbot, based at Oban from 1909 to 1911. Talbot describes looking north from the top of a hill above Oban and seeing "clusters of peaks, of every shape and form, 3,000 to 4,000 feet high, wooded to the summit and forming the watershed of the country between the Cross River and the sea."[4]

Talbot walked extensively around the hills, averaging seventeen hundred miles a year, but he did not penetrate to the center of the range. In March 1912, soon after his explorations and probably at his urging, a large part of the hills was declared a forest reserve. Talbot described the reserve as "a stretch of land nearly 400 square miles in extent, which has been set aside by the wish of Government as a sanctuary for all wild bush things. Here one evening we came upon a great herd of elephants, which melted silently into the shadows on our approach." Talbot collected many plant and animal specimens, which were sent to the Natural History Museum in London; he provided the museum with its first adult skulls of the drill (a forest-dwelling baboon), and by the time he wrote his memoir 150 new genera and species of plant had been found in his collection of two thousand different plants (his name is enshrined in the specific name *talbotii* given to several of these new species). But in the sixty years following the publication of Talbot's book, very little was written about this region.

D. R. Rosevear of the Nigerian colonial forestry service visited Oban in 1924, soon after his arrival from Britain. He recalls that he found in the villages a general atmosphere of decay, and that he spent some of his nights in village juju houses, "the like of whose earthy gruesomeness I never again in 30 years came across." Rosevear was impressed by the "dark, gloomy and continuous forest" on his first visit, but returning with a more experienced eye in 1946 he realized that much of the forest he had seen was secondary, and perhaps a hundred years old.[5] On his revisit he noticed that the largest trees were species used by people for food and poison (and therefore probably nurtured or even planted by people). These observations led him to the conclusion that the area had once been much more heavily settled, and he guessed that the "atmosphere of decrepitude" in villages was a consequence of the proximity of the area to the major slave-trading port of Calabar, which he thought had drained the countryside of people over hundreds of years. Whether the Oban region became depopulated primarily because of slave raiding is not proven, but there is growing evidence that many African forests once regarded as ancient and pristine are actually quite young and grow in areas that at times in the past supported much larger human populations. There is certainly no evidence to support the claim made by WWF in several publicity and planning documents for Korup that the forest is "over 60 million years old."[6]

Even Rosevear appears not to have penetrated the Oban forests in any deep or extensive fashion; he describes his first visit as a three-week trek round the area, during which he often stayed in villages, and his second visit as a "quick special inspection" by a senior officer. This is a pattern frequently repeated in the conservation history of Oban, and it seems that Petrides, during his 1962 survey of potential national parks, also touched only the edge of the forest, despite recommending it as a park.

A TREK THROUGH THE OBAN HILLS

When I came to Nigeria in 1966 and reviewed my research program with the Eastern Region Forestry Department, the importance of the Oban forests became clear. With an area of 1,445 square miles, the Oban Group of Forest Reserves (which comprised the original Oban Hills reserve, together with later additions such as Ikpan) constituted by far the largest forest tract in the region. But the area was remote from my Nsukka base and therefore inconvenient as a long-term study site. For repeated sampling of the small mammals I was focusing on, Mamu River Forest Reserve (see chapter 2) was a much more accessible place. I was still eager, however, to get some samples from Oban, and an opportunity arose when Peter Jewell and I learned through the Forestry Department that an inventory of these forests was being conducted by a Canadian forestry consultancy company working under a technical assistance agreement between the Canadian and Eastern Region governments. The stimulus behind this inventory was a large new plywood and veneer mill then nearing completion in Calabar. The mill was being built by the Calabar Veneer and Plywood Company (Calvenply), owned by the U.S. Plywood Corporation (with 51 percent of shares), the Eastern Region government (25 percent), and several other groups, including the local timber company Brandler and Rylke.[7] The plans for Calvenply had grown out of a logging operation initiated in the Cross River forests in 1955 by Brandler and Rylke on the recommendations of Rosevear (who was now Chief Conservator of Forests for the Federation of Nigeria) and the Eastern Region Forestry Department. When planning began for the Calvenply operation, there had been no sound inventories of the reserves that would supply the mill. The Canadian consultants were therefore brought in to help with inventories, with the idea that these could be used to plan sustainable harvesting of the forests.

I was not pleased to learn of the plans to turn the Cross River forests into plywood, but I was glad of an opportunity offered to me by the Canadians to join one of their enumeration teams on a trip to the Kwa River headwaters in the center of the Oban Hills.

On January 8, 1967, I drove my Land Rover from Nsukka to the riverside port of Oron. Today there is a bridge over the Cross River, but in those days there was no direct road access to Calabar from the rest of eastern Nigeria, and the last stage of the journey involved taking a ferry from Oron across the mangrove-fringed estuary of the Cross and then up the Calabar River. I spent the day after my arrival in Calabar meeting Forestry staff and getting organized for our trip. At the end of the day I found myself with one of the Canadian foresters in the Calabar Club, a relic of colonial days that was still frequented by a collection of exotic expatriates; these included a one-armed man, Charles Cooper, who had recently arrived in Calabar after an eleven-month bicycle journey from Scotland. On January 10 we drove out of Calabar on the Cameroon road, crossed the river Kwa on a ferry, and headed for Oban. Fifty miles from Calabar we stopped at the "twinned" villages of Aking and Osomba and began our trek into the forest reserve.[8]

My fifteen days in the Oban Hills were a memorable experience. We progressed by a series of five camps to a point near the headwaters of the river Kwa. We spent a few days at each of the last three camps, deep in the forest, while the Canadian team leader John Austin ("Oz") supervised enumeration teams. Although I was struck by the small stature of many of the Oban trees, none of the forest we passed through had recently been disturbed by logging or agriculture, and we pitched our camps by cool, clear, fast-flowing streams and rivers running on rocky beds. I spent the daylight hours setting and checking small mammal traps, collecting frogs, and searching the forest for wildlife. Most evenings I would walk out of camp after dinner with a headlamp in order to scan the trees for bushbabies. Larger mammals were scarce in the forest, however. I managed to spot a few groups of monkeys and I saw the footprints of forest elephants, bushpigs, and duikers. This scarcity of larger mammals was probably a result of largely unregulated hunting. We encountered hunters and fishermen and their camps, and the forestry crew had their own hunter who occasionally shot monkeys and duiker antelopes for the crew's evening meal.

Inevitably our trek into Oban ran into logistical problems. A few days into our trip, Oz discovered that we had been given the wrong set of aerial photographs, which made it impossible to ever establish our exact position in a poorly mapped area, and we found that half of our food had been left behind. The large yam that was supposed to sustain us for several days had been carried in the same box as a leaking kerosene container, and nothing could disguise the taste of kerosene in many of our meals. But after a week new food supplies arrived, and the forest and its streams were always enchanting, especially near our last camp where there were no signs of humans. I returned with the conviction that Petrides was correct, and that some of this forest should be protected from logging and hunting as a national park; I subsequently argued this case in an article in *Animals* magazine.[9] The Nigerian civil war caused these plans to be set aside for many years, but the war also gave the Oban forests a temporary reprieve; during the war, logging plans were suspended and the Calvenply mill lay idle for three years.[10]

In October 1985, more than fifteen years after the end of the civil war, the Nigerian Conservation Foundation and the International Council for Bird Preservation arranged for the ornithologists John Ash and Robert Sharland to visit Nigeria to investigate potentially significant areas for bird conservation. One of the sites Ash and Sharland visited was Oban. On November 22 they traveled up the same road I had used in 1967, and they spent the next two days mist-netting near the road. They found only degraded forest near the road, and this observation, together with conversations they had in the area, led them to the conclusion that "only 200–300 ha (of forest) remain untouched in the centre of the area, far from the roads, of this once large area of lowland rain forest. The remainder had either gone (probably mostly through logging, but also by clearing for replanting or for farming) or was in the process of going, as we witnessed."[11] Ash briefly revisited the area in February 1987 and again came away with a gloomy view of conservation prospects, noting that "the last remaining area of primary forest is under concession to the Calabar Veneer & Plywood Company." After this second visit, however, Ash did at least recommend that the NCF carry out more detailed surveys to identify significant areas of remnant forest, and particularly suggested a survey of the forest area (Ikpan) close to the Cameroon border and the Korup National Park, with a view to giving it protection.[12] But Ash had not penetrated deeply into the Oban forests and was therefore misled into believing that the scale of destruction in Oban was greater than it in fact was.

In response to this latest report, and because NCF's affiliate WWF was becoming interested in extending its project in Korup across the border into the Oban area, Philip Hall of the NCF asked Lee White to take a leave in January 1988 from managing the Okomu project to carry out more detailed surveys in Oban. White conducted these surveys over a period of three weeks with Jon Reid, a zoologist at the University of Calabar. Their findings were a surprise. After combining road journeys with extensive surveys on foot, they concluded that in the main western forest block (the Oban Hills themselves) at least 550 square miles of unlogged forest remained, of which 400 square miles were within the forest reserve. In the eastern, Ikpan, block of the forest—that adjacent to Cameroon—they estimated that unlogged forest survived over an area of 250 square miles, with 195 square miles within the forest reserve. The heavy exploitation noted by Ash occurred only within a few miles of the road. In the Ikpan block, White and Reid found some magnificent forest with a high density of large trees. They also saw some Preuss's red colobus monkeys here, the first definite record from Nigeria of this rare monkey that had been assumed to be restricted to a small area of southwest Cameroon, mostly within Korup. In their report, White and Reid recommended the immediate establishment of strict conservation areas in the unlogged forests, even though timber concessions had already been granted. They also recommended further surveys and the setting up of a conservation project similar to that under way in Korup, combining ecosystem protection with rural development in the surrounding area.[13] This recommendation was to set in train the Cross River National Park project. Because of the influence of the Korup project on subsequent conservation planning in Cross River, I will briefly review the history of the Korup project before returning to the story of Oban.

KORUP, AND THE RISE AND FALL OF EARTHLIFE

Stephen Gartlan obtained his Ph.D. from the University of Bristol in 1967 for his thesis on the behavior of a population of vervet monkeys on Lolui Island in Lake Victoria. He was awarded a postdoctoral fellowship by the British Medical Research Council, and went to Cameroon to study rain forest primates. This study led to a long-term involvement with Cameroon, which has continued to the present day; Gartlan now directs WWF-Cameroon's operations from the country's capital, Yaoundé.

Gartlan's earliest work in Cameroon was concentrated in the English-speaking southwest of the country, where he met Thomas Struhsaker, who had begun forest primate studies there in 1966. Struhsaker surveyed many forests in southwest Cameroon, including the Banyang-Mbo Forest Reserve near Nguti; here, he was told of a forest farther to the west, on the Nigerian border, where "red monkeys" were present. At that time he did not visit this forest to the west, nor did he see any red colobus monkeys. But in March 1970 Struhsaker returned to Cameroon in the course of a pan-African survey of sites that might be suitable for a behavioral study of red colobus, and he visited the forest on the Nigerian border that he had been told about. This was the Korup Forest Reserve, established in 1937 when this part of Cameroon was administered from Nigeria by the British colonial government.

In 1970 Korup could not be reached by road, so Struhsaker took a boat through the coastal mangrove swamps and up the Ndian River. He spent two weeks in the forest and found that the rare Preuss's red colobus was indeed present.[14] Although he eventually decided to base his long-term study of red colobus monkeys in Uganda's Kibale Forest Reserve (where I was to join him later in the year), Struhsaker reported his Korup observations to Gartlan, noting that some of the Korup forest was very old, that no commercial timber exploitation had occurred there, and that primates were abundant in spite of some hunting.[15] In June 1970, Gartlan himself visited Korup for the first time, also saw red colobus, and agreed that the forest deserved more attention. In 1971, Struhsaker and Gartlan made a proposal to the government of Cameroon, arguing that Korup be declared a national park, along with the Douala-Edéa Reserve, which lay just south of the Sanaga River and was at that time a focus of Gartlan's research.[16] The Cameroon government had no immediate reaction to Struhsaker and Gartlan's proposal.

In 1977 Phil Agland traveled to Cameroon from England to make a documentary film about the country's forests and their wildlife for conservation purposes. Gartlan was one of the few people in Cameroon who had responded positively to Agland's inquiries before his visit, and it was with Gartlan's help that he began his work at Lake Tissongo in the Douala-Edéa Reserve. During the 1970s, hunting and trapping greatly increased in Douala-Edéa, and oil prospectors began seismic surveys in the reserve, opening it up to further exploitation.[17] When attempts to halt this exploitation failed, Gartlan shifted his major research and conservation efforts in 1978 to Korup;[18] when the project moved to Korup, Agland followed.[19] Agland's filming project was to extend over more than five years, and in the process, the filmmaker fell in love with Korup and became determined to do something to protect its future. The threat to Cameroon's forests from logging was growing, but loggers could not easily get into Korup, and although the reserve supported a very diverse rain-forest ecosystem it did not have large numbers of valuable timber trees.

Korup's days of isolation were coming to an end, however. The Cameroon government targeted the Mundemba area south of the reserve for development because of its proximity to offshore oil fields and the Nigerian border; road-building was given a high priority. Gartlan felt that if Korup was to survive, conservation efforts would have to be integrated with this development planning.[20] In 1981 Gartlan and Agland therefore prepared a new proposal for the Cameroon government, urging the development of three forest national parks: Korup, Dja (in southern Cameroon), and Pangar-Djerem (on the forest-savanna boundary in central Cameroon). The proposal suggested that these parks be created in conjunction with rural development projects that would include efforts to provide alternative sources of animal protein to people living around the forest, so reducing hunting pressure.[21] The initial cost of the projects was estimated to be at least $3 million, and sources of funds considered were international oil companies and international development agencies. This proposal came a year after the launching of the World Conservation Strategy, which, as I described in chapter 3, had made the integration of conservation and development the formal policy of IUCN and WWF.

On completion of his filming in 1982, Agland returned to England, where his enthusiasm and concern for the Cameroon forests encouraged a group of his friends and associates to launch a new not-for-profit corporation, "Earthlife," of which he was made a director. Earthlife's main initial goal was to raise funds to create the three new parks proposed by Gartlan and Agland. Earthlife used the first screening of Agland's film, in 1982, to launch its campaign, which focused primarily on Korup. Earthlife was conceived as a new kind of conservation organization, no doubt in part because most of its directors were not professional biologists or conservationists. Its founder, Nigel Tuersley, was a London real-estate developer who planned to raise large sums of money by purchasing run-down buildings in central London, rehabilitating them, and selling them at a profit. As he put it in a subsequent Earthlife publication, "We are no longer talking of Victorian institutions operating out of dingy offices with antiquated technology. Today's charities and non-profit organisations are essentially businesses with a particular product and a particular market, and they are operating in an increasingly competitive market place."[22] To run its operations and raise money for conservation, Earthlife solicited financial support from British businesses, and the organization sought and received the backing of an array of rich and famous people.

In 1984 Earthlife launched a subsidiary company, Bioresources Ltd., whose stated goal was to link science and business in developing sustainable alternatives to the destructive exploitation of tropical rain forests; for instance, by promoting the development of new crop varieties and agroforestry techniques that would allow agricultural intensification on already cultivated land, and by searching for and developing new drugs from forest plants.[23] Clive Wicks, the agricultural-extension manager mentioned in the last chapter, was appointed as General Manager of Bioresources.

Within Korup were several villages that, because of their farming and hunting, were seen as an obvious impediment to the operation of an effective national park. Early in the planning of the park it was proposed to resettle the people of these villages outside the forest. Wicks and Bioresources therefore became involved in surveys of the agricultural suitability of resettlement sites, and in studies of ways to intensify agricultural production in existing settlements close to the park, on the rationale that this would reduce the possibility of encroachment on the forest. The British Overseas Development Administration had recently launched its joint-funding scheme, under which ODA would pay for 50 percent of the cost of an approved project if a nongovernment organization raised the other 50 percent.[24] It was through this scheme that the agricultural development component of the Korup project was initially to be funded; Wicks noted that this development would be designed to "provide a much higher standard of living for those being resettled and other villages who already live in the resettlement area."[25] Nothing was said about the possible consequences of an increase in numbers of people if these improvements occurred.

Wicks's statement was made during an important workshop on the future of Korup, held in December 1985 in Mundemba, near the forest. In their report, the workshop participants urged the government of Cameroon to establish the national park as a matter of urgency. In addition to proposals for resettlement and agricultural development, the report recommended the establishment of research, environmental education, and tourist facilities.[26]

Earthlife reached its apogee in 1986. In that year it submitted its funding proposal to the ODA for assistance with the development of "an agricultural buffer zone to support the Korup National Park," and it arranged with the influential British Sunday newspaper the *Observer* to publish a special full-color supplement entitled "Paradise Lost?" dealing with tropical rain forests and their conservation. In addition to articles about rain forests around the world, this publication contained information on a variety of products and schemes by which readers could donate to or otherwise assist Earthlife. Later that year, on October 30, Korup National Park was established by presidential decree. But Earthlife's success did not continue; in March 1987 the company collapsed after its new Chairman, Peter Smith, studied its accounts and concluded that its assets were significantly overvalued.[27] Roger Hammond, Earthlife's Director of Education, negotiated to take over some of the company's assets, and he established a new foundation, "Living Earth," which was to have an emphasis on conservation education. Clive Wicks joined WWF-UK, along with another Earthlife staff member, Francis Sullivan.

The World Wildlife Fund (which, as noted earlier, had in 1986 changed the name of its international organization and many of its national operations to the "World Wide Fund for Nature") had provided limited support to the Korup project since the 1970s. Now, WWF-UK assumed Earthlife's position in the joint-funding project with the ODA, and Wicks set about organizing work on a master plan for the park. The project was funded in 1988 with a grant of £378,000 sterling (about $680,000 at that time) from ODA, while WWF pledged to raise £390,000 (about $700,000) over the following five years.[28] As the project developed it acquired additional support from GTZ (the German technical assistance agency) and the European Commission (the commission is the administrative arm of the European organizations that in 1993 became the European Union).

From the outset, then, the Korup project included agricultural and rural development as a major component of its conservation activities. Efforts at directly protecting wildlife from hunting were not given a particularly high priority, although it was the wildlife of the forest that had most excited the project's instigators. It was hoped that the development initiatives would lead local people to reduce their dependence on the forest, but as the consultant Mark Infield, contracted to study hunting in Korup, said in a 1989 report, "Development . . . is a slow process and, in the meantime, hunting continues unabated."[29]

In 1989 Wildlife Conservation International (WCI), a division of the New York Zoological Society (today known as the Wildlife Conservation Society), began a program of ecological research on the fauna of Korup through an agreement with WWF-UK and with funding from the U.S. Agency for International Development. James ("Buddy") Powell managed this project for WCI from a base at Nguti, east of the park. A field station and intensive research area were set up in the park at Ikenge, and a biological inventory commenced; Powell's own studies focused on the ecology of forest elephants. The problems caused by hunting soon became apparent. Powell reported that twenty-seven elephants were shot in the park in the September–December 1990 period alone; hunters threatened research project staff if they tried to work outside the research area, and some hunting occurred within this area. WCI personnel and students using the site were an easy target for any feelings of resentment against the conservation project because they were living and working right inside the park. Tensions also increased over the issue of village resettlement.[30]

So as to be able to put biological data on Korup into a regional perspective, Powell had initiated comparative surveys in other nearby forests, including the Banyang-Mbo Forest Reserve to the east of Nguti. As tensions grew around the research project in Korup, WCI focused more of its effort on Banyang-Mbo, and eventually research was transferred there in 1993.[31]

After WCI pulled out of Korup, there seems to have been little systematic study of the park's wildlife, and the present status of the fauna and the extent of antipoaching efforts are unclear. When I visited Nguti in March 1996 I was told that hunting in Korup had decreased, but the guards for the northern section of the park were all based in Nguti town, ten miles from the park boundary. I have been told that the situation is better in the south, where apparently most visitors now see some animals.[32]

Although wildlife protection does not seem to have been a high priority in Korup, at least the vegetation and smaller animals have been spared the ever-increasing logging pressure that is rapidly eroding Cameroon's other forests. In 1989, Cameroon exported 525,187 metric tonnes (476,345 U.S. short tons) of timber, 80 percent as raw logs,[33] and in 1996 I found that a Malaysian company had moved into the area immediately northeast of Korup and was felling indiscriminately.

WWF COMES TO OBAN

White and Reid's optimistic report from their January 1988 reconnaissance of Oban soon found its way from the Nigerian Conservation Foundation to WWF-UK, and a further study was organized. This was conducted by Francis Sullivan of WWF and Ibrahim Inaharo of the NCF. This second survey formed the basis of a preliminary proposal for a national park project, organized along the lines of what was being done in Korup.[34] One major rationale given in this proposal for a park in Oban was that the linked parks of Oban and Korup would not only constitute one of the most important biotic reserves in Africa but also provide the basis for a cooperative regional program; such regional cooperation was being encouraged by development-aid donors, such as the European Commission, which had made special funds available for transfrontier projects. Wicks traveled to Nigeria with Gartlan in May 1988 to discuss this proposal with officials of the Cross River State and Federal Forestry Departments. The proposal was approved in principle by the governments, and in August 1988 work began on a more detailed funding proposal.

The next proposal for the Oban project was drawn up in England by Julian Caldecott, who had done his Ph.D. research on the behavioral ecology of pig-tailed macaques in the forests of peninsular Malaysia from 1979 to 1981.[35] After completing his doctoral degree, Caldecott spent four years in the East Malaysian state of Sarawak, studying bearded-pig ecology and human hunting patterns.[36] Much of that work focused on the region drained by the Upper Baram River, and in 1986 he obtained support from Earthlife to survey the population of endangered Sumatran rhinoceroses in this area. Not long before Earthlife collapsed, Caldecott joined the organization on a full-time basis, and his survey developed into a conservation planning exercise for the entire Upper Baram region. He wrote a master plan for the sustainable use of the Upper Baram forests, but this was eventually vetoed by the Sarawak government, which had allocated logging concessions in key areas.[37]

The initial proposal for Oban had led WWF and ODA in Britain to jointly fund a pilot project, and this allowed Caldecott to take up an appointment as WWF's Oban Project Manager in September 1988. Given the importance of the area and the complexity of the conservation challenges that it presented, it is remarkable how quickly these plans were made and that they were formulated in large part by people with little or no prior knowledge of the area.

Caldecott has described some of the history of the Cross River National Park Project up to 1993 in his book *Designing Conservation Projects*. From its inception, the project took a rational, economics-based view of conservation: "It was proposed that Nigeria and CRS [Cross River State] should invest in protecting natural forests in order to obtain future economic benefits, for example in the form of tourism and research revenues and by avoiding floods and damage to fisheries. Because of uncertainty over the scale of costs and benefits resulting from either preserving or destroying the forest . . . external donors were . . . to be asked to subsidize Nigeria's and CRS's investment in the Park."[38] According to the plan, people living near the proposed park would be provided with incentives to conserve the forest. A support zone was conceived, which would include people who were judged to have some degree of economic dependence on the forest (for instance, through hunting or the gathering of forest products). In this zone, projects would be initiated that would increase agricultural productivity, promote economic development and lessen people's direct dependence on forest resources; such a program, it was argued, would relieve pressure on the park and give people a vested interest in defending it.[39]

Funding for the preparation of an Oban master plan was obtained not only from ODA and WWF, but also from the European Development Fund, which is administered in Brussels by the European Commission. To provide information for the plan, a team of consultants under Caldecott's direction undertook surveys in the first half of 1989, giving particular attention to a review of land use and agricultural development options in the support zone and to logistical and administrative issues. Only one consultant, Goetz Schuerholz (a Canadian wildlife ecologist), undertook field studies on the ecology of the park itself; these studies were brief and looked mostly at the periphery of the forest reserves. No one returned to the Kwa headwaters area in the center of the proposed park, the area I had visited in 1967.

Although the Oban master plan that emerged from this process at the end of 1989 was ostensibly written for the federal government of Nigeria, it was essentially a project funding proposal to the European Commission. The plan concentrated on development activities, laying out a seven-year program involving agricultural intensification in the support zone and the establishment of a number of mechanisms to provide financial incentives to villagers: for instance, a revolving credit fund that would provide loans to individuals for agricultural and small-scale industrial activities, and a Village Conservation and Development Fund (VCDF) that would dispense grants to villages for development and education projects. Over seven years the VCDF was expected to spend 1.70 million European Currency Units (in January 1990, one ECU was equivalent to $1.21). By far the largest projected cost envisioned, however, was to be the payment of 5.61 million ECU to a core management team, a group of foreign consultants who would advise on project management, including finance, research, park protection, support zone development, and training. Only one short paragraph of the ninety-eight-page plan dealt directly with park protection, noting that this would be undertaken by a ranger section.[40] In its conclusions, the Oban master plan acknowledged that increased incomes among people living around a forest generally lead to increased pressure on the forest, but it argued that the specific economic incentives proposed for the Oban Support Zone could encourage conservation.

EARLY ATTEMPTS TO PROTECT NIGERIA'S GORILLAS

As the Oban project was beginning at the end of 1988, I was in Nigeria to survey the status of a rare forest monkey, Sclater's guenon. Some months before I had written to WWF-UK about my interest in Oban, and my letter was eventually answered by Julian Caldecott. We arranged to meet in Calabar soon after Christmas to discuss the project. By this time, Caldecott was aware that the Cross River Forestry Department had a long-standing proposal for a conservation area in the Obudu region in the north of the state, which it considered more significant for wildlife conservation than Oban.[41] Caldecott had persuaded WWF to devote some resources to extending its park planning project to the Obudu area, and he thought that I might be interested in helping with surveys there.

After his 1962 visit, Petrides had made a strong case for a national park at Obudu, a park whose primary purpose would be to safeguard the gorilla population living there, along with a montane ecosystem unique to Nigeria. Petrides felt that the pleasant resort hotel at the Obudu Cattle Ranch would be a good base from which tourists might one day be able to venture to see wild gorillas. The ranch occupies most of the Obudu Plateau, which undulates between altitudes of about 5,000 and 5,500 feet and is an extension of the Bamenda Highlands of Cameroon. The plateau is largely covered by grassland, and long before the establishment of the ranch this grass was burned annually by Fulani cattle grazers. But the plateau has a high rainfall (exceeding 150 inches per year) and its natural vegetation would almost certainly be montane forest in the absence of tree cutting and frequent burning. Although they are now much degraded, many strips of this forest still survive along watercourses on the plateau.

The Obudu Cattle Ranch was developed by the colonial government of the Eastern Region of Nigeria following a 1949 visit by a veterinary officer, a Mr. McCulloch, who found the plateau grasslands to be free of tsetse flies. The ranch was formally established in 1951, and a road up the escarpment to the plateau was completed in 1955.[42] In 1959 a hotel was built at the ranch headquarters, and by 1966 this was a popular recreational destination, particularly among expatriates eager to escape the heat and humidity of the southern Nigerian lowlands.[43]

Below the Obudu Plateau to the south and west are closed-canopy forests. The first published report of gorillas in these forests was by James Allen in 1931, who tracked a group for three days in February 1930.[44] Ivan Sanderson collected a few specimens of gorillas across the border in Cameroon in 1932–33, and for five months kept as a pet a young female that was apparently brought to him from Nigeria.[45] In 1934, Collier's report, referred to at the beginning of this chapter, was published. For the next twenty years, no doubt in part because of World War II, little more was heard about the gorillas of Nigeria. But in 1955 and 1956 the Chief Conservator of Forests for the Eastern Region of Nigeria, Eric March, visited the Obudu area to gather more information on the gorillas and make plans for a game sanctuary to protect them; he estimated that one hundred to two hundred gorillas probably remained.[46] As a result, the forests on the rugged terrain immediately to the west of the Obudu Plateau were gazetted in 1958 as a reserve that could act as a gorilla sanctuary; this was the Boshi Extension Forest Reserve.[47] In 1964 the Eastern Region government proposed a game reserve that would combine Boshi Extension with the contiguous Boshi and Okwangwo Forest Reserves, but this reserve was never formally established.

When I arrived in Nigeria for the first time in 1966, my supervisor, Peter Jewell, had a copy of Petrides's recently published report, and we consulted it in planning our own research. In the course of this planning we also sought the permission and cooperation of the Eastern Region Forestry Department, for my mammal studies were to be predominantly in government forest reserves. The department proved very helpful, and they explained that they had a particular interest in establishing a game reserve at Obudu. This led us to make a reconnaissance visit to the area with Arikpo Ettah of the Forestry Department (see plate 21); Ettah had studied forestry and wildlife management at Michigan State University, where he had met Petrides.

So it was that on November 3, 1966, the day after arriving at the Obudu Cattle Ranch Hotel, Ettah and I set off on horseback in cool, misty weather to reach the edge of the Boshi Extension reserve. We had planned only a day trip, and this gave us no time to search properly for gorilla signs, but at the forest edge we did see possible leopard tracks and we located a good potential campsite. Enthusiastically, we began making plans for more thorough studies of the area's wildlife, and especially of the gorillas. We devised a plan for a joint scientific expedition of students from the University of Nigeria and University College London, supervised by Ettah and me, to visit Obudu in July–September 1967. The expedition would undertake a biological survey of the plateau and adjacent forests and formulate more precise recommendations for a protected area.

Jewell and I revisited the Obudu Plateau from May 19 to 22, 1967, to finalize arrangements for the expedition. The British expatriate manager of the ranch, Wally Cranfield, told us that there should be no problems, except for the weather, which would be exceedingly wet. It was around this time that I first learned, from Cranfield, about Tom Struhsaker's work in Cameroon. Struhsaker had visited the Obudu Cattle Ranch in December 1966 and trekked down from the plateau into Cameroon's Takamanda Forest Reserve, where he surveyed primates, finding fresh gorilla nests in the Mava area.[48]

But our Obudu expedition never took place. The rising political tensions reached a head when the federal government, led by Yakubu Gowon, announced the division of the country into twelve new states on May 26, 1967; the Calabar and Ogoja Provinces of the Eastern Region of Nigeria were designated as South-Eastern State (later renamed Cross River State). As noted in chapter 2, the military government of the Eastern Region defied Gowon and on May 30 announced its secession from the federation, as the Republic of Biafra. On that day a representative of the Security Division in the office of the Military Governor of the Republic of Biafra wrote to me at Nsukka, saying that "in view of the present troubled situation in the country your proposed visit to Obudu now would not be advisable."

The outbreak of the Biafran war on July 7 put an end to our plans, and for the next decade Obudu received little attention. Many people in the outside world assumed that Nigeria's gorillas were extinct; for instance, a 1978 review of the status of all gorilla populations in Africa cast doubt on the presence of any resident gorillas in Nigeria.[49] But in 1979 a UNESCO team recommended Obudu as a World Heritage site, and soon afterward the Nigerian federal government encouraged the Cross River State government to launch "Operation Locate Gorillas."[50] Arikpo Ettah, with whom I had planned the 1967 Obudu survey, was now Chief Conservator of Forests for Cross River State; as a first step in developing the long-mooted Obudu Game Reserve, and in an effort to learn more about the gorillas, Ettah put his senior wildlife officer in charge of a Wildlife Conservation Unit in Obudu Town. This officer was Clement Ebin, who had recently returned from training in the United States.

"REDISCOVERY" OF THE EXTINCT GORILLAS

In the early 1980s, staff of the Obudu wildlife unit found gorilla signs in surveys of Boshi Extension Forest Reserve, and the unit also turned up evidence of gorillas at a previously undocumented site, the Mbe Mountains, about twenty miles southwest of the Obudu Plateau. A new road had recently been completed from Ikom to Obudu, passing through the settlement of Kanyang at the foot of the mountains. This road opened up a remote and poorly known area. In 1983, a Kanyang hunter, George Ocha Abang, brought a baby gorilla to Ebin in Obudu, after shooting its mother. The gorilla was sent to Calabar Zoo, where a special ceremony was held at which Abang, despite having killed a protected animal, was praised by the Commissioner for Natural Resources for his "patriotic gesture."[51] This young gorilla (which did not survive) generated excitement in Cross River because it was such clear proof of the local survival of a celebrated and much feared animal.

Following the confirmation of the continued existence of gorillas in Cross River, Ebin submitted a report to the Nigerian Conservation Foundation in which he argued for an expanded sanctuary in the Obudu area and for an in-depth gorilla study.[52] Soon after this, the NCF began to develop a major program of field surveys and conservation projects across Nigeria; the driving force behind these surveys was A. P. Leventis, head of NCF's Scientific Committee, whose involvement at Okomu I described in the previous chapter. Among these surveys was that of ornithologists John Ash and Robert Sharland regarding potential bird conservation areas. Ash and Sharland were much more impressed by the conservation potential of forests in the north of Cross River State than in the Oban area (which they had surveyed only superficially), and they recommended immediate action to create a national park including the Obudu Plateau, and the Boshi, Boshi Extension, and Okwangwo Forest Reserves.[53]

The NCF arranged for Ash to pay two further visits to Cross River State in 1987. On these visits Ash found that no action had yet been taken by the Cross River State government to improve protection of the Obudu and Boshi-Okwangwo areas, and he noted that farming and burning were causing serious deterioration of the remaining forest patches on the Obudu Plateau. In the lowland forests he found mammal populations reduced to very low levels by excessive hunting. But Ash also saw some rare birds previously unknown from Nigeria: the green ibis, gray-necked Picathartes, and violet-backed flycatcher. And he obtained many reports about the continued presence of gorillas in the area, from people both at Kanyang near the Mbe Mountains and at Buanchor below the mountains in the northwest of the Afi River Forest Reserve. The evidence for a gorilla population surviving in Afi was a particular surprise, for the only published report of gorillas there was Collier's 1934 article, in which he said that "when a Boji hunter was hurt in the Afi Forests in 1927 by one [gorilla] he had wounded, the opinion was expressed by the local people that the animal was a wanderer from the hills in the Umbaji direction and that there were no gorilla on the Boji group."[54] Yet Collier guessed that there might be a resident gorilla population in Afi that had little connection with that in Boshi, for there has long been extensive human settlement and forest clearance across the twenty miles between the Afi massif and "Umbaji" (the Bumaji group of villages near the Boshi Extension reserve).

In the reports he produced following his 1987 surveys, Ash argued again for a very serious conservation effort to save the forests of northern Cross River State and their wildlife, and he reiterated that national park status should be sought for the area. He also recommended particular attention to the gorillas at Kanyang and Buanchor, calling for an assessment of their status and for the institution of protection measures.[55] As a result of Ash's recommendations, Leventis began making inquiries in England about people who could carry out a more thorough gorilla survey. Roderick Fisher at University College London put Leventis in touch with Alexander ("Sandy") Harcourt at the University of Cambridge. Harcourt had carried out long-term studies of the mountain gorillas of the Virunga Volcanoes at Dian Fossey's site in Rwanda and had surveyed gorilla populations both in the Virungas and in the Bwindi Forest of Uganda.[56] Harcourt and Leventis agreed a plan to begin a Nigerian gorilla survey at the end of 1987, in the dry season. Meanwhile, NCF sent two of its technical officers, John Mshelbwala and Ibrahim Inaharo, to Kanyang to learn more about the gorillas. In July, Mshelbwala saw only gorilla nests, but in August Inaharo managed to see a group of the apes.[57] In discussions with Inaharo, the Kanyang hunters agreed to suspend their hunting on a temporary basis, until NCF started a project in the area; Inaharo hired two hunters as game guards and suggested that NCF help the community to develop alternative sources of protein and improved farming techniques. This was the beginning of the Kanyang gorilla project.

Harcourt undertook his survey between December 1987 and January 1988, accompanied by his wife Kelly Stewart (who had also studied gorillas in the Virungas) and by Inaharo. Through the evidence of nests and dung they confirmed the presence of gorillas in three areas besides the Mbe Mountains. These other areas were the Afi Mountains, the Boshi-Okwangwo Forest Reserves, and two sites on the edge of the Obudu Cattle Ranch.[58] Based on their survey, which concentrated on Mbe and Afi, Harcourt and his colleagues estimated that 150 gorillas might survive in this part of Nigeria, but they noted that the gorillas' habitat was threatened by cultivation and that it was likely the animals themselves were being killed by hunters at a rate that might be higher than their birth rate. They recommended conservation measures that they felt would protect the gorillas and bring development to the region. These included advertising and enforcing existing laws prohibiting the killing of gorillas, gazetting a strict sanctuary in the core of each gorilla population's range where no hunting of any kind would be allowed, promoting conservation awareness among the local people, and (based on experience in Rwanda) establishing gorilla-based tourism.[59] Harcourt did not favor a complete ban on hunting throughout the area, nor the establishment of a national park, because he felt that such moves could alienate local people, many of whom gained significant income from commercial hunting.

Publicity about this new NCF-sponsored survey finally brought much wider attention to Nigeria's gorillas, including coverage in a front-page article in the *New York Times*.[60] And, building on the groundwork laid by Ash, NCF started a conservation project in the Mbe Mountains, based at Kanyang, which implemented some of the recommendations of Inaharo and Harcourt. This project began in September 1988 under the management of two American volunteers, Elizabeth ("Liza") Gadsby and Peter Jenkins.

It was soon after this that I arrived in Calabar to meet the WWF Oban project manager, Julian Caldecott. Caldecott suggested that I could contribute to the plan to extend the Cross River National Park into the Obudu area by carrying out a study of the conservation needs of the gorillas and other primates. He proposed that we make a short reconnaissance of the area and so, at the very end of December 1988,

Caldecott and I set off for the north of Cross River State. We visited the NCF gorilla project at Kanyang, as well as the Obudu Cattle Ranch, where we met a man from Anape village who was familiar with the gorillas in what he called the "black bush" of Boshi Extension. I was excited both to be back at Obudu and to finally have a chance to undertake a study I had first considered in 1966. But I had misgivings about the approach of the conservation project outlined to me by Caldecott, an approach emphasizing development and economics. However, it seemed that the project would go ahead whether I participated or not, so I agreed to undertake the primate study, feeling that through participation I might at least have a chance of influencing the project's course.

THE 1990 GORILLA SURVEY

In January 1990 I had my first view of gorilla nests in Boshi Extension, as I described at the opening of this chapter. For the next five months I surveyed the Obudu Plateau and the forests of Boshi, Okwangwo, and the Mbe Mountains with my assistants, Paul Bisong and Dominic White; we not only tried to estimate the status of populations of primates and other large mammals, we also investigated conservation problems and possibilities for tourism. Meanwhile, Liza Gadsby and Peter Jenkins conducted systematic questionnaire-based interviews with hunters in all the villages in and around the park area, gathering information both on the hunters' knowledge of local wildlife and on their hunting practices.

Our senior local counterpart on this survey was Clement Ebin, who by then was in charge of Cross River State's National Parks and Wildlife Development Project. Ebin's aim was not only to see the Boshi-Okwangwo area upgraded to national park status but to incorporate the Mbe Mountains into the park. The boundaries of the Boshi and Okwangwo reserves were already demarcated, but for Mbe to be incorporated, new boundaries would have to be established that took into account both conservation concerns and existing land use by Kanyang and other villages. The isolated gorillas in Afi River Forest Reserve were not to be included in the national park; they were still little known, and their habitat had never been the subject of any proposal for a wildlife protection area. Even so, Caldecott asked us to include the Afi gorillas in our survey, but not to give them highest priority.

Some of the findings from our fieldwork were uplifting, but most were depressing. Within the hearts of the Boshi and Okwangwo reserves and in the rugged hills of Mbe and the Afi massif there were some magnificent forests that showed no sign of recent disturbance by farming, logging, or fire. On the other hand, one or another of these factors was eating at the edges of each forest. This part of Cross River State experiences a longer dry season than Oban, and the forest is therefore much more vulnerable to fire.

Except in parts of the Mbe Mountains, where the NCF project had succeeded in limiting hunting activity, we saw very few large animals. Over a period of five months, we located forty-seven clusters of gorilla nests, but except for one possible distant sighting by Bisong, no gorillas were seen or definitely heard. Most gorilla nests were found in the Mbe and Afi Mountains and a few in the Boshi Extension Forest Reserve. Only one gorilla nest site was found in the Okwangwo Forest Reserve, and that was in the eastern hills of the reserve, not far from Takamanda; we concluded that the Okwangwo animals were probably part of a population centered in Takamanda. The rugged terrain in most of the areas in which we found gorilla signs made it almost impossible to lay out census transects through the forest. We were therefore forced to estimate the gorilla population from the nests we had seen, and our best guess was that in 1990 there were 110 gorillas in Nigeria; we acknowledged, though, that the total population might be as low as 75.

We encountered monkeys less frequently in these forests than in any forest I had ever visited in Africa. Between us, Dominic White and I spent 116 days in the field, surveying about three hundred miles of forest trail at slow walking speeds; we heard fifty-two calls from guenon monkeys, but during our walks we had only one clear view of monkeys—a group of putty-nosed guenons in the Mbe Mountains. Twice, monkeys were seen from campsites. All the hunters interviewed knew the large, terrestrial baboonlike drill ("keshuom"), and we occasionally saw signs of their foraging paths in the leaf litter, but only Jenkins, going out with experienced hunters specifically to find drills, actually sighted the animals.[61]

In interviews, hunters agreed that populations of monkeys and apes were declining, and they usually cited hunting as the main reason for this decline. Two species that hunters had names for, the crowned guenon and the gray-cheeked mangabey, seemed to be already extinct in this part of Nigeria, though they might still occur in the adjacent Takamanda forest in Cameroon. Amid this gloom was one bright spot; we heard the calls of Preuss's guenons in the hills of Boshi Extension and saw carcasses of this monkey killed by hunters. These were the first definite records from Nigeria of this rare species that is otherwise restricted to the montane forests of Cameroon and Bioko Island.

Everywhere we went, except in the Mbe Mountains, we observed abundant evidence of hunting: camps, trails, snares, shotgun cartridges, and piles of spent carbide from acetylene headlamps. We found that much of the hunting in the Boshi-Okwangwo forests was commercial. A common pattern was for small groups of hunters to travel deep into the forest to semipermanent campsites at which they had a shelter (or "shed"). From their shed they made forays over several days. The carcasses of the animals they killed would be smoked and then carried out to market at the end of the hunting trip. Judging by the spent cartridges we collected, most hunters were using ammunition suitable for small game, including monkeys. Hunter interviews confirmed that chimpanzees and gorillas were killed only occasionally. Buffalo and elephant, best hunted with rifles—which ordinary hunters did not possess—were very rarely killed, at least at the time of our survey. Indeed, we found that forest elephants were abundant in parts of the Okwangwo Forest Reserve, and White and I had one direct encounter with them.

One of the most disturbing of our observations was the extent of forest destruction on the Obudu Plateau. With the development of the cattle ranch in the 1950s, people had moved to the plateau to work on the ranch, bringing their families with them. But as the human population on the plateau expanded, the fortunes of the ranch declined, along with the employment opportunities the ranch presented. People turned increasingly to farming to support their families. The watercourse forests and the other small areas of montane woodland on and around the plateau offered the best soils for farming, so these biologically fascinating forests (shown in plate 21) had come under more and more pressure. In addition to farming, the forests were also exploited for fuelwood and damaged by the fires that annually swept the grasslands. Elgood had foreseen these problems in 1965, and in 1981 Hall had observed the dangerous trend of forest destruction.[62] After their visit in November 1985, Ash and Sharland noted that "it is probably not possible to find undisturbed forest within 10 km of ranch headquarters."[63] By the time I surveyed the plateau in 1990, I found that hardly any undisturbed forest remained anywhere and that many of the valleys had lost the majority of their trees. About fourteen hundred people were living on the plateau and, not surprisingly, there was no evidence of gorillas still using the area. Older men in some of the plateau settlements told me that up till 1960 they had seen gorillas quite often, but that with the development of the ranch the animals had stopped using the plateau.

Almost as disturbing as the destruction of the plateau forests was the size of the village "enclaves" of Okwa and Okwangwo within the Okwangwo reserve (shown in map 7). These enclaves were the sites of villages that existed when the forest reserves were gazetted, and where villagers were allowed to remain on their land and to farm. We estimated that these enclaves now supported more than twenty-five hundred people. A major path connected the enclaves to villages and a roadhead west of the reserve, and this path continued east to the settlements known as Balegete on the Cameroon border, immediately below the Obudu Plateau. Farms from Okwa and Okwangwo were beginning to spill out into the surrounding forest reserve, where the villagers hunted and gathered many plant products. It was obvious that if these villages remained where they were and continued to grow, they would slice the Okwangwo forest into two separate pieces and progressively deplete its wildlife.

Based on these observations, one of the main recommendations in our final report was that if the Boshi-Okwangwo area were to be an effective national park, the villages of Okwa and Okwangwo would have to be relocated outside the forest. We also proposed that the Mbe Mountains and Obudu Plateau be made part of the new park, and that the extensive farming and uncontrolled burning on the plateau be halted before the forest loss became irreversible. And for the park as a whole we proposed a zoning system, with strict protection for conservation and tourism given to the Mbe Mountains, the two Boshi reserves, and the eastern part of the Okwangwo reserve. We suggested that the collection of some plant products be allowed to continue in a "traditional use zone" in the western part of Okwangwo, and we proposed special measures to stabilize the Obudu Plateau ecosystem, including a restriction on cattle raising, the encouragement of market gardening, and the resettlement of some inhabitants. Given the difficulty of seeing any gorillas at all, we suggested that a tourism program lay emphasis not on gorilla viewing but on hiking through the rain forest on networks of trails connecting campsites and simple rest houses. Meanwhile, we recommended that efforts be made to learn more about gorilla ecology and behavior; we thought that such studies would increase the chances that in the long term visitors might be able to see gorillas. We also recommended the constitution of a wildlife sanctuary in the northwestern hills of the Afi River Forest Reserve to protect the isolated gorilla population there.

The recommendations of our wildlife survey team formed appendices to the master plan for developing the northern sector of the proposed Cross River National Park.[64] Seeking one name for this sector, the plan called it the Okwangwo Division, after its largest and most central reserve component; to the south of the Cross River, the Oban Group of forest reserves would be the centerpiece of the Oban Division of the park. As at Oban, the master plan proposed that a support zone would border the Okwangwo Division. Several teams of consultants had been employed to examine economic development issues in this zone, and they had come up with proposals for a variety of agricultural development projects.

Like the separately published Oban plan, the Okwangwo master plan was presented by WWF to the Nigerian federal government, the Cross River State government, and the European Commission (EC). Again, the plan was designed as a funding proposal to the EC for assistance in the establishment of the park. As with the Oban plan, most of the proposed spending would go to development projects around the park and to support foreign consultants; Nigeria would be left to find most of the money needed to protect the park itself. While the Oban plan had called for spending a total of 18.43 million European Currency Units over a seven-year period (of which 3.08 million would be contributed by the Nigerian government and the rest by the EC), the proposed budget for Okwangwo was 21.00 million ECU over seven years (with 2.36 million to be contributed by Nigeria).[65] The cost of the Okwangwo support zone program (including a revolving credit fund) was put at 4.67 million ECU (.75 million ECU to be contributed by Nigeria), with an extra 1.86 million ECU to be allocated to a Village Conservation and Development Fund, and 1.44 million ECU to be spent on the resettlement of Okwa and Okwangwo villages. For constructing offices and accommodation and visitor reception facilities at a divisional headquarters, 1.68 million ECU was budgeted, and for the consultancy team that would advise on management, 1.70 million ECU. The seven-year cost of a ranger force, to be paid for by the Nigerian federal government, was estimated as the equivalent of 1.29 million ECU. The Okwangwo and Oban master plans gave little attention to how such expenditures (a combined total of about 5.6 million ECU per year [over $7 million]) could be sustained in the future in the absence of foreign aid, although it was suggested that debt-for-nature swaps be explored.

Why were such large expenditures proposed? As a participant in this project, I perceived that large budgets gave potential benefits to the European and Nigerian planners involved, whether or not the expenditures made good conservation sense in the long run. The people involved in the planning process gained greater kudos in their organizations when they discussed the spending of large sums of money, and should the funds be awarded, some of the money would be likely either to flow through the organizations in which the planners themselves worked, or to be paid to consultancy groups with which they were affiliated. This was an actualization of Nigel Tuersley's vision (described earlier in the chapter) of modern conservation operating as a business in a competitive marketplace.

THE CROSS RIVER NATIONAL PARK IS CREATED:
PROBLEMS SOON ARISE

By September 1990, WWF's master plans for both Oban and Okwangwo
had been completed. But for the plans to take effect and for major funds
to be committed, the national park and some rudimentary administrative structure had first to be created. Creation of a park was a relatively
straightforward matter, for Nigeria was being run by the highly centralized military administration of Ibrahim Babangida; a presidential decree
was promulgated in October 1991, establishing Cross River and several
other national parks. In the desire to quickly establish a park, its boundaries were defined as being identical to those of the existing Oban Group
and Boshi-Okwangwo Forest Reserves; these boundaries were already
identified in legislation, so no great difficulty arose in redefining the forest reserves as a national park. But this expediency excluded from the
park several crucial areas recommended in the master plans: the Mbe
Mountains and Obudu Plateau in the Okwangwo Division, and a major
area of "community forest" north of the Ikpan block in the Oban Division that would have provided a link between the central Oban Hills
and Korup in Cameroon. Long and possibly difficult negotiations would
have been needed to include these areas in the national park without
alienating existing land users, and their inclusion would also have required the professional surveying of new boundaries. Prior to the release of funds by the EC, no one seemed prepared either to pay for
proper boundary surveys, or to give priority to negotiating the transfer
to the federal government of the nonreserve lands. As a result, three
areas of key biological importance were excluded from the Cross River
National Park. I suspect that one of the reasons this was allowed to
happen is that some park planners perceived that the release of
development-aid funding would be delayed if creation of the park were
held up by attempts to include these extra lands. If this is true, the urge
to secure funding overrode some of the original conservation goals for
the area: safeguarding the unique Obudu Plateau, protecting a majority
of Nigeria's remaining gorillas, and linking the Korup National Park to
the Oban Hills.

Having overseen the completion of the Cross River National Park planning exercise, Caldecott had left Nigeria in October 1990. For the next
three years a series of project managers appointed by WWF-UK followed
Caldecott in Calabar, while conservation organizations, Nigerian federal
and state governments, and the European Commission debated the implementation of the expensive and complex proposals in the master plans,
which involved creating new and multifaceted organizational structures.
When I visited Calabar in January 1992, WWF's new project manager was
Nick Ashton-Jones, who had been a professional plantation manager in
New Guinea and Southern Africa. I learned that his highest priority was
to increase the well-being of people in the park support zone; without
such development, Ashton-Jones felt, no conservation efforts could succeed. Although the Oban and Boshi-Okwangwo forests now had national
park status (making all hunting technically illegal) antipoaching efforts
and research were given low priority; the newly recruited ranger force
was not armed, despite the usually well-armed and aggressive nature of
poachers in these forests,[66] and research was regarded as a luxury that
could be indulged in once the park was fully institutionalized.

Villagers had become concerned to learn that the creation of a national park would curtail some of their traditional use of the Oban and
Okwangwo forests. These people, and many from farther afield, had
been hunting in the forest reserves and gathering a variety of plant products for a long time, with few controls. During Caldecott's tenure, WWF
had begun to appoint village liaison assistants in the project area as a
way of improving communication with villagers and dealing with some
of their concerns. Appointed on the recommendation of their village
councils, the part-time village liaison assistants were responsible for explaining the park project to their fellow villagers and for reporting back
to project staff with questions and problems. This system was expanded
by Ashton-Jones, so that by April 1992 there were forty-five village liaison assistants in Oban and twenty-five in Okwangwo.[67]

Expectations among local residents that major development aid was
on the way had been raised since 1989, when consultants and government officials first began appearing in long-neglected areas in brand-
new Land Rovers, gathering information and talking about a project that

from its inception had placed special emphasis on development. When I talked to Clement Ebin at the start of my Okwangwo survey in early 1990, he stressed the importance of not discussing issues of compensation with villagers because of the danger that this would raise expectations difficult to fulfill. During my surveys I therefore tried not to suggest that any particular benefits were to accrue to villagers from the park project (I said that the main aim of my work was to learn more about the animals) but I found that I was following in the wake of many other consultants, some of whom were only concerned with development issues. None of us could do our work without revealing something of its purpose, and the cumulative effect of the visits was inevitably to engender hopes of a major foreign "project" that would bring development to rural backwaters.

The appointment of the village liaison assistants in 1991 added to the effects of consultants' visits. At the same time, the published master plans began to circulate widely, making no secret of proposals for multimillion-naira development projects and credit funds. Then the national park was decreed and rangers deployed, theoretically to enforce park laws. These events, along with the expansion of the village liaison assistant program in 1992, inevitably produced widespread expectations that the park was going to lead to significant improvements in villagers' living standards.

It was not long before these great expectations began to crumble. No major European funds had yet been released, and so there was little money to spend on either village development or park protection. A disagreement over management policy between Ashton-Jones and WWF resulted in Ashton-Jones leaving the project in May 1992, and his successor abandoned the village liaison assistant program.

COLLAPSE OF THE OBAN PROJECT

While little was being done in Nigeria to protect the wildlife of the new Cross River park, negotiations continued in Europe on its financing. In their book on conservation policy in Africa, *The Myth of Wild Africa,*

Jonathan Adams and Thomas McShane have noted that the European Union's planning process for conservation and development projects is murky and secretive. Although, in response to European citizens' concerns, the European Union (like its predecessor the European Community) has made substantial funds available for conservation, these funds are disbursed through a structure that, in the words of Adams and McShane, seems designed "to ensure jobs for the bureaucrats in Brussels and EC consulting firms, rather than successful conservation and development initiatives in Africa."[68] In the case of the Cross River National Park, a long period of discussion and revision of the master plan proposals took place in Brussels at the European Commission headquarters before final project documents were ready that could be used as the basis for contracts between the EC and European organizations and consulting companies. Clive Wicks of WWF-UK appears to have been closely involved in these discussions in Brussels.[69]

Although the Oban master plan had been accepted by the Nigerian federal government in December 1989, it was not until March 1992 that an Oban Hills Programme contract document was finalized in Brussels. This document proposed that the Oban Division of the Cross River National Park be developed under a management contract to a European consultancy team, a contract that would be cofunded by the European Development Fund (EDF) and the German Development Credit Agency (Kreditanstalt für Wiederaufbau [KfW]). Meanwhile, the next phase in the development of the Okwangwo Division would be funded by WWF and ODA in the United Kingdom and by a European Commission fund specifically targeted to tropical forest conservation; this funding for Okwangwo would be part of a package that also included support for Korup. Although WWF-UK would continue to be actively involved in the management of Okwangwo, they would relinquish their management role in Oban, where they would retain control only of a subprogram in research and education.[70]

Although the Oban contract was subsequently put out for competitive bidding, KfW never fully committed themselves to funding the project. They were concerned both about arrears on earlier loans to Nigeria and by the fact that the Oban Division boundaries had not been decreed according to the recommendations of the master plan. Disagreements also arose about whether KfW funds would be managed by the Nigerian national parks authority, or by the office of the European Commission in Nigeria.[71] Despite these problems, the EC selected a British consultancy company, Hunting Technical Services, for the Oban management contract in October 1993, and WWF appointed a German ecologist, Klaus Schmitt, as the Oban research biologist. These specialists began arriving in Calabar in early 1994, but their work was very slow in getting off the ground because of delays in the release of funds. Some money was released from the EDF, and this at least covered the salaries of the foreign consultants, but KfW money was not released; the KfW funds were supposed to cover the cost of many project activities, in particular the support zone development program.

During 1995 the Oban research program under Schmitt did get some work done.[72] In a butterfly survey, Torben Larsen collected almost 600 species, and estimated that the Oban Hills probably supported around 950 species, and the Cross River National Park as a whole more than 1,000—the highest number reported from any locality in Africa.[73] However, the central parts of the Oban Hills, around the headwaters of the Calabar and Kwa Rivers, were apparently not explored by any scientist, and no effort was made to look for red colobus in the Ikpan area adjacent to Korup. No project personnel seemed aware that the presence of the rare Preuss's red colobus monkey had been a significant factor in initiation of the Korup conservation project, which in turn had led to the Oban conservation program; or, if these people were aware of this, they showed little interest in the monkey.

By the middle of 1995, when KfW funds still had not been released, serious concern about the future of the Oban project arose in Calabar. Then came a fatal blow to the project's limited outside support. In November 1995 the Nigerian government executed political activist Ken Saro-Wiwa and eight associates, following the deliberations of a secret tribunal. There was an international outcry, and Nigeria was suspended from the Commonwealth. The European Union, under public pressure to demonstrate that it was taking sanctions against the military regime, suspended support to several projects. The Oban project,

Plate 1. Gerald Durrell on his first collecting trip to Cameroon (1947–48), with his chief assistant, Pious. The picture was probably taken in Eshobi. (Photo courtesy of Lee Durrell.)

Plate 2. Elias Abang (left) and Andreas Ncha (right) in Eshobi in March 1996. They were Durrell's hunters on his first expedition to Cameroon.

Plate 3. A new logging road extending north from Eshobi, March 1996. Roads began to open this area to loggers after a large bridge was built over the Cross River at Mamfe in 1991.

Plate 4. Jack Lester (left) and David Attenborough (right) search for the nests of *Picathartes* in a Sierra Leonean forest in 1954. The birds build their mud nests on rock faces like this one. (Photo courtesy of David F. Attenborough.)

Plate 5. Members of the University College London expedition to Fernando Po cross the Iladyi River in montane rain forest below Moka in 1964. A primary aim of the expedition was the collection of zoological specimens.

Plate 6. The author with field assistant Joseph Ekumson at a camp in the Mamu Forest Reserve, Eastern Nigeria, in April 1967. Much of this twenty-five-square-mile reserve had already been converted to plantations and farms. (Photo by Peter Jewell.)

Plate 7. Tom Struhsaker watching monkeys in the Kibale Forest in 1985 with (from left) John Kasenene, Isabirye Basuta, and Jeremiah Lwanga. These students from Uganda's Makerere University went on to complete doctoral degrees based on their studies in Kibale. (Photo by Lysa Leland.)

Plate 8. A lion-tailed macaque in the Kalakkadu forest, Tamil Nadu, South India, in 1976. At that time the main threat to this rare monkey's survival was fragmentation of its habitat through clearance of forest for plantations.

Plate 9. A view looking over the Singampatti tea estate's golf course at Kakachi toward the Agastyamalai hill range of the Western Ghats, South India, in 1976. In the middle distance, once-forested land is being cleared by the tea company.

Plate 10. Max Nicholson (right) with Julian Huxley on an expedition to the Coto Doñana, southwestern Spain, in 1957. Nicholson was later recruited by Huxley to lead the group that planned the formation of the World Wildlife Fund. WWF helped the Spanish government purchase land in Coto Doñana, which became a national park in 1969. (Photo by Eric Hosking, courtesy of WWF.)

Plate 11. Pa Luseni Koroma of Kambama, photographed at Tiwai Island, Sierra Leone, in 1983. Pa Luseni, the oldest man in the village, remembered the first arrival of Europeans in this district.

Plate 12. First encounter: the Moa River seen from Kambama waterside in August 1989. The man on the right is bailing water from a canoe that the party will use to reach Tiwai Island (in center background).

Plate 13. Olive colobus monkeys in the Taï National Park, Côte d'Ivoire. The crest of hair on the crown of the head is a characteristic feature of this monkey. (Photo by Noel Rowe.)

Plate 14. George Whitesides (left) and Lee White inspect the carcasses of black-and-white colobus monkeys killed by a hunter near Kambama, Sierra Leone, in 1984. We were told that the monkeys' meat was destined for Liberia.

Plate 15. The author's transport to Potoru en route to Tiwai in 1979. The motto on the back of this *poda-poda* is a Creole version of "Do not bite the hand that feeds you."

Plate 16. Sierra Leonean soldiers in the ransacked Tiwai research building in January 1992. Rebels had passed through the area in the previous year, bringing an end to ecological research at Tiwai Island.

Plate 17. A hunter in Okomu Forest Reserve with a recently shot white-throated guenon, 1982. A wildlife sanctuary was established at Okomu in 1986, but hunting of primates and other wildlife has continued.

Plate 18. A logging truck hurtles across the Okomu River in the Okomu Forest Reserve, disturbing Pius Anadu (right, foreground) and University of Benin students on a field trip, 1982. Logging has been so intense at Okomu that few large trees now survive in the forest.

Plate 19. A *taungya*-farming area in Okomu Forest Reserve. Although the farmers are supposed to plant trees to replace their food crops, very few trees were planted at Okomu and many *taungya* areas have become permanent farmland.

Plate 20. Forest clearance for a new rubber plantation in Okomu Forest Reserve just north of the wildlife sanctuary, January 1984. Many areas outside the reserve could be planted with rubber trees, but it is generally cheaper for plantation companies to negotiate for the lease of government land in reserves.

Plate 21. Surveying the Obudu Plateau in November 1966. Second from the left is Peter Jewell and second from the right is Arikpo Ettah. The Boshi Extension Forest Reserve, established to protect a gorilla population, lies behind the high ridge in the background.

Plate 22. A Cross River National Park guard inspects the contents of a sack of bushmeat dropped by a man we encountered in the Oban Hills in January 1997. Sam Ettah is on the left, with a still-living forest tortoise near his feet. The shirtless man, who was accompanying two men who ran off into the forest, claimed that he had nothing to do with the meat or its poaching.

Plate 23. A farm demonstration plot at the Butatong headquarters of the Okwangwo Division of Cross River National Park, photographed in 1998. No signs at the headquarters mentioned wildlife conservation.

Plate 24. The Suhien River, southwestern Ghana, near the site of our 1995 camp. Nini-Suhien National Park is on the right bank and the Ankasa Resource Reserve on the left bank.

Plate 25. A large open area in the Kakum National Park, the result of past logging, photographed in 1993. The ground is blanketed by an exotic weed, *Chromolaena*, which inhibits tree regeneration. Elephants further slow forest regrowth in these clearings by browsing on saplings that manage to emerge through the weed blanket.

Plate 26. Ewe farmers from eastern Ghana near the southern edge of the Ankasa Resource Reserve, in far western Ghana, August 1993. In the foreground is cassava harvested from their farms.

Plate 27. Peter Scott, founder of the Wildfowl Trust and first Chairman of the World Wildlife Fund, with Hawaiian geese at Slimbridge, 1951. The geese are a well-known example of the captive breeding of a species endangered in the wild. (Photo by Philippa Scott.)

Plate 28. A golden lion tamarin wearing a radio transmitter is prepared for release at Poço das Antas by James Dietz. Sixteen years elapsed from the beginning of the tamarin reintroduction project at Poço das Antas until a thorough survey of wild tamarin populations in other forests was undertaken in 1990. (Photo by Jessie Cohen, courtesy of the National Zoological Park, Smithsonian Institution.)

Plate 29. A caged black howler monkey is rushed to a waiting RAF helicopter for translocation to the Cockscomb Basin in Belize in 1993. Translocation of wild animals from an area of abundance to an area where they have gone extinct can be a more effective conservation strategy than captive breeding. (Photo by Fred Koontz.)

Plate 30. The author's Nilgiri langur study area in the Kalakkadu Reserved Forest, Tamil Nadu, in 1976. In that year the forest became a wildlife sanctuary.

Plate 31. Nilgiri langur study area in 1995. As a result of careful protection, the forest changed little over twenty years.

with its financial and managerial wrangles unresolved, was a convenient target, and its European Development Fund support was withdrawn. The Hunting consultancy and WWF research program came to an end, and by January 1996 most of the foreign consultants had left Calabar. Now there was only Nigerian federal funding to maintain limited park management, which was in the hands of Clement Ebin, who was now the General Manager of the park. No funds were available for support zone development activities, and the people living in this zone, who had been led to believe that new prosperity was to be theirs, now became thoroughly antagonistic to the national park.

THE CROSS RIVER PARK TODAY: POACHING CONTINUES

I tried to learn what was happening to Oban during a visit to Cross River State in January 1997. I thought it would be enlightening to retrace my journey of January 10, 1967, from Calabar to Aking-Osomba and then into the edge of the Oban Hills forest. I discussed this plan with Clement Ebin, but he was not enthusiastic and would not give me official support. He said that feelings in Aking were running high against the park project because almost none of people's expectations about what the park would bring had been fulfilled. Indeed, villagers had seen little concrete action beyond the distribution of some oil-palm seedlings. Meanwhile, logging concessions had been revoked when the park was declared, and this had probably had adverse effects on the local economy. Previously, some of the larger logging operations had provided employment opportunities, brought cash into local markets, and opened up the forest for farming; village headmen in particular benefited from this opportunity, for they were able to lease farming concessions to migrant Ibibio farmers from overcrowded Akwa Ibom State. These migrant farmers now posed a problem for park management because many of them were farming inside the boundaries of the original forest reserve and, therefore, technically inside the national park.[74]

Because Ebin said that a visit to Aking by a foreigner on any official basis might revive unfulfilled hopes and lead to further complaints about the park, I decided to travel there privately, as a tourist. On January 16, I hired a taxi and traveled north up the road to Aking, accompanied by Sam Ettah from the Pandrillus primate rehabilitation project in Calabar (a project run by Gadsby and Jenkins, who had previously worked on the Kanyang gorilla project). Thirty years before, the journey to Aking had involved taking a ferry over the Kwa River and then following a narrow dirt road (the "MCC Road") that led to Oban town before meandering through hilly terrain into Cameroon. Now a bridge spanned the Cross, and the road was paved. Before, forest in places had edged the road; now, the road was entirely bordered by farms and plantations. After two hours in our rattling taxi, we reached Aking village. In 1909, P. Amaury Talbot had described Aking as "a small place nestling at the base of beautiful purple hills";[75] the village is of course larger now than in Talbot's day, but its setting is still attractive.

At Aking, we visited the new national park office on the edge of the village. This was a renovated building originally erected by the logging company, Seromwood, that had been active in the area before the park was established. Accompanied by two of the twenty park staff based here, we drove a few miles back along the MCC Road to the village of Mango and then followed an old Seromwood logging track northwest toward the forest. In 1967 we had also driven south from Aking before leaving our vehicles and trekking into the forest, which then grew right up to the road. Now we had to drive for about three miles through farmland before meeting secondary forest, where we parked our taxi and walked. The muddy track we followed displayed fresh tire marks, and we passed several stacks of recently sawn timber piled by the roadside. After about forty-five minutes we approached the river Imeh, where I had camped with the forest inventory team on our second night in the Oban Hills in 1967. Then, the forest had struck me as cool and dark and showed no signs of recent disturbance. Now, the forest canopy was broken from logging, and as we approached the Imeh we heard not only the sound of water running over rocks but also the sounds of a vehicle and men talking. We spotted three men on the road ahead of us; the park guards shouted; two of the men ran off, leaving one man and a large package behind (see plate 22). We inspected the package. It contained a live hinge-backed tortoise and several pieces of smoked animal meat: the body of a monkey, two monkey heads, a duiker head, a small pangolin, and two small carnivores. The man who had not escaped said he was from Akwa Ibom State, and he claimed the meat did not belong to him.

Leaving the guards to question the man further, and carrying the tortoise to release in the forest, Ettah and I followed the sound of the vehicle. We crossed the Imeh and soon met a continuation of the logging road on the other side. Here, stuck on a hill, was a farm tractor pulling a trailer, and seven men working on the road. The tractor belonged to the Akwa Ibom State government. We questioned the men, who said they were from Akwa Ibom, that they were going far into the forest to collect timber that was being cut, and that their boss (apparently a former university professor who lived in Oban town) had hired the tractor in Akwa Ibom State. The men claimed they did not know that this was a national park, or that logging was illegal.

It was now almost 1 P.M. and, because I had hired our taxi for only one day, I turned back. We reported our observations to the park office in Aking, and then returned to Calabar. What I had witnessed, while saddening, was not surprising. I knew that although a park ranger force existed, low priority had been given to protection since the Cross River National Park had been established, and that other visitors had witnessed similar evidence of poaching. In August 1994, Liza Gadsby had trekked to the river Imeh from Aking, encountered several Ibibio hunters and fishermen, and shared her taxi back to Calabar with five sacks of smoked bushmeat and several loose carcasses.[76] In November 1995, Klaus Schmitt reported to the park authorities that during twenty-six field trips into the park by his research staff in 1994 and 1995, signs of logging, hunting, and/or farming had been seen on all but one trip.[77]

Poaching, therefore, appears to have continued unabated in the Oban Division of the national park since the park was established, and with the knowledge of the park authorities. The Aking park offices I visited had been functioning for three months and were just a few miles from where I saw evidence of active logging and hunting.

Before I left Calabar in January 1997, I met another visitor who added an additional piece to this picture. Kim Drasler, a young American tourist, had heard of the park before coming to Nigeria and wanted to see it for herself. In December 1996 she took a taxi to Oban town and contacted national park staff, one of whom escorted her to a camp on the edge of the park. This camp was occupied by several men, three of whom were hunters and one of whom came from Cameroon. Drasler stayed at the camp for four nights; every night, the hunters brought back animals that they had killed in the park. On Drasler's last morning in the park, the Cameroonian hunter returned with a dead female drill and its still living infant, which he wanted to sell in town.[78] That an ordinary visitor to the Cross River National Park should be directed by park staff to stay with hunters who were openly killing endangered species in the park is a clear indication of the lack of a strong commitment to wildlife protection by the park authorities at that time, and a telling indictment of the development-oriented approach that had dominated park planning.

The Okwangwo Division of the Cross River National Park did not experience the abrupt withdrawal of outside support that afflicted Oban in 1996. Until 1998, WWF-UK kept a small team of expatriate advisers at Okwangwo to help with park development activities that were supported from 1994 by a 4.08 million ECU grant from the European Union[79] (considerably less than the 18.64 million ECU over seven years proposed in the original Okwangwo master plan). Even so, little urgency has been attached to the control of illegal hunting in the Okwangwo forests. My student Kelley McFarland saw no mammals and found many signs of poaching on a trek right through the former Okwangwo Forest Reserve at the end of 1993. A review of the Okwangwo Division project carried out at the request of WWF in June and July 1994 concluded, "The performance of the National Park Rangers lacks any real conviction, their motivation and training is poor. However, the current activities in the support zone covering agricultural extension and rolling credit are successful."[80] When I visited the headquarters of the Okwangwo Division of the park in February 1996, I asked a senior ranger about the disposition of protection staff. He told me that rangers were based in villages around the park, patrolling (without guns) from the villages by day and returning to the villages at night. Obviously, this would not allow the patrol staff to reach deep inside the park and would make it almost impossible for them to arrest or even deter any serious poachers. The WWF project manager told me that longer patrols were in the process of being organized, but this was more than five years after we had reported to WWF: "The control of poaching must be a high priority in the management of the Okwangwo Division. Staff will need to be highly-motivated, well-trained and well-equipped."[81]

Not until 1998 were buildings completed for the Okwangwo divisional headquarters at the village of Butatong, three miles from the park, where a farm demonstrating new crop varieties has also been established (see plate 23). And virtually no progress has been made in resettling the villages of Okwa and Okwangwo from the center of the park. In July 1996 the emphasis placed on development as opposed to protection activities in Okwangwo was indicated by a notice I saw outside the Park General Manager's office in Calabar: "The Okwangwo Programme of Cross River National Park has initiated another major move in its people-oriented development and conservation activities. The programme has successfully concluded a four day conference on the potential resettlement of the communities of Okwangwo, Okwa I and Okwa II." Although this showed that resettlement was still being considered, the notice also indicated that any agreement was far away. The communities' representative, Gregory Mbua, was reported as having declared that "while the enclave communities are willing to be resettled, the issue should be approached with considerable dexterity. According to him [Mbua], 'we are proud of our homes and will not want to be treated like refugees escaping from hunger, war or epidemic . . . ', therefore a situation where the people will be exposed to avoidable hardship will not be entertained."

When I discussed park management issues with Clement Ebin in January 1998, he openly acknowledged that the support zone development program had been a failure and had led people to expect that the park authorities would provide much more material assistance than was possible. He agreed on the need to give much greater priority to protection, and he told me that efforts were now being made to obtain rifles to arm the protection force.

LOGGING THREATS GROW

Creation of the Cross River National Park has improved forest conservation in one significant way. The declaration of the park was accompanied by the revocation of commercial logging concessions over large areas of the Oban Group of forest reserves. This action required no foreign advisers and no money was paid; the loggers were offered concessions, however, in other reserves. Although small-scale logging has not ceased in the Oban forests and larger animals are being indiscriminately hunted, the forests themselves are presently protected from major disruption. But fears are growing that large-scale mechanized logging could return to Oban.

Following the designation of the Cross River National Park, a planning team from the British ODA worked with the Cross River State Department of Forestry (soon to be renamed the Department of Forestry Development) to produce a plan to improve the management of those state forests remaining outside the park, which were now going to come under more intense logging pressure. Of an estimated 3,900 square miles of forest in Cross River State, about 1,390 lie in the national park, 965 in state government forest reserves, and 1,545 on community land. In the community (or "protected") forests, the state government theoretically has some control over the removal of timber or the reallocation of land for commercial use, but otherwise the forests are largely managed by village communities, who may give leases to loggers.[82]

After the ODA review, new logging concessions were approved by the Cross River State government. Among the concessionaires, one newcomer to the state had much greater resources than the established logging companies; this newcomer was the Western Metal Products Company (WEMPCO), a company based in Lagos but whose owners are

Hong Kong Chinese. The company, which has made much of its money in the manufacture of roofing sheets, obtained concessions to log 209 square miles of forest in five forest reserves close to the Cross River National Park; the largest concession is in the Cross River South Forest Reserve, immediately adjacent to the Oban Division of the park. WEMPCO has also been negotiating deals with many village communities for access to timber on their land. As part of its agreements with village communities, WEMPCO has offered to build clinics and schools, provide college scholarships, and support football teams.

Most disturbingly, WEMPCO has constructed a large sawmill with associated plywood and veneer production plants on the banks of the river Cross, close to the town of Ikom. This factory was completed in 1996, following planning that apparently began in 1992. The factory is said to have cost $5 million to construct, and it is strategically located within twenty-five miles of the boundaries of the five forest reserves where WEMPCO has concessions, and midway between the Oban and Okwangwo Divisions of the national park.

The Nigerian federal government now requires environmental impact assessments (EIAs) for projects such as this. An EIA of WEMPCO's plans was produced, and it concluded that the operations would not have adverse environmental consequences. But this assessment (done for profit by a Lagos consultancy firm) was widely regarded as superficial and probably tailored to WEMPCO's needs; it was produced after the completion of the wood-processing plant. In response to an outcry from a coalition of local environmental groups, Nigeria's Federal Environmental Protection Agency has not allowed WEMPCO's logging operations to proceed and the agency is conducting its own EIA of the logging plans. However, the operation of the wood-processing plant has been approved, and to feed this plant WEMPCO has been buying timber from communities and illegal loggers, whom the company is said to have provided with chain saws and other assistance. Meanwhile, WEMPCO has made threats against conservationists in the state and taken some of them to court on trumped-up charges.[83]

The expansion and intensification of logging in Cross River State poses an obvious threat to the large area of community forest that lies along the Cameroon border, adjacent to Cameroon's Ejagham Forest Reserve and contiguous with the Ikpan sector of the Oban Division of the park; although this area was recommended for inclusion in the park, it has yet to be formally gazetted as parkland. If this community forest is seriously degraded by logging there is little likelihood that it will become an effective component of the park in the future, and a forested connection between Cameroon's Korup National Park and the central forests of the Oban Hills will have been broken. Conservationists in Nigeria fear that once community forests and forest reserves have been depleted, WEMPCO and other major commercial loggers will threaten the park itself, which has the most valuable timber remaining in the state. Already, some people in Cross River State are expressing the view that the state should take the parklands back from the federal government, and logging interests are suspected to be behind these arguments. Such views could gain wide support in the Oban area, given the complete failure of the large-scale development project that the government and the local people had come to expect from the time the WWF program commenced in 1989.

WERE THERE ALTERNATIVES?

Julian Caldecott has argued correctly that delays between the completion of the Cross River National Park master plans and the release of implementation funds by the European Commission and associated donors caused a local loss of credibility in the value of the park program.[84] But these delays must have been aggravated by the novelty, complexity, and expense of the plans, factors bound to slow the process of approval by the European bureaucracy. In my view, the overriding problem in WWF's design of this national park project was that it was conceived of by outsiders who, consciously or unconsciously, were pursuing a philosophy laid down by the founder of Earthlife: that conservation should function as a business.

Since the 1950s the governments of first the Eastern Region of Nigeria and then of Cross River State had considered proposals for a game reserve or national park to include at least part of the Obudu Plateau and the adjacent Boshi-Okwangwo Forest Reserves. But no administration had been prepared to give sufficient attention to this idea or to release sufficient funds to make it a reality. National park status for Oban had also been suggested by a number of foreign scientists visiting the area, but the potential value of the Oban forests to local logging interests had meant that the proposal received little support from the state government.

The situation changed dramatically once WWF came on the scene and began talking about a large conservation and development project. Such a project appeared to suit many interests. On the part of WWF, the project followed the policy adopted in the late 1970s, that of linking conservation with economic development, and it held the promise of major financial support from the European Commission, which had expressed itself as particularly in favor of transborder, regional projects. Like other big internationally active conservation organizations at this time, WWF could expect large contracts with foreign-aid donors to provide substantial overhead for administrative expenses at its home office, and so help keep its own organization running and its staff employed. The project also provided obvious advantages to the Nigerian and foreign consultants employed by the project; some of these consultants worked for the U.K. Overseas Development Natural Resource Institute, an offshoot of the U.K. ODA, another project sponsor. And the Cross River State government must have perceived that a large foreign-aid project could bring some badly needed resources to the government, quite apart from the potential advantages to the people of the state from development. All these people had an interest in seeing that whatever project was initiated was as large and expensive as possible; in other words, they were major "stakeholders."

In consequence, many project participants lost sight of some of the original reasons for seeking designation of a national park in Cross River State. The park planners had been affected by a phenomenon seen in other conservation and development projects, which frequently come to function mainly as development projects to which conservation goals are subordinated.[85] In Cross River, concern for protecting the forests and their interesting animals because of their intrinsic value came to be rather unimportant. During my involvement with the project I was often struck by the fact that few of the administrators and consultants responsible for establishing the park and planning its management ever showed a strong interest in penetrating deeply into the park simply to enjoy nature for its own sake, even though it was expected that "rain forest tourists" would wish to do this.

Given the project's increasingly overt emphasis on people and their economic development, it is hardly surprising that little serious effort was made to control hunting or strongly encourage research on some key species. I did meet a biological survey team when I visited the Okwangwo Division in February 1996, and learned that the team were collecting butterflies and looking for evidence of mammals, particularly buffalo. This latter fact was surprising, as buffalo are most typical of the forest edge, such as the forest-grassland interface along the northern edge of the park; they had never been considered a conservation priority in Okwangwo. The survey team told me that they were not paying any special attention to gorillas, although gorilla conservation had been the original primary incentive for a national park in this area. As far as I was able to discover, no one had tried to learn anything about the status of the gorillas in the original Boshi Extension Gorilla Sanctuary since the last visits by Dominic White and me in 1990.[86]

It is perhaps too easy with the benefit of hindsight to criticize a pioneering project in a country like Nigeria that provides many obstacles to efficient progress. Could any better outcomes have been reasonably expected from a different project design? From the time I first learned of the design of the Cross River project, I had misgivings about the emphasis on big money and development. Perhaps in part because of my knowledge of earlier conservation plans for the area, but also given my experience at Tiwai and in other parts of West Africa, I was more disposed to an approach that involved building modestly on existing structures and that laid emphasis on reducing the very high levels of hunting.

How could such an alternative approach have been supported? It is difficult to estimate the total foreign financial contributions to the Cross River National Park project from its initiation by WWF in 1988 up to the end of 1996, but my guess is that these contributions (used in large part to pay for expatriate managers and consultants and for equipment) have totaled well over $8 million. A sensible alternative would have been to invest this money in a trust fund, which could have yielded a moderate but steady return in perpetuity; this income could have been used for sustained education and antipoaching efforts and for improvements in the management of the existing protected areas. In Cross River the national and state governments already had embryonic plans for a national park, at least in the Obudu area. If effective conservation rather than an increase in the wealth and power of international conservation organizations and consultancy firms had been the first priority, the most sensible course would have been to build slowly and incrementally on the existing plans and organizational structures. Such an incremental approach surely holds more promise of sustainability, but no gradual, relatively small-scale efforts appear to have been contemplated.

To the best of my knowledge, no mechanism currently exists for European development funds to be deposited into a trust. This is unfortunate, but a trust fund is not the only option that might modestly support conservation in places like Cross River. Much could be achieved by raising relatively small sums of money through conservation organizations (on the order of a hundred thousand dollars annually), sustaining this support, and making renewal of the funding contingent upon satisfactory accounting. Foreign staff would not need to hold long-term appointments; outside experts could instead make regular advisory visits.

Despite what I see as the better sense of such small-scale, incremental approaches to conservation, I concede that it might have been more difficult to establish a national park in Cross River State if it had not been for the active engagement of an organization like WWF and the assurances that large development funds were on the horizon. It was probably this "carrot" that persuaded state authorities that logging permits could be revoked.

The revocation of the concessions for logging that were threatening to seriously damage the forest of the Oban Hills is perhaps the most positive effect that the declaration of the Cross River National Park has had for conservation. The declaration has also brought some federal government funds to the state to be used in park management. But at least up till 1997, the creation of a national park had not led to any major reduction of hunting in Oban, nor had it ended all logging. Logging pressures are mounting all around Oban, and there is no guarantee that its national park status will protect it in the long term. Meanwhile, having had their expectations raised and then dashed by a conservation project, people living around the Oban Hills will almost certainly be less sympathetic to conservation initiatives in the future than they were before the WWF project began.

The situation is slightly better in the Okwangwo Division of the park, where a combination of small-scale development projects, protection efforts, and biological surveys continued under WWF auspices until 1998. But even at Okwangwo there have been many signs of a half-hearted commitment to the control of poaching. For instance, when I was camped on the Obudu Plateau near the park boundary in January 1998, I met hunters coming out of the park carrying loads of animals they had trapped in wire snares. And when I spent three days in the park forests below the plateau in January 1999, the only mammal I observed was one flying squirrel; snares were abundant in the forest.[87] At Okwangwo, as at Oban, people living around the park have shown overt hostility to park staff, apparently because they do not see themselves receiving all the material benefits they had expected.[88]

Relative to the amounts of money spent, therefore, the achievements of the Cross River National Park project are small. And of the primates that first drew international conservation attention to these forests, the future of the gorillas is not secure and the status of the red colobus monkeys is completely unknown. As hunting in the park continues with little regulation, its forests (which WWF had once called "the most important biotic reserve in Africa") are becoming as empty of wildlife as the forests of Ghana that I describe in the next chapter.

SEVEN

The Empty Forests of Ghana

After celebrating Christmas Eve with some Ghanaian brandy, Michael Abedi-Lartey and I left our camp on the Suhien River at 7 A.M. on December 25, 1995, and set off with our two game-guard assistants into the Nini-Suhien National Park. We planned to complete the cutting of a transect line through the forested hills in the heart of the park, a transect specifically designed to census primates. Since entering the forest three days before, we had not seen or heard any monkeys, or any other mammal larger than a squirrel, although we had noticed a few antelope and elephant tracks. On Christmas Day we met only squirrels, birds, and a green tree viper, and during our next eight days in the forest, while quietly walking our transects and following hunters' trails, we detected monkeys on just two occasions. Once, we heard monkey calls not far from our camp. On the second occasion we were walking slowly down a trail when we heard monkeys moving toward us through the forest canopy; we crouched in the undergrowth and managed to glimpse a mixed group of three species, until a Campbell's monkey spotted us and gave an alarm call, causing all the animals to crash rapidly away through the trees in evident terror of the humans they had met. Near the Suhien River were some magnificent ironwood and mahogany trees, and the forest was among the most impressive I had seen in West Africa. But it was a forest that seemed to be virtually empty of many of the medium-sized animals (such as monkeys, small antelopes, and guinea fowl) that are the favorite quarry of hunters.

During our survey, we found many old snare traps and several poachers' camps, which were apparently being used by men who were not only gathering rattan canes and chewing sticks in the forest but also hunting game. On Christmas Eve we had found one very recently vacated camp with a fire still smoldering; scattered around this camp were empty boxes of shotgun cartridges and the remains of several birds (including a hornbill) and a small forest pangolin. Hunters in these forests generally start shooting hornbills and other large forest-canopy birds when mammals have become scarce. Such an "empty forest" has been discussed by Kent Redford, who has described how populations of game animals have been reduced or extinguished in a great many areas of Amazonia as a result of subsistence and commercial hunting, producing a severely disrupted ecosystem lacking the species richness valued by naturalists.[1]

In this chapter I summarize the history of efforts to conserve Ghana's forests and their wildlife in the face of growing exploitation, and I explain how these efforts have been affected by national political and economic forces. I describe how I came to be in Nini-Suhien National Park at the end of 1995 during a series of surveys to establish the status of forest monkey populations. These surveys revealed the devastating impact on wildlife of uncontrolled illegal hunting and suggested that a local form of red colobus monkey had probably gone extinct. I discuss how, coincident with the revival of Ghana's economy, foreign consultants and organizations (such as IUCN and the European Union) have become involved in plans to improve the management of the forest national parks of Bia and Nini-Suhien. These plans have called for expensive integrated conservation and development projects like those in Nigeria that I have described. Since 1989, when this planning began, and 1997, when a project finally commenced, no extra effort was made to protect the wildlife of the parks or of other Ghanaian forests. As I had found in Nigeria, no special attention was given in the planning process to the implications of the fact that many of the pressures on Ghana's forest parks were coming from immigrants rather than long-term residents. As colobus monkeys and other wildlife disappeared, simple low-cost measures available to protect them were ignored, and attention was instead focused on designing a large, high-cost project that would pay handsome salaries to foreign consultants.

FOREST CONSERVATION IN GHANA: A SHORT HISTORY

The Nini-Suhien National Park, where Abedi-Lartey and I had spent Christmas 1995, is the northern part of a protected rain forest area of two hundred square miles in the southwestern corner of Ghana, not far from the Côte d'Ivoire border. The southern part of the forest, separated from the national park by the Suhien River (see plate 24), is designated as the Ankasa Resource Reserve, formerly known as the Ankasa Game Production Reserve. Both areas were once part of the Ankasa River Forest Reserve established in 1934. They gained their status as special wildlife protection areas in 1976 following the declaration of another forest national park at Bia in 1974. At that time Emmanuel Asibey was Chief Officer of Ghana's Department of Game and Wildlife, and he fought to improve the protection of wildlife not only in the savanna regions in the north of the country, but also in the southern forest zone.[2]

The need to take measures to protect Ghana's forests and wildlife had become increasingly apparent in the decades leading up to Asibey's initiatives. People had inhabited the forest zone of this part of West Africa for hundreds of years,[3] practicing bush-fallow cultivation. One group of Akan-speaking people, the Asante (or Ashanti), became politically predominant in the early eighteenth century. By that time, Europeans had been actively trading with people at the coast—for gold, ivory, and slaves—for more than two hundred years; the rich deposits of gold in the territories controlled by the Asante gave this coastal region the name "Gold Coast." By the early nineteenth century the British had become the dominant foreign trading power on the coast, while the Asante had consolidated their power over a large area of the interior. Tensions between the two increased, especially after the British outlawed the maritime slave trade in 1807. Like those of the Mende in Sierra Leone, the Asante economy and farming system relied heavily on slavery, and the abolition of the overseas trade disrupted parts of the economy and made it more difficult to dispose of surplus slaves. Subsequent friction resulted from British attempts to control the trade in arms to the Asante, and Asante restrictions on the movement of palm oil to the coast. The first battle between the Asante and the British occurred in 1807, but the Asante were not finally defeated until 1900—"by far the longest" African military resistance to European conquest, according to one writer.[4] With peace established, the development of the Gold Coast colony and protectorate began.

Some rain forest logging had occurred near the coast of Ghana in the 1800s, but the logging was restricted to sites near rivers, down which logs could be floated. British colonial rule brought railways and roads to the interior, and the economy developed. Cocoa farming expanded, and the demand for pit props grew as gold mines became mechanized. Although this led to an increase in deforestation, logging in the first half of the twentieth century was largely unmechanized and, when not associated with farming, was of relatively low intensity.[5]

Along with roads and railways, colonial control led to land use planning and the establishment of forest reserves in uninhabited forest areas. As early as 1887, Alfred Moloney of the colonial administration in Lagos had argued the need for forest conservation measures in all British territories in West Africa.[6] In the Gold Coast colony, a Forestry Department was formed in 1909; the main program of forest reservation began in 1919 and was largely completed by 1939. The reserves were established particularly to protect water supplies, to secure the supply of forest produce to villages, and to "assist the well-being of the forest and agricultural crops."[7] Although some recent accounts imply that the main original purpose of setting forest aside in reserves was to aid the colonial power in the exploitation of timber, little evidence exists for that view. The reservation initially met with considerable resistance from many people in the forest zone, because controls were placed on some of their traditional use rights.[8] But this resentment declined over the years; a rising population and more farming led to the loss of much of the forest outside the reserves, and the benefits of the reserves came to be better appreciated.[9]

World War II heightened the pressure on the forests inside and outside the Gold Coast's reserves. German actions interfered with the supply of timber to Britain from North America and Scandinavia, and this led to a great increase in demand for West African wood. Sawmills and mechanized logging proliferated in the Gold Coast colony, and sawn timber exports jumped from 18,806 cubic feet in 1939 to 7 million cubic feet in 1956.[10]

In 1957, the Gold Coast became the first British colony in tropical Africa to achieve real independence (as a "dominion" of the Commonwealth), and in 1960 it declared itself the Republic of Ghana, under President Kwame Nkrumah. Nkrumah's government began distributing large numbers of logging concessions to small Ghanaian-owned businesses, further intensifying the pressures on the remaining forest.[11] As the scale of logging increased and forests in the most remote areas were opened up, the hunting of forest animals for meat also escalated. Although forest reserves had been designed to regulate forest use and the felling of trees, their purpose was not seen as the protection of untouched wilderness, and little had been done in colonial times to control hunting or enforce the game laws that ostensibly protected rare animal species.[12] Angus Booth, whose studies of olive colobus monkeys I described in chapter 4, witnessed the effects of hunting on forest primates during his surveys in Ghana in the early 1950s, and he suggested that the extinction of one species, the red colobus monkey, was probable "in the near future" unless special measures were taken to protect it and its habitat.[13]

Prospects for wildlife conservation improved in 1965 when Emmanuel Asibey, who had joined the Game Branch of the Forestry Department in 1960, was appointed as head of a new Department of Game and Wildlife, which had been separated from Forestry. In 1968 Kai

Curry-Lindahl, Vice Chairman of IUCN's Species Survival Commission and of its International Commission on National Parks, visited Ghana to advise the government on wildlife conservation and on the organization of the new department. In his subsequent report, Curry-Lindahl recommended a ban on hunting in some forest reserves.[14] Soon after this, Sonia Jeffrey, a resident of western Ghana, described vividly how timber roads had brought large-scale farming and intense hunting pressure to the previously remote forests near the Côte d'Ivoire border. Jeffrey, writing in *Oryx*, echoed Curry-Lindahl's call for the establishment of some no-hunting forest-and-game reserves that would allow animal populations to increase and repopulate surrounding areas.[15] The forest-and-game-reserve concept appears to have been the idea behind the system of "Game Production Reserves" that was to develop in Ghana.

Although Jeffrey saw such conservation action as fraught with difficulties that would take many years to solve, surveys to locate the best site for a forest national park began in the early 1970s. The Bia Tributaries South Forest Reserve was eventually chosen, in part because Peace Corps volunteer Michael Rucks, working with the Department of Game and Wildlife, reported that red colobus monkeys were relatively abundant there but were no longer found in the nearby Krokosua Hills Forest Reserve, the first area considered for park status.[16] Reports by Booth and others had stressed that of Ghana's rain forest primates, red colobus monkeys were the most susceptible to both logging and hunting, and so the choice of Ghana's first forest national park was made in part to provide a refuge for this species, an interesting parallel to the influence that the presence of red colobus had on the establishment of the Korup National Park in Cameroon.

Thus was the 120-square-mile Bia National Park declared in 1974 (see map 8). Probably because of Curry-Lindahl's status in IUCN and his recommendations for Ghana, assistance was forthcoming from both IUCN and WWF for the establishment of Bia. Under this WWF-IUCN program, the Swiss biologist Claude Martin was appointed as Senior Warden of Bia Park in 1975.

Kwame Nkrumah had been deposed in a military coup in 1966, and after a brief period of civilian rule, Ghana came under the military government of General I. K. Acheampong, who had come to power in another coup in 1972. In 1977 the Acheampong government, regarded as

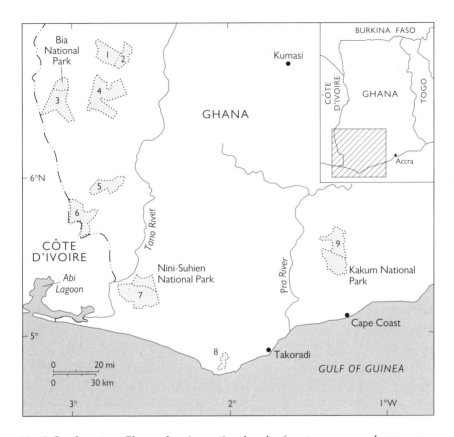

Map 8. Southwestern Ghana, showing national parks, forest reserves, and resource reserves mentioned in the text. Key to reserves: 1, Subim Forest Reserve; 2, Ayum Forest Reserve; 3, Bia Resource Reserve; 4, Krokosua Hills Forest Reserve; 5, Yoyo Forest Reserve; 6, Boin River Forest Reserve; 7, Ankasa Resource Reserve; 8, Cape Three Points Forest Reserve; 9, Assin Attandanso Resource Reserve.

particularly corrupt, was persuaded by timber companies to reduce the area of Bia National Park to only thirty square miles, with the remainder becoming a so-called Game Production Reserve.[17] While the national park was supposed to be strictly protected against exploitation, controlled and supposedly sustained-yield logging was permitted in the production reserve. At least initially, animals were not to be hunted there, although in the long run the government apparently envisaged such reserves as sources of animals for meat and sport hunting.[18]

Despite this early threat to the integrity of Bia, wildlife protection in what remained of the national park appears to have been relatively good. Asibey and Martin encouraged the study of primates by an American group that included Meredith and Michael Rucks (studying guenons and red colobus), Dana Olson (black-and-white colobus), and Sheila Hunt-Curtin (Diana monkeys). Unfortunately, the studies ended in 1977, and only a very few of their results were ever published.[19]

The pressures on Bia led to a search for another forest area, one less threatened by logging, in which wildlife could be safeguarded. As a result, Claude Martin surveyed the Ankasa River Forest Reserve in 1976 and recommended its conversion to a national park.[20] Ankasa appeared to have little commercially valuable timber, and its rugged terrain had hampered the little exploitation that had been attempted up to that time. The protection of Ankasa added to the park system an additional forest type, wet evergreen forest, complementing Bia's moist deciduous forest. However, only part of Ankasa was given full protection, as the Nini-Suhien National Park; the southern portion of the forest reserve was designated as a Game Production Reserve, following the Bia model.

CONDITIONS IN GHANA DETERIORATE

By the late 1970s, Ghana's prosperous economy had been reduced to a shambles by government corruption and mismanagement, and by huge rises in the world price of oil. Logging continued to increase, but the production of cocoa (the mainstay of the economy) slumped 61 percent between 1972 and 1978,[21] and severe fuel shortages made long-distance travel difficult and expensive. In this crisis, few resources were devoted to conservation. The files of the Department of Game and Wildlife contain some revealing quarterly reports made by the officer in charge of Ankasa in 1979. In March he reported that a lack of equipment was hindering protection, and he noted that an influx of Asante farmers in recent years was destroying forest right up to the reserve boundary as farms were cleared; in June he pointed out an immediate need for firearms for protection work, and by September he was complaining of transportation difficulties resulting from the fuel crisis.[22]

The Ghanaian economy gradually stabilized and then improved after Jerry Rawlings's second military coup against the government on December 31, 1981. Earlier that year, Stephen Gartlan (then Vice President for Conservation of the International Primatological Society) visited Ghana at the invitation of Asibey and reviewed forest primate conservation issues, concentrating on Bia and Ankasa. Among Gartlan's recommendations following his trip was the suggestion that the Ankasa Game Production Reserve and Nini-Suhien National Park be consolidated into one national park. He felt that production reserve status left the Ankasa ecosystem too vulnerable to damage from logging and, potentially, hunting. Gartlan also encouraged foreign scientists to take greater advantage of primate research opportunities in Bia and recommended that external assistance be found to develop a conservation education program aimed at schoolchildren.[23]

Gartlan's report did not, however, express alarm about the status of forest primates, and little was done to follow up on his recommendations. Emmanuel Asibey, who had played a key role in creating the protected areas at Bia and Ankasa, was appointed as the Chief Administrator of a new Ghana Forestry Commission in December 1980 and therefore became less directly involved with wildlife conservation; in 1989 he took a leave of absence from the Forestry Commission and went to the World Bank in Washington, D.C.

Bia and Ankasa were neglected for most of the 1980s, and little more was heard of them until 1988, when a team of students from Cambridge University made a survey of the birds of Ankasa and Nini-Suhien. Among rare and threatened birds seen from a base on the Suhien River were the white-breasted guinea fowl and the yellow-throated olive greenbul. However, the expedition's report noted seeing many signs of poachers and "alarmingly low" numbers of primates; just two groups of Diana monkeys and one group of black-and-white colobus were seen over a one-month period, and there were no sightings at all of red colobus.[24] By contrast, during just fourteen and a half hours of censusing in Ankasa in 1976, Martin's team had encountered seven groups of Diana monkeys and three groups of black-and-white colobus, and claimed to have once heard red colobus calls.[25] By 1988, however, Ankasa had probably had no serious protection for ten years.

GHANA TRIES INTEGRATING FOREST
CONSERVATION AND DEVELOPMENT

By 1990 the Ghanaian economy was recovering, international concern for the fate of tropical rain forests had grown, and development-aid money had begun to flow to conservation projects in significant quantities. In that year Joshua Bishop, an economist employed by the Environment and Development Group (EDG) of Oxford University, made four visits to Ghana under a consultancy contract to the Department of Game and Wildlife funded by the European Commission. His main brief was to consider improvements in the management of Bia and Ankasa, giving special attention to community conservation (integrating protected areas "in the process of rural economic development and in the lives of local communities").[26] This project had its origins in the concern for elephant conservation that had brought Stephen Cobb of EDG to Ghana in 1989. Bishop was in Ghana for a total of thirty-six days; most of his time was spent in Accra and Kumasi, but he did make brief visits to the edges of Ankasa and Bia in June 1990. In addition, Yaa Ntiamoa-Baidu of the University of Ghana at Legon, in Accra, interviewed people in two villages near Ankasa and two villages near Bia about their attitudes toward wildlife and conservation. But no effort appears to have been made to survey the interiors of the parks and reserves. The final EDG report was submitted to the Department of Game and Wildlife and to the EC in 1992. It recommended a three-year program costing 3.46 million European Currency Units (about $4.6 million), of which 1.30 million ECU was to be for consultants and 245,000 ECU for community development. This report was not immediately accepted by the European Commission, which apparently felt that the community development component was inadequate.[27] A revised proposal therefore was produced in 1993 by the Department of Game and Wildlife with the help of John Grainger, an IUCN consultant working with the department on developing protected-area management plans as part of a larger Forest Resource Management Programme funded by the World Bank. The final version of the proposal, recommending the expenditure of 4.6 million ECU over three years, was approved by the EC in July 1995; in this approved version, community development expenditures had risen to

653,500 ECU and included allocations for the construction of schools and health centers.[28]

Meanwhile, development funding for forest conservation in Ghana was also being sought in the United States. In 1989, the U.S. Agency for International Development (USAID) approached the Midwest Universities Consortium for International Activities (MUCIA) to provide technical assistance on a project formulated by the government of the Central Region of Ghana. The project's key idea was to boost the economy of this region by stimulating tourism. The chief elements of the project were the development of hotels and beach resorts, refurbishment of historic coastal forts, and development of the existing Kakum and Assin Attandanso Forest Reserves into a national park that could be used for ecotourism.[29] Kakum had been considered in the past for game reserve or park status in large part because it contained a relatively healthy population of forest elephants.

By 1991, Conservation International (CI) of Washington, D.C., had become involved through MUCIA as the American agency that would provide technical assistance for development of the new park. In the same year Kakum (eighty square miles) was gazetted as a national park, and Assin Attandanso (fifty-four square miles) as a game production reserve; they are generally considered to be a single conservation area, "Kakum." In 1992, Russ Mittermeier, President of CI, approached Tom Struhsaker and me to provide an evaluation of primate conservation needs at Kakum, and in March and April 1993 we carried out surveys in the forest.

Neither Struhsaker nor I had heard of Kakum before. The site had not been featured in reports about Ghanaian primates or in lists of priority forests in West Africa for conservation, but the CI planning documents we consulted suggested that Kakum contained nine species of primate. During our initial surveys over a period of thirteen days, we spent forty-eight hours in the forest and were disappointed to get direct evidence for the presence of only five primates species: the spot-nosed, Campbell's, and olive colobus monkeys (all small animals, typical of disturbed forest), and, seen at night in the beams of headlamps, the potto and Demidoff's bushbaby. We also received several seemingly reliable reports about the presence of black-and-white colobus in Kakum. A few people said that Diana monkeys also were present, but these accounts were less convincing, and none of our guides or other naturalists we talked to had any knowledge of red colobus monkeys, mangabeys, or chimpanzees in the forest (three species that in the past had been reported in Bia and Ankasa). The monkeys we did encounter were very shy, suggesting that they had been hunted, and we found that the forest itself had been heavily logged (see plate 25). We were unable to learn of any surveyed trails or campsites in the center of the conservation area, and so our observations were restricted to the periphery. We therefore arranged for a trail into the center of the park to be surveyed, for a campsite to be located there, and for a transect line to be cut that we could census later in the year. We also advised that surveys should be made of other forests in the southwest of Ghana to assess the status of red colobus, mangabeys, and Diana monkeys. Each of these species is represented in western Ghana and eastern Côte d'Ivoire by a distinct subspecies found nowhere else in Africa; these are Miss Waldron's red colobus monkey (*Procolobus badius waldroni*), the white-naped mangabey (*Cercocebus atys lunulatus*), and the Roloway form of Diana monkey (*Cercopithecus diana roloway*). Our Kakum experience and conversations with naturalists and Game Department staff in Ghana led us to think that these monkeys were threatened with extinction.[30]

I returned to Ghana to make further surveys in August 1993, and Struhsaker followed in November. In Kakum I conducted careful censuses on two prepared transects, one at Antikwaa near the western edge of the forest and one near the Obuo River in the center of the park. I saw the same three monkey species we had encountered in March and April, but I also heard the calls of black-and-white colobus monkeys. At Obuo in November, Struhsaker had similar findings, and he managed to see one group of black-and-white colobus. But neither of us saw or heard any sign of red colobus, mangabeys, or Diana monkeys. We also made visits to Ankasa and Bia. In the course of three days at Ankasa, I saw one group of Campbell's monkeys and I heard monkeys calling or moving in three other places; in one of these places I heard the distinctive call of a male Diana monkey (a species I had known at Tiwai). Over five days in Bia, Struhsaker encountered only five monkey associations; he could not get clear views of any individual monkeys but he heard the distinctive calls of spot-nosed and Campbell's monkeys, and once he heard a chimp calling in the far distance. Although game staff told Struhsaker that they sometimes saw black-and-white colobus and Diana monkeys, none knew of red colobus monkeys or mangabeys. In Bia and Ankasa, Struhsaker and I found many signs of poaching.[31]

WIDER SURVEY EFFORTS

Struhsaker and I were shocked by our findings. They suggested that Ghana's three locally endemic forest primates were close to extinction, and we began to fear that Miss Waldron's red colobus might already be extinct. We recommended to Conservation International that top priority be given to a survey in western Ghana extending over several months and examining other forests, to better ascertain the status of the endemic primates and to identify conservation measures that might be taken to protect them. During his November 1993 visit, Struhsaker discussed the need for this survey with USAID officials in Accra, and we both discussed it with the Chief Game Warden, Gerry Punguse.

When no funds were committed by CI or USAID to the further efforts we recommended, Struhsaker wrote in April 1994 to Claude Martin, who had now become Director General of WWF International in Gland. Struhsaker suggested creating an emergency fund of ten thousand dollars annually that could be used to pay bonuses to protection staff at Bia and Ankasa. We had found the staff in these conservation areas to be demoralized and poorly paid, and it seemed that bonuses paid to guards for arrests leading to convictions might improve their performance. This was proposed as an emergency measure until a larger and more comprehensive conservation program, such as that being considered by the EC, could become effective. Martin responded somewhat positively, but said that he would require a letter from Punguse explaining how the bonus system would be run; we tried to arrange for such a letter through CI, but it was not forthcoming.

Meanwhile, in the absence of other initiatives, I began planning a broader survey of the western Ghana forests. This was finally conducted in July and August 1995, in collaboration with George Whitesides (my colleague from Tiwai days), Bryan Dickinson of the Ghana Association for the Conservation of Nature, and Michael Abedi-Lartey of the Ghana Department of Game and Wildlife (which had now been renamed the Department of Wildlife). Whitesides and I began the survey with Dickinson, and after I left to undertake other primate surveys in Bénin and Togo, Whitesides completed it with Abedi-Lartey.

The survey in July and August 1995 only heightened our concerns about the status of Ghana's forest wildlife. In addition to further visits to Bia and Ankasa, the survey included visits to the Ayum, Boin River, Krokosua Hills, and Subim and Yoyo Forest Reserves, as well as the Nini-Suhien National Park. These forest reserves (shown on map 8) were chosen either because of their proximity to the sites at which the monkey we considered most threatened—the red colobus—had been collected in the past for museums, or because Forestry staff claimed that these reserves were good places to see monkeys.

Near the Suhien River, where the Ankasa Resource Reserve meets the Nini-Suhien National Park (see plate 24), Whitesides and Abedi-Lartey saw one group of Diana monkeys and heard a male Diana calling; otherwise, the only species of monkey we detected in our extended survey were those that Struhsaker and I had found at Kakum: spot-nosed monkeys, Campbell's monkeys, olive colobus, and black-and-white colobus. No red colobus, mangabeys, or chimpanzees were seen or heard anywhere, although the chief of the settlement of Nkwanta within the Ankasa reserve gave Whitesides a description of a monkey that could have been a red colobus; this man, Edele Kwao, was a hunter, and he said that he had recently seen mangabeys.[32]

We saw evidence of uncontrolled hunting and trapping in all the forests we visited. And although the Ghana Forestry Department had clearly been successful in preventing encroachment on forest reserves by farmers, the timber in many of the reserves had been overexploited, and in some places we saw signs of illegal logging. In a project supported since 1985 by Britain's ODA, the Forestry Department has been trying to institute a more careful management system for its forest reserves, a system designed to allow long-term sustainable harvesting. Among other things, the new management system extends the felling cycle from twenty-five to forty years, specifies when particular forest areas can be logged, and designates certain areas (particularly hills) as sanctuaries protected against logging.[33] We saw several abuses of this system, which was supposed to be in effect at the time of our survey. For instance, in part of the Krokosua Hills we encountered logging by a company called G.A.P., whose concession to the area had lapsed one year previously, and we witnessed extensive illegal logging in the Bia Resource Reserve by the Mim Timber Company. We reported these infringements to the Forestry Department in Kumasi.

ANKASA: A LAST HOPE?

Of all the forests that Struhsaker, Whitesides, and I visited in Ghana, the Ankasa/Nini-Suhien area appeared to offer the best hope for long-term conservation of a rain forest ecosystem and its primates. It was the least disturbed of all the forest areas we had visited; some logging had taken place in the Ankasa section, but this ceased in 1975, and in recent times no logging at all had occurred in Nini-Suhien. This was the only site where we had detected Diana monkeys and where (based on the Nkwanta chief's report to Whitesides) a slight possibility remained that red colobus still existed. The 1988 Cambridge expedition had found Ankasa to be an important site for birds, and botanical surveys by the Ghana Forestry Department had found it to be outstanding in terms of the number of rare tree species present.[34]

Given Ankasa's evident significance, I decided to make another visit to this forest at the end of 1995, both to look again for red colobus and other primates and to help formulate conservation plans. As had Whitesides and the Cambridge expedition, I camped at the Suhien River. From here, Michael Abedi-Lartey and I cut the transect lines that I described in the introduction to this chapter. Although we did see Dianas in the only monkey association that we encountered during twelve days inside the forest, we found no sign of red colobus monkeys. In addition, further questioning of Edele Kwao in Nkwanta convinced me that he was not truly familiar with red colobus—for instance, he did not recognize a tape recording I played of some of their distinctive calls. I concluded that red colobus were not present in the forest, and I began to suspect they might not have lived there at any time in the recent past.[35] Martin's team had reported seventeen encounters with monkeys in Ankasa in 1976, but only one of these was with red colobus, which was not seen, but heard. The chief of Nkwanta (the father of the chief present in 1995) told Martin that "red colobus was not represented some 15–20 years ago but migrated into the Reserve from Ivory Coast."[36] This seems unlikely, and the report that red colobus was heard calling in 1976 should be regarded with some skepticism since the red colobus call repertoire is complex, and some of these calls can be confused with those of other animals.

As Michael Abedi-Lartey and I moved north into Nini-Suhien on our Christmas 1995 survey, we found that small footpaths were converging into larger ones that were clearly leading to the northern boundary of the park. This confirmed my view that we should inspect that boundary area, but first we had to pack up our camp and trek back to the southern edge of Ankasa, where we had arranged for our vehicle to meet us. On January 2 we emerged from the forest, and the next day we set off to drive as close as we could to the northern edge of Nini-Suhien. We were accompanied by two game guards, one of whom, we were told, knew the area better than any of the other wildlife department staff at Ankasa. For five hours we followed the directions of this man, and of people we met on the road. In late afternoon the dirt track we were following became so rutted and muddy that it was impassable to our small truck; dusk was approaching, and our guide seemed to be lost. We turned back to the nearest village and pitched camp. Using a survey map and a GPS unit, I concluded that we were now some distance to the east of the park boundary and traveling south, away from the northern park boundary.

Even the best informed of the wildlife staff clearly knew little about the Nini-Suhien Park. They could not find its northern boundary, which they seemed never to have visited. Whitesides and I had each had similar experiences in trying to find our way to the Suhien River on the park's southern boundary; wildlife staff did not know the path to the river, and we had to rely either on the hunter-chief Edele Kwao to lead us, or on following a compass bearing through the forest. If the protection staff knew little about the park, it is hardly surprising that the area contained so many poachers' camps and so few large animals.

The village where Abedi-Lartey and I finally stopped on January 3 was called Asomase. It was a village of immigrants who had come from at least five different areas of Ghana to this frontier area to farm and to plant cocoa and oil palms. The local Nzema people were few and far between, and we did not meet any of them; I was told that the immigrants made payments to Nzema chiefs (many of whom now lived in towns outside the area) and in return were given farming rights, but not ownership of the land.

The following morning we consulted several people about how to reach the forest, and when we set off again we paid close attention to our GPS unit and our map. After two hours, we reached the village of Ayensukrom and were evidently close to Nini-Suhien. But again we were among immigrants: Asantes, Fantes, and Krobos, who were growing cocoa, plantains, and pineapples. The road beyond Ayensukrom was impassable, but the villagers directed us to a man who would lead us on foot to the edge of the forest. Early that afternoon we walked into the compound of Yaw Mensah, an Asante cocoa and pineapple farmer who had come to the area in 1973, just after the African Timber and Plywood Company had finished logging forest outside the reserve. Yaw Mensah was surprised to see a European and wildlife staff on his farm. He had heard a rumor in the Ayensukrom market two days before that there was a white man in the forest, but he had not believed it (the story probably originated with one of the poachers we had disturbed); he also said that he had seen no personnel from the Department of Game and Wildlife since they last cleared the park boundary ten years previously. Mensah led us to the park boundary on the edge of his farm, and we walked down it to meet the Nini River. Mensah told us of the many different people who were living in settlements along the northern edge of the park: Akwapims, Krobos, Ewes, Kwahus, and Fantra. He said that he used to see monkeys in the area, but that none were there now (our guide told Abedi-Lartey that Mensah himself was a hunter and had Diana monkey beards hanging in his house).

THE SIGNIFICANCE OF IMMIGRANTS

These observations, although anecdotal in nature, reinforced the impression I had gathered from traveling along the southern boundary of Ankasa in 1993: that people lived all around the Ankasa/Nini-Suhien conservation area, and that the vast majority of these people had migrated from other parts of Ghana (see plate 26). They had little interest in the long-term productivity of the system they were exploiting, but rather were attempting to maximize their income in the short term, sending much of it out of the area to build houses in distant towns and to educate their children. Such migration is not a new phenomenon in Ghana. A recent demographic report by the Ghana Statistical Service notes that migration has been going on since before the advent of a market economy, and that since 1970 the movement of population has been "tremendous."[37]

The situation around Ankasa and Nini-Suhien reminded me very much of the migrant farmers I had encountered at Okomu in Nigeria, and it led me to question even more the wisdom of including community development as a major component in the conservation of Ankasa, as envisaged in the plan still being considered for funding by the European Commission. Surely, Abedi-Lartey and I told ourselves, if some of the immigrants we had met were able on their next visit home to tell their friends and relatives that an aid project was now providing better schooling and health services near the park, even more migrants would be attracted to the area and pressures on the forest would increase.

Our suspicions were corroborated the following month by Kojo Mbir of the Kakum project. In February 1996 he made a one-week survey of villages around Ankasa and Nini-Suhien and reported that most people interviewed had moved there only in the last twelve years. He noted that most farmers near the northern boundary could not tell the name, origin, or family size of their neighbors.[38] He confirmed the high incidence of poaching and recommended that wildlife staff strength be increased, especially in the northern area. Although he still recommended community development efforts (citing IUCN publications), he did acknowledge that such efforts would have to be undertaken carefully to discourage further immigration.

The fact that most people living near Ankasa and Bia today are settlers from other parts of Ghana was acknowledged in an appendix to the EDG consultants' report to the EC in 1992. That appendix presents the results of interviewing people in two villages near Ankasa and two near Bia, and comments on the fact that there were settler farmers from all over the country in all four villages.[39] Even so, most of the people interviewed said they were in favor of protecting the forest and its wildlife, and only 16 percent claimed to have used the reserved areas prior to reservation. They did not express confidence in wildlife staff, however, accusing them of bribery and corruption, of connivance with poachers, and of misuse of power. This report recommended conservation education efforts, but did not specifically recommend providing schools or clinics; such development measures seem to be an EC requirement for a conservation project rather than a Ghanaian one.

THE EUROPEAN PROJECT BEGINS

In the reports of our 1995 and 1996 surveys, Whitesides and I argued strongly for an immediate increase in the protection effort at Ankasa and Nini-Suhien, given the area's biological importance, the high level of poaching we had witnessed, the small number of staff posted there and their lack of equipment, and the likely harmful impact of a new road that we learned was being constructed near the western edge of the conservation area.[40] We suggested that the budget of the upcoming EC project be reallocated to give more weight to Ankasa, because we now viewed this site as being considerably more important to conservation than Bia was (the budget proposal we had seen allocated much more to Bia than to Ankasa; for instance, 402,500 ECU for infrastructure at Bia versus 195,500 ECU at Ankasa, even though Bia already had better buildings and access roads). I also argued that the few people who remained at Nkwanta in the center of the conservation area at Ankasa should be relocated outside the area (as recommended by Martin in 1976), and that the whole area, including the Ankasa Resource Reserve, should be given the status of national park (as recommended by Gartlan in 1981). We presented these recommendations directly to the Department of Wildlife, and I also discussed them with Henning Bosüner, the European Commission's Rural Development Adviser in Accra and the person responsible for overseeing the "Protected Areas Development Programme" for Bia and Ankasa. He appeared sympathetic, but indicated that he was simply administering an existing program in which there was little scope for significant modification. I followed up the meeting with letters asking about progress, but I received only a formal project status report in September 1996 from the head of the EC delegation in Accra. This noted that five European consultancy companies had tendered for the technical assistance contract worth 1.4 million ECU (now about $1.8 million), and that this contract was to be awarded in December; the report also noted that there were delays in the separate tendering processes for buildings and vehicles.

Our recommendations had more obvious impact on the Ghana Department of Wildlife itself. Chief Officer Punguse accepted the recommendation for better protection efforts at Ankasa, and he authorized the employment of seven new guards. New patrol camps were established, including one on the northern boundary of the park and two on the eastern boundary, and in August 1996 Michael Abedi-Lartey himself (who had been a junior officer working in the Kumasi Zoo) was put in charge of protection efforts at Ankasa. Patrols began to be organized deep into the park, where poachers were arrested. As an indication of the small size of prey being taken by the hunters, following the reduction of larger game, Abedi-Lartey reported that among the smoked animals at one poachers' camp were thirty rats. These new efforts were accomplished not through the intervention of a foreign-aid program, but with local resources and a very small budget. However, the efforts have not proved entirely successful; Abedi-Lartey has told me that the wildlife staff soon became dependent on people in the hamlets where their new camps were based and were therefore not eager to arrest lawbreakers from these communities.[41]

When I returned to Ghana in June 1997, I found that the Protected Areas Development Programme had at last begun, two months previously. Some of our concerns about the project's design had been addressed, though it was unclear to what extent this was the result of our reports. The project was now giving rather more attention to Ankasa than to Bia. I was told that protection activities were going to be given strong emphasis, and that development efforts near the protected areas were now to be handled under a separate European Union "microproject" program. On the other hand, some common features of foreign-assisted conservation projects were strongly in evidence. The technical assistance contract (using European Development Fund money) had been awarded to a British consultancy company, which was to receive 90 percent of the contract in pounds sterling (£865,915, about $1,429,000 at a mid-1997 exchange rate); for a thirty-month contract, the team leader was to get about $317,000, and a community development specialist was to get about $246,000.[42] By contrast, the Department of Wildlife's entire 1996 budget for Ankasa and Nini-Suhien was 52.6 million cedis (about $26,000), including all salaries, vehicle maintenance, and building repairs; the annual salary of the most senior professional Ghanaian officer at Ankasa was 2.1 million cedis (less than $1,000).

In June 1997 the new consultants were just settling into their houses in the town of Takoradi, about seventy miles west of Ankasa and more than half a day's drive from Bia. They had visited Ankasa and Bia, but not Nini-Suhien Park, and their Land Rover Discovery vehicles were being used mostly for driving in and around Takoradi. The Wildlife staff at Ankasa were still relegated to using public transport; their new vehicles had not yet arrived, and their old truck had been impounded by a local court as part of the proceedings of an eight-year dispute over the dismissal of two former game guards accused of conniving with poachers.

LESSONS FROM GHANA

My experiences in Ghana reinforced four lessons I had learned from my work in Nigeria:

1. Local hunters can quite readily extirpate populations of some mammals from African rain forests, even when the forest itself

remains little disturbed; indeed, the results of further field surveys in 1997 by Michael Abedi-Lartey in Ghana and Scott McGraw in Côte d'Ivoire suggest that Miss Waldron's red colobus monkey is now extinct.

2.   An emphasis on large projects, linking conservation with rural development and relying on large amounts of foreign money, leads to the neglect of relatively simple, low-cost, and more sustainable conservation solutions.

3.   Development-orientated conservation projects often ignore the implications of the fact that much forest exploitation is conducted by recent immigrants who have no long-term commitment to the area they are exploiting.

4.   Conservation policymakers and senior managers tend to be motivated more by the material rewards that they or their organizations may obtain from a project than by a deep concern for the future of threatened nature.

The devastating impact of low-technology hunting on forest wildlife was brought home to me on a visit I made in July 1997 to the Cape Three Points Forest Reserve near Takoradi in Western Ghana with Abedi-Lartey. During parts of three days we spent in this eight-square-mile forest we did not detect a single sign of a monkey or any other large mammal. In daylight hours we saw one mouse, and at night we saw one potto and heard a bushbaby. As well as seeing many spent shotgun cartridges along the forest paths we followed, we found (and dismantled) dozens of wire-snare traps, two of which held the remains of rats and one of which held the leg of a live and loudly squealing cusimanse mongoose, which we released. Yet the forest itself was little disturbed and had suffered hardly any logging or encroachment by farmers since it was reserved in 1950. A remarkably similar story has been told recently by WCS's Alan Rabinowitz, following a visit he made to the interior of the largest protected forest in Laos. He describes a beautiful but silent forest, devoid of large animals, and he reports finding a massive trap line in which a few snares contained the carcasses of long-dead victims.[43]

Among the many problems associated with large conservation and development projects, one that had serious effects both on Nigeria's

Cross River Park and on the Ghanaian forest parks, is the slow pace at which such projects proceed between inception and initial implementation. Eight years elapsed from the inception of the plan to obtain European money to improve conservation in Ankasa and Bia before a management project actually commenced. While plans to spend millions of ECUs were drafted and redrafted, and arguments took place over the extent to which the project would involve rural development in addition to forest protection, little effort was made to prevent hunting or (in the case of Bia) the expansion of logging. When the foreign consultants eventually began work in 1997, few large animals were left in Bia and the forest there had been devastated; in Ankasa, mammal densities were precariously low. If in 1989 the equivalent of $1 million (less than 25 percent of the final project budget for just three years) had been allocated for the conservation of Ankasa and Bia, and if the funds had been put in trust in an interest-bearing account, the annual interest from these funds would have been sufficient (if accompanied by vigorous management) to have produced radical improvements in the protection of the two forests. If, in consequence, more animals were likely to have been seen by visitors, visits by tourists and scientists to these forests would have been more frequent; this in itself would surely have increased staff motivation and helped build a constituency who would have opposed continued logging in Bia. More successful management would have meant that any trust fund would have had a good chance of attracting more donations, allowing conservation efforts to be sustained indefinitely.

Even if no donor had been found willing to make a onetime investment of $1 million to secure a better future for Bia and Ankasa, just twenty thousand dollars granted each year for wildlife protection during the eight years of project planning would very likely have prevented some mammal species from becoming extinct in these forests, would certainly have saved many thousands of individual animals from the cooking pot, and would have laid a good foundation for any more ambitious later efforts.

Although the consultants involved in preparing the initial proposal for European Union funding were aware of the large numbers of immigrants near Ankasa and Bia, no special allowance for this fact was made in the project design. Both my own conversations with some of these settlers and the earlier study by Yaa Ntiamoa-Baidu suggested that the immigrant farmers did not see themselves as having special rights to exploit the protected areas, and indicated that they would respect laws against poaching if these were enforced.[44] In a situation like this it is counterproductive for a foreign-sponsored project to enter the scene and suggest that poachers should expect benefits (such as development assistance) in return for not breaking the law. The main rationale for pursuing such a course seems to be that the funding sought from agencies such as the European Development Fund requires that a project have a strong community-development component, even when this is not in the best interests of conservation.

Andrew Noss has described a project in the Central African Republic that has several similarities to Ghana's protected area program and to the Nigerian projects I described in earlier chapters. The Central African Republic project, focused on protected areas in the Dzanga Forest, is administered by WWF-US and involves the integration of conservation with development activities. Noss explains that in the Central African Republic, as in Ghana, people are highly mobile and attracted to economic opportunities such as a commercial logging operation promoted by the Dzanga conservation and development project. The immigration encouraged by this development is increasing pressure on the area's wildlife by, for instance, raising the local demand for bushmeat. Noss's perception is that the hunters have little concern about the sustainability of their hunting, expecting to switch to other resources or move elsewhere if the local wildlife is exhausted.[45]

In the Ghana examples I have described, much of the planning for forest and wildlife conservation was handled by economists, geographers, agriculturalists, and professional bureaucrats; few people who cared deeply about nature or who had much knowledge of it were involved. While considerable attention was paid to designing programs that would combine conservation and development, little importance was attached to safeguarding the very animals that had been the chief original reason for establishing protected areas in Ghana's rain forest zone: the rare and unique rain forest primates. And when individuals like Struhsaker, Whitesides, and myself (who have had many years of research and conservation experience in African forests) made recommendations designed to mitigate the threats to these primates, our recommendations produced more reaction from within the local wildlife department than from the foreign organizations ostensibly concerned with conservation in Ghana. This, it seems to me, strengthens the argument that many people in the international conservation community have come to have more concern for the development of their own careers and for doing what is politically expedient than for the future of threatened ecosystems and species.

EIGHT

Can Zoos Be the Ark?

One response by some conservationists to the kinds of crises facing primates and other animals in West African forests has been to suggest that effective protection in the wild may be impossible at the present time and that, before it is too late, colonies of endangered species should be established in captivity where they may be bred and husbanded until such time as conditions in the wild have improved, when captive animals may be returned to their natural habitat. For instance, in an analysis published in 1987, Thomas Foose, Ulysses Seal, and Nathan Flesness, some of the leading proponents of this idea, wrote, "Captive propagation can and must be a part of the strategy to preserve endangered primates from extinction. The more traditional philosophy and strategy of conservation by protecting the habitat, and presuming its inhabitants will also be preserved, are becoming increasingly difficult or unfeasible."[1] The site usually recommended for captive propagation is a zoo in a rich, industrialized country. For obvious reasons, such zoos have been described as "Noah's Arks."

The Noah's Ark concept, sometimes described as ex situ conservation (in contrast to in situ conservation in a natural habitat), has acquired considerable popularity in the last twenty-five years and has been especially promoted by people involved with zoos in North America and Western Europe. It is a concept that has become almost as popular in international conservation circles as the idea that wild animal populations and their habitats are best protected by involving local human communities in integrated conservation and development projects. In this chapter I review the history of the Noah's Ark concept and discuss its relevance to conservation. I argue that captive breeding and reintroduction are expensive and ineffective techniques relative to the protection of wild animals in their natural habitat, and that they can deflect resources and attention from such protection efforts. I suggest, as have others before me, that zoos can make their greatest contribution to conservation not through the captive breeding of endangered species but through their role in public enlightenment.

CAPTIVE BREEDING RESCUES PÈRE DAVID'S DEER

The idea of captive breeding as a conservation strategy has its roots far in the past. For instance, medieval hunting parks—the historical antecedents of modern national parks—protected both managed populations of wild animals and their habitat.[2] One famous medieval hunting park provides an interesting link between ancient and modern captive breeding. The Chinese Imperial Hunting Park, on the edge of Beijing, survived into the nineteenth century; it reportedly covered more than a hundred square miles and was surrounded by a high wall. It was strictly private, and no foreigner was supposed to see inside it. But in 1865 Jean Pierre Armand David, a French missionary and enthusiastic naturalist, managed to look over the park wall by climbing on a pile of workmen's sand. Just a hundred yards away he saw a herd of unusual deer. By bribing Tartar soldiers he managed to get some skins and skeletons, and eventually he obtained live animals, which he sent to European zoos.[3] The deer, known in China as Mi-lu, proved indeed to be a new species, which was named *Elaphurus davidianus*—often called Père David's deer in English-speaking countries. No truly wild population has been found since Père David looked over the wall of the Imperial Hunting Park.

The walls of the hunting park were breached by severe floods in 1894, and all but 20 of the deer escaped and were drowned, or eaten by starving peasants. Most members of the remaining herd were killed or captured in 1900 by the foreign troops sent to Beijing to quell the Boxer Uprising, and by 1921 all the Père David's deer in captivity in China had died. In England, meanwhile, the eleventh Duke of Bedford had gathered the animals that survived in several European collections into his own deer park at Woburn Abbey. The Woburn herd was now the last surviving population of Père David's deer. It numbered 20 animals in 1901 and gradually grew (despite serious mortality from food shortages in World War I), so that at the end of World War II the Woburn herd had 250 animals. Small groups began to be returned to zoos, including some sent to Beijing in 1956. In 1985, 22 deer sent from Woburn to China were placed in an enclosure in the central part of what remained of the old hunting park at Nan Haizi, and in the following year a further 39 animals from seven British collections were released in the Dafeng Mi-lu Protected Area, 4 square miles of beach-marsh habitat 235 miles north of Shanghai, and within the species' presumed original range. Subsequently, the deer have been released in at least two other reserves, including a 6-square-mile area of wetland beside the Yangtze River at Shishou in Hubei Province where they are not fed at any time of year.[4]

The case of Père David's deer provides a good, though rather rare, example of a species that went extinct in its original habitat but survived in a captive-breeding program. A truly wild population of the deer has not, however, been restored.

THE JERSEY WILDLIFE PRESERVATION TRUST

Modern enthusiasm for the role of zoos as arks owes much to the charismatic personality of Gerald Durrell, whose early books about animal collecting in Cameroon provided such a strong impetus to my own odyssey through the West African rain forest. Although it was Durrell's descriptions of Africa that most fascinated me, his own greatest interest seems always to have been the keeping of wild animals in captivity, especially in zoos. As he acknowledged, he had "zoomania."[5] He began his career as a student keeper at the London Zoo's country park, Whipsnade, and it was apparently the experience of caring for Père David's deer at Whipsnade that first made him think about the role of zoos as sanctuaries for threatened species.[6]

On his first expeditions to Africa and South America, Durrell was collecting animals to sell to a variety of British zoos. Increasingly, though, he came to want his own zoo. In his book *A Zoo in My Luggage*, published in 1960, he recounted how the idea of starting a zoo of his own grew from a combination of sadness from parting with animals he had come to know well, and of growing concern with the extermination of wild animals.[7] He felt that many rare and threatened species were getting little protection in the wild because they were small-bodied and of low touristic value, and he thought he could keep them from extinction by establishing breeding colonies.

Durrell's zoo began with his third expedition to Cameroon in 1957; according to his own account, he decided to obtain the animals first and find the zoo later. So it was that he returned to England with a large collection of animals that initially had to be kept in the garden of his sister's house in Bournemouth; the collection then became a temporary menagerie in a department store, before being loaned to Paignton Zoo in Devon. Finally Durrell's publisher, Rupert Hart-Davis, gave him a contact in the British Channel Islands and provided him with a loan. This led Durrell to rent an old manor house (Les Augrès Manor) on the island of Jersey, to which he moved his animal collection. In March 1959 the Jersey Zoo was founded, and in January 1964 it evolved into the Jersey Wildlife Preservation Trust (JWPT).[8]

In 1966 Durrell defined the objectives of the JWPT to be:

- To build up colonies of species threatened with extinction in the wild.
- To show the public animals which are in urgent need of conservation.
- To create public interest in the need for conservation, "both in the wild and in captivity."[9]

Although Gerald Durrell's personality seems to have contributed strongly to the popularity of the concept of the zoo as an ark, by 1960 this idea was already quite widely accepted among zoo administrators in Western countries. That year, for instance, Solly Zuckerman, Secretary of the Zoological Society of London, stated his view that there was little or no difference between conserving species in the wild and maintaining them in captivity, as specimens in a living museum.[10]

By the early 1970s, captive breeding had moved into the mainstream of conservation thinking. In May 1972 a conference was held in Jersey on the breeding of endangered species; this meeting was organized jointly by the JWPT and the Fauna Preservation Society. At the end of the conference, Peter Scott, Chairman both of the Fauna Preservation Society and of the meeting, announced a six-point declaration:

1. The breeding of endangered species and subspecies of animals in captivity is likely to be crucial to the survival of many forms. It must therefore be used as a method of preventing extinction, alongside the maintenance of wild stocks in their natural habitats.

2. The technique must be learnt, improved, extended and published.

3. All who keep endangered species have a responsibility to carry out breeding programmes and to cooperate both with other zoos or collections for this purpose and with conservationists in returning them to the wild.

4. Such programmes will reduce the demands being made currently on wild populations and may serve to reinforce them, or, if they have disappeared in the wild, to re-establish them.

5. Even if reintroduction ultimately proves to be impossible, maintaining a captive population is obviously superior to the irrevocable alternative of extinction.

6. Where feasible, breeding programmes should be encouraged in the natural habitat of the species.[11]

This declaration encapsulates the new view that zoos had developed of themselves: they were much more than interesting menageries of exotic beasts, and they would play a major role in conservation. That Peter Scott should have taken a significant part in this process is not surprising, for he had devoted much of his own life to the captive breeding of ducks and geese and had been a strong advocate of such breeding as a conservation tool. In his autobiography, *The Eye of the Wind*, Scott describes how his initial enthusiasm for wildlife lay chiefly in hunting it, a common pattern among many conservationists of that era. As a young man at Cambridge University in the 1920s he delighted in wildfowling, enjoying the beauty of the marshes and estuaries where he hunted, the thrill of the chase, and the satisfaction of good marksmanship.

But by the 1930s, Scott had become less interested in shooting; he wanted instead to catch birds, to keep them in captivity, and to learn more about them. He began to build up a collection of captive waterfowl, but gave it up during his naval service in World War II. After the war he began to construct observation posts at Slimbridge on the Severn Estuary in Gloucestershire, after seeing the very rare lesser white-fronted goose there in December 1945. In November 1946 he formed the Severn Wildfowl Trust for the scientific study and conservation of waterfowl, and this soon became the Wildfowl Trust.[12]

RELEASING CAPTIVES TO THE WILD

In their early pronouncements on the value of keeping rare animals in their collections, zoos said little about reintroducing these animals from the zoo to the wild, but in the annual report of the JWPT in 1967 Durrell wrote, "If successful breeding colonies of certain species are built up, then at some future date (when conservation in their country of origin is an established fact) they can be re-introduced."[13]

The case of Père David's deer shows that, under certain circumstances, a species can be "saved" from extinction by captive breeding and eventually returned to at least a semiwild state. Saving Père David's deer required tremendous effort and expenditure, however, over a long period of time, during which there was no option for attempting to conserve a wild population. A consideration of two other well-known examples— the Hawaiian goose and the golden lion tamarin—shows that, where a wild population still survives, a captive-breeding program may distract from efforts to conserve the wild animals.

When Peter Scott established the Wildfowl Trust in the 1940s, the Hawaiian goose, or Nene (*Branta sandvicensis*), was thought to be on the verge of extinction in the wild. In 1950, Scott sent his curator, John Yealland, to Hawaii, where a captive colony had been maintained since 1918. Yealland (who had accompanied Durrell on the 1947–48 collecting trip to Cameroon) returned to Slimbridge with a pair of geese from the Hawaiian colony. The new Slimbridge colony grew (see plate 27), and in 1960 some captive-bred geese from both the Hawaiian and Slimbridge colonies were returned to the wild. Over the following twelve years some eighteen hundred birds were released.

When the first captive-bred Hawaiian geese were released in 1960, the size of the wild population was not known, although a flock of twenty-eight is reported to have been seen in 1955. The original decline of the wild population had not been studied, so the causes of its decline are unclear; it is thought that introduced predators, the destruction of vegetation by introduced domestic animals, and shooting probably each played a role. In a review of the captive-breeding and release program, Janet Kear and A. J. Berger concluded that it is therefore unknown whether the money spent on captive breeding would have been better spent on conservation measures in the wild, such as predator control. Kear and Berger note that if more had been done earlier for the wild population, it might well have recovered without additions from captivity, especially as only a few of the released birds seem to have survived and bred. It is even possible that the numbers of geese were rising before the release.[14]

Another well-documented case, particularly relevant to my account, is the captive-breeding and reintroduction program featuring a small, endangered tropical forest primate, the golden lion tamarin (*Leontopithecus rosalia*) of Brazil.[15] Concern for the future of this monkey was raised by Adelmar Coimbra-Filho and other Brazilian scientists in the 1960s, as the impact of the uncontrolled destruction of the species' restricted Atlantic forest habitat was appreciated.[16] The original range of the tamarin probably extended along much of the coast of Rio de Janeiro State (including the area that is now the city of Rio) and into the southern part of neighboring Espírito Santo, but by 1973 it was estimated that no more than 350 square miles of tamarin habitat remained, and this habitat was still shrinking. In addition to drastic habitat loss, golden lion tamarin populations had been decimated by trappers, who had captured the attractive animals for the pet trade and for zoos; as recently as 1960–65, two to three hundred of these tamarins were thought to have been shipped from Brazil annually.[17] In consequence, there was a relatively large captive population.

Recognizing in 1965 the precarious position of the golden lion tamarin, Clyde Hill, then with the San Diego Zoo, initiated efforts to ban importation of the monkeys to the United States, and by 1967 the International Union of Directors of Zoological Gardens agreed that its members would end imports of the tamarin and publicize its endangered status. During the early 1970s the zoo tamarins, most of them in the United States, became the object of an international captive-husbandry program coordinated by the National Zoological Park in Washington, D.C., which had the largest collection of golden lion tamarins outside Brazil (twenty-two of ninety-five animals). Meanwhile, a captive colony was also established in Tijuca National Park (1.3 square miles) within the city of Rio de Janeiro; of thirty-one golden lion tamarins in this "Tijuca Bank" in September 1975, twenty-four had been captured in the wild, fifteen of these since the completion of the cages in early 1974.[18]

In a major review of lion tamarin conservation prospects published in 1977, Coimbra-Filho and Russell Mittermeier concluded that the establishment of well-protected reserves for wild populations of the golden lion tamarin (along with the related golden-headed lion tamarin) should be a primary conservation concern. They viewed the successful breeding of captive stocks as a secondary goal, "just in case attempts to save wild populations fail."[19]

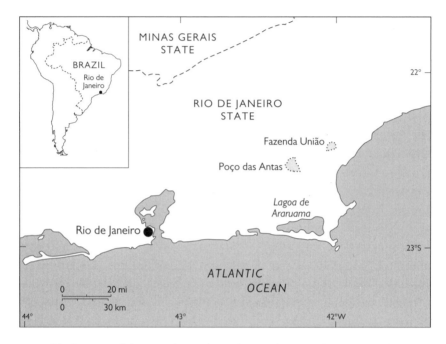

Map 9. The location of the Poço das Antas and Fazenda União forests in Rio de Janeiro State, Brazil.

By 1981, the international husbandry program, under the expert direction of Devra Kleiman, had been so successful that there were more than three hundred captive tamarins and "measures had to be taken to control the burgeoning numbers."[20] In 1982, Kleiman therefore began discussions with Coimbra-Filho, WWF-US, and Brazilian organizations about a reintroduction program, which was viewed in part as a way to cope with an excess of captive animals. The program was initiated with field studies on wild tamarins in 1983 in the Poço das Antas Biological Reserve (see map 9), which had been established in 1974 specifically to protect wild golden lion tamarins, and expanded in 1975 from about twelve square miles to twenty-one square miles. Two more preferred sites for tamarin reserves, identified by Coimbra-Filho and his colleagues in the late 1960s, had been deforested before these privately held lands could be purchased or expropriated.[21]

Even after a reserve had been established at Poço das Antas, its forest continued to be destroyed, so that by the time the tamarin reintroduction project began, 40 percent of the reserve had been deforested; it was also occupied by squatters, exploited by poachers, and damaged by annual fires. The project therefore sought not only to study the wild tamarin population (estimated to number about 150 animals at that time) but also to rehabilitate the reserve. These efforts were complemented by public relations exercises designed to educate people around the reserve about the tamarins and their reintroduction.[22] In 1984 the first batch of captive tamarins was released, and further batches have been released in every subsequent year (see plate 28). The animals have apparently been released not in the Poço das Antas Biological Reserve itself, but on nine square miles of private ranch lands around the reserve.

The tamarin reintroduction program has had mixed success. Of 15 captive-born tamarins sent to Brazil from the United States in 1983, 4 died during quarantine in Rio, and 11 died after release near Poço das Antas; causes of presumed death included disease, predation, and starvation. Survivorship improved with later releases, but out of a total of 147 animals released between 1984 and 1996, only 24 were still present at the end of 1996; theft and killing by humans have been the leading known causes of loss of reintroduced animals. However, those released animals that survived have bred, and the wild-born offspring have done better than the captive-born tamarins; of 268 documented to have been born alive, 176 survived to the end of 1996.[23]

Kleiman and colleagues have estimated that the total cost of the reintroduction program in its first six years was about $1.08 million (including a proportion of the salaries of senior personnel). This is equivalent to more than $22,000 for each tamarin that survived, compared with an estimated cost of $1,657 per year for maintaining each of about 500 captive animals.[24] The cost of protecting each wild tamarin in the Poço das Antas Biological Reserve has been estimated as $389, and in 1997 there were about 290 tamarins in the reserve.[25]

Although there were some preliminary field surveys in the 1960s, it was not until 1990 that a major field survey was initiated throughout the golden lion tamarin's original range to assess its distribution and status. This eighteen-month survey by Brazilian graduate student Cecilia Kierulff refuted the long-held view that Poço das Antas "is the last hope for the survival of *L. r. rosalia* in its natural habitat."[26] The survey located thirty-nine tamarin groups living in other parts of Rio de Janeiro State: nine areas of less than one square mile and four larger areas. This survey has led to a plan to translocate the twelve groups living in the small, isolated forests to the nine-square-mile forest on the Fazenda União, a ranch originally owned by the Brazilian Federal Railway Network; after Poço das Antas, the Fazenda União forest is the largest in the lowlands of Rio de Janeiro.[27] Translocation to the Fazenda União began in 1994, and by early 1998 six groups of tamarins had been moved there. In April 1998 Fazenda União became a federal biological reserve, and its tamarin population had grown to fifty individuals.[28]

There is no doubt that the zoo-led golden lion tamarin captive-breeding and reintroduction program has focused a great deal of valuable attention on this species. This attention has helped to stimulate efforts to conserve not only the golden lion tamarin but also three related species. The program has brought considerable resources to the Poço das Antas Biological Reserve, resources that have helped to better protect the forest and its wildlife, expand the forested area, and promote support for conservation among local people. However, it is unclear whether the process of reintroduction in itself has promoted the survival of golden lion tamarins in the wild. It may have increased slightly the genetic diversity of the population in the Poço das Antas region, but how important this might be is unclear; there are reasons to think that low levels of genetic variation are typical of marmoset and tamarin populations, and that low genetic diversity has been given undue emphasis as a risk factor in extinction.[29]

Thus, the golden lion tamarin reintroduction case has several features in common with that of the Hawaiian goose. The primary impetus for tamarin reintroduction came from those holding the animals in captivity, and during the initial captive-breeding and reintroduction efforts the ecology and status of the wild population as a whole were largely ignored. If 50 percent (or less) of the funds and resources devoted to the tamarin reintroduction program had instead been used in a project that, from the early 1970s, had paid greater attention to all surviving wild tamarin populations and their problems, the result might have been a larger wild population than presently exists. Until very recently, most of the tamarins outside Poço das Antas seem to have been almost completely neglected. The zoos and conservation organizations concerned with the reintroduction program would probably argue that significant funds would not have been forthcoming for purely wild conservation measures. This may be correct (and if so it is a sad indictment of conservation priorities), but since an alternative program was not attempted there is no way to be sure.

In my view, the greatest benefits of the golden lion tamarin project (and of similar zoo programs) lie in their effects on the captive rather than the wild population. Until the 1970s, zoos had had little success in second-generation breeding. But following the establishment of the international captive management program there has been a marked improvement in the viability of the zoo population, and this has removed one of the original pressures on the wild animals, which was the demand for animals by zoos.

ZOO MANAGEMENT EXTRAPOLATED TO THE WILD

The increasing success with which zoos were able to manage small captive populations appears to have strengthened the opinion of some people in the zoo world that their institutions could be more effective conservation tools than were efforts to protect wild populations, many of which seemed to be regarded as doomed. Writing in 1986, Ulysses Seal, Chairman of IUCN's Captive Breeding Specialist Group (CBSG), referred to conservation efforts in natural habitats as providing only "temporary relief" for some populations, and referred to the "sanctuary" provided by "captive habitat."[30] This approach assumed (as had Zuckerman back in 1960) that there was little difference between zoo and wild populations. Indeed, the CBSG pioneered the application to wild populations of numerical, computer-based models that had been developed in part for the management of small populations of zoo animals, in which inbreeding was considered a problem. Such an approach also owed a good deal to the thinking of academic conservation biologists such as Michael Soulé, who in 1980 used evidence of declining survival in captive populations (apparently the result of inbreeding) to warn of the threats to wild animal populations that would arise purely as a consequence of small size and isolation.[31]

By 1991, Seal's colleague Thomas Foose had become Executive Director of the CBSG (he subsequently left the group) and was espousing the view of the wild as little different from a zoo, saying that "natural sanctuaries are becoming megazoos that will require intensive genetic and demographic management of much the same kind as must be applied in captivity."[32] It was at this point that I got some direct experience of the zoo-based conservation planning being promoted by Foose and Seal. I had been serving as coordinator of the African section of the IUCN/SSC Primate Specialist Group (PSG), and I had compiled for the PSG an *Action Plan for African Primate Conservation*, published in 1986.[33] As compiler of this plan I was invited in March 1991 to a meeting arranged by Foose and Seal at the headquarters of the CBSG at the Minnesota Zoo, on the outskirts of Minneapolis. The meeting was to be in the form of a workshop, whose recommendations would be used to produce a Conservation Assessment and Management Plan (CAMP) for primates, which was envisaged as the first step in the production of a Global Captive Action Plan (GCAP) that would guide zoos in captive-breeding programs. I was one of a few members of the PSG invited to this workshop, along with Ardith Eudey (coordinator for Asia), Bill Konstant (PSG Deputy Chairman), Russ Mittermeier (PSG Chairman), and Tom Struhsaker. I traveled to the meeting prepared to discuss, among other things, the general relevance of captive breeding to conservation. But on arrival in Minneapolis, I found that the workshop agenda provided no time for such discussion and was organized as if it were the meeting of a corporation dealing with a technical problem that had already been identified.

The problem and the form of its best solution were to be considered as follows:

- Many wild primate species or subspecies have been reduced to sets of small, isolated subpopulations in danger of extinction; these primates will be best conserved by active management (rather like the zoo population of golden lion tamarins), and this management might involve not only the exchange of individuals between wild subpopulations but also between captivity and the wild.
- Planning the management of such "metapopulations" is best achieved using computer models and an analytical framework known as a Population and Habitat Viability Assessment (PHVA), an outgrowth of the more simple Population Viability Analysis.

For such a numerical, computer-based modeling process to work, numbers were required. As our Minnesota workshop proceeded, those of us with some knowledge of wild primate populations found that the main reason we were invited to participate appeared to be that the organizers wanted us to provide estimates of the size, distribution, and rate of decline of these populations. We were asked to report the status in the wild, with a numerical estimate of abundance, of all the species and subspecies of primates recognized by the CBSG. We were also asked to suggest appropriate conservation options, including various kinds of captive breeding. In the limited time available, this meant that we could devote only a few minutes to each species and subspecies on the CBSG list. We pointed out that the population sizes of the great majority of wild primates had not been estimated with any degree of accuracy, and that using inaccurate estimates in conservation planning was dangerous. But under pressure from the workshop organizers, we reluctantly made some crude estimates (such as "less than a million"), on condition that these estimates would not appear in print and so be given the semblance of established fact.

To my chagrin and that of some of the other PSG participants in this workshop, the draft document that appeared a few months later included numerical estimates of the population sizes of 385 taxa (species and subspecies) based on the guesses we had made in Minnesota.[34]

These estimates persisted into the final version of a primate CAMP presented to the Fourteenth Congress of the International Primatological Society at Strasbourg in August 1992. This plan recognized 512 primate taxa, of which 137 were recommended as subjects of a habitat and viability assessment, and 229 for captive-breeding programs.[35] At an open meeting at that congress, the members of the Primate Specialist Group reached a consensus that they could not endorse the plan. The PSG members felt that the major emphasis in primate conservation should be on improving the survival prospects of existing wild populations, without the emphasis on captive breeding given in the plan.

The CBSG, renamed the Conservation Breeding Specialist Group in 1994, continues to hold workshops that seek to apply its computer-based viability models. Although it is still closely associated with the planning of captive-breeding programs, it has announced that it is moving away from a focus on taxonomic groups of animals to a more regional approach, and that it is exploring the incorporation of the fashionable concept of the "rapid rural assessment" of human populations into Population and Habitat Viability Assessments. It is probably one of the most expensive to operate of the World Conservation Union's Specialist Groups; it raises about $290,000 annually (mostly from zoos) and is constantly seeking new funds.[36]

CRITICISMS OF THE CAPTIVE BREEDING PARADIGM

Captive breeding as a primary conservation tool is subject to increasing critical evaluation. Even in the early days of enthusiasm for zoo arks, some contrary opinions were expressed. Speaking at the Second World Conference on Breeding Endangered Species in Captivity, held in London in 1976, K. S. Sankhala of India's Project Tiger said, "When the time comes to make a full appraisal of the Indian conservation effort, the recovery of the tiger, rhinoceros and crocodile in my belief will justify the view adopted by the Indian authorities that the strict protection of the species' natural environment is by far a more effective conservation measure than to dislodge the animals for breeding in zoos, be it under the most expert care."[37]

At the time, Sankhala's argument seems to have fallen on deaf ears, at least in the zoo community. Zoos as a whole had larger resources than conservation organizations, and zoo managers must have found appeal in the idea that their animal collections fulfilled a higher ethical purpose than the entertainment of the public. But in recent years a growing number of voices have been heard supporting the view expressed by the primate conservationists in Strasbourg in 1992, that captive breeding programs can divert attention and resources from the conservation of animal populations in their natural habitats.

In his book *The Last Panda*, published in 1993, George Schaller explains his distress at realizing that an international giant panda conservation project in which he participated during the 1980s may have harmed pandas more than it helped them.[38] During this project, supported by WWF, large sums of money were spent on captive-breeding facilities; 108 pandas were captured and brought to these facilities, where 33 of them soon died and many languished without breeding. Meanwhile, little was done to control poaching, the most immediate threat to wild pandas.

In 1995, Alan Rabinowitz published in the journal *Conservation Biology* an incisive analysis of efforts to conserve the endangered Sumatran rhinoceros. He pointed out that more than $2.5 million had been spent between 1987 and 1993 to capture Sumatran rhinos and breed them in captivity, resulting in the deaths of twelve animals; no captive births occurred, except to one female who was pregnant when she was captured. Meanwhile, the wild rhino population continued to decline, and little was done to implement obvious in situ measures such as the control of poaching and the establishment of new reserves. Such measures brought less publicity, and involved more political difficulties, than the glamorous capture program.[39]

In his critique of the Sumatran rhino conservation program, Rabinowitz noted that population and habitat viability assessments, metapopulation analysis, and similar computer-based approaches to conservation are almost completely removed from the real world, and he suggested that they were designed from the beginning to point to the conclusion that captive breeding is the only solution to save endangered species.[40] In his paper, Rabinowitz cited an important review of currently popular approaches in conservation biology that had been published in the previous year by Graeme Caughley, an Australian ecologist who died shortly before his review was published. Caughley pointed out that there is no evidence of any wild population going extinct as a result of some genetic problem, such as inbreeding, despite the emphasis placed on genetics in the small-population paradigm that became popular through the work of Soulé and others in the 1980s.[41]

Also in 1995, Andrew Balmford and colleagues used information from a range of conservation projects involving threatened mammals (including the golden lion tamarin) to show that in all cases where data were available, it has proved cheaper to conserve a mammal in the wild than in captivity. They suggested that captive breeding might be a conservation solution where a threat to a wild population (such as war or introduced predators) cannot be eliminated in the near future, but they pointed out several general advantages of in situ over ex situ conservation, including the fact that in situ programs are usually designed to conserve whole ecosystems. They concluded that the most important contributions zoos can make to conservation lie in raising public awareness of conservation issues and helping to finance in situ conservation.[42]

The growing tide of criticism about the use of captive breeding as a tool to restore the health of threatened wild animal populations is well summarized by Noel Snyder and colleagues in another *Conservation Biology* article, published in 1996.[43] In a wide-ranging review, this article covers many of the points I have mentioned above and adds others. The authors note that few animal species continue to breed successfully in captivity over long periods of time, and that the majority of reintroduction programs have not managed to establish viable wild populations. Like Balmford and colleagues, they also discuss both the risk that reintroduction will bring novel diseases to wild populations and the danger that captivity tends to select for traits, such as tameness, that are disadvantageous in the wild. Finally, after noting the problem of maintaining effective administrative continuity in a captive-breeding program over decades, Snyder and his colleagues echo the conclusion reached by Balmford that zoos can most effectively contribute to wildlife conservation not by captive breeding, but through public education, research, and the support of in situ programs. A good example of a zoo performing one of these other roles is provided by the work of George Schaller and Alan Rabinowitz, which I referred to above; they are both employed by the Wildlife Conservation Society (formerly the New York Zoological Society), which runs the famous Bronx Zoo and other smaller zoos in New York City.

RETHINKING THE ROLE OF ZOOS IN CONSERVATION

Fortunately, some influential voices in the zoo world itself are now being heard that raise doubts about the ability of zoos to act as arks. As early as 1980 William Conway, Director of the New York Zoological Society, pointed out that zoos have finite and limited physical space, and that American zoos could perhaps maintain only 100 species of mammal at 150 specimens per species.[44] Conway later increased to 250–300 his estimate of the number of individual mammals needed to maintain viable populations for two hundred years in captivity, and suggested that international zoos could (as of 1986) maintain 330 species at that population size.[45] Even so, that is only 7 percent of the more than 4,600 presently recognized species of mammal, of which 25 percent are judged to be vulnerable to or endangered with extinction.[46] In other words, only with a huge increase in capital and recurrent expenditure could zoos act as an ark for the majority of threatened animal species. Citing this point, along with the problems and expense of reintroduction programs, Conway and Michael Hutchins (Director of Conservation and Science for the American Zoo and Aquarium Association) have added their voices in support of the view that zoos can make important contributions to conservation in directions other than captive breeding.[47] They agree that zoos can play significant roles in educating the public about wildlife and the threats to it, in increasing biological knowledge through the study of zoo animals, in developing husbandry techniques that may have applications in the management of wild populations, and in fund-raising in support of conservation. Hutchins and Conway argue, though, that zoos should not abandon the captive breeding of endangered species, in part because these animals bring people to zoos and therefore encourage public support for conservation, and in part because captive breeding and reintroduction are still the best conservation option for some species.

This critical self-analysis of the role of zoos by some of the zoo community's leaders is a healthy sign, and in my view Hutchins and Conway have given sensible signposts for the future of zoos. But the notion of zoos as arks is now so widely and firmly entrenched that it will probably take some time for a majority of zoos to adopt a fundamentally different view of their role. My own observations suggest that even some of the world's best zoos still have a long way to go in changing their philosophy. During a visit I made in 1996 to the London Zoo (a place that encouraged much of my own early interest in animals), I found a notice in the Reptile House informing the public that the large Nile crocodiles (which had intrigued generations of visitors) were to be sent to another zoo, to be replaced by an exhibit of "endangered" Chinese alligators, which are much smaller reptiles. Visiting London Zoo later in the year, writer Susan A. Toth noted the insistence with which placards announced that the zoo was acting as a conservator of its captive colonies of golden lion tamarins and other species.[48] Earlier in the same year, the members' newsletter of the Zoological Society of London reported on an October 1995 expedition to the Mauritius archipelago (conducted in conjunction with the Jersey Wildlife Preservation Trust), in which the head keeper of the Reptile House had participated, and which had brought back to London Zoo "a significant collection of live specimens of . . . day geckos . . . for inclusion in future captive breeding programmes."[49] Whether during its short stay the expedition thoroughly assessed the status in the wild of the three species they brought back is not made clear.

Although there are signs of change, my perception is that a primary motivation for the actions of many zoo personnel and managers is still the fascination of acquiring and keeping rare and exotic animals, just as it was for Gerald Durrell. This is not an unusual motivation; it is surely the same motivation that leads many people to acquire exotic pets, and it is closely related to the universal human interest in collecting and keeping any object. If a consequence of this motivation is that zoo visitors acquire a greater interest in wildlife and its conservation, that is a good thing for conservation, at least if the zoo collection has caused little harm to wild populations. But all too often, captive breeding for conservation has been used glibly as a justification for new acquisitions, with little sober thought given to the consequences of depleting a wild population and distracting attention and resources from the protection of those populations.[50]

While many zoos in rich countries are now relatively good at animal husbandry, a great majority of the world's zoos, and especially zoos in poor or developing countries, are a clear drain on wild-animal populations, constantly acquiring new stock, which are incarcerated in poor conditions, rarely breed, and often die after a short time.[51] One of the most valuable and appropriate roles that good zoos could play in nature conservation would be in helping to change attitudes and management in the many low-quality zoos around the world, especially in places like West Africa, where wild mammals are so seriously threatened. From the point of view of conservation and animal welfare, it would be best if bad zoos were simply closed down, but there is often no local consensus for closure. In these cases, it would be worthwhile for zoos in rich countries to help make these bad zoos into better places that exhibit healthy, breeding animals; such zoos would be more likely to inculcate respect for nature among children.[52]

After all, it is through stimulating a fascination with animal life that zoos have always had their most significant positive impact on conservation. In the *New York Times* article in which Susan Toth noted the abundance of placards in the London Zoo proclaiming that the collection was conserving species, Toth makes clear that, since her childhood in Iowa, zoos have had their most profound impact on her by inspiring a sense of wonder in the variety of animal life and by invoking images of distant and intriguing lands.[53] Zoos can continue to provide this inspiration, and to strive to do it as well as possible. To do this job well, zoos do not have to be filled with rare and endangered animals; a Nile crocodile can inspire as much awe as a Chinese alligator, and just because wild baboons are common enough to be pests in some place does not make a group of baboons less interesting to a child than a group of endangered leaf-monkeys. Indeed, many of the animals that children most enjoy seeing in zoological collections are not among the rarest and most threatened species. By concentrating on keeping and breeding the rarest species, zoos may actually decrease rather than increase the effectiveness of their role in public education.

THE FUTURE OF CAPTIVE BREEDING AND ITS RELEVANCE TO WEST AFRICAN PRIMATE CONSERVATION

I think it is now well established that captive-breeding programs have many drawbacks, and that they are usually much more expensive and less effective conservation tools than strategies applied directly to improving the protection and management of wild populations. But there may still be circumstances where captive propagation is the best or only option available. In a few cases where wild populations are already extinct, or where there is no realistic hope of protecting remaining wild animals, captive breeding may be the only means to ensure the survival of a species. If appropriate husbandry techniques can or have been developed for the species, eventual reintroduction to the wild may be possible if part of the species' original range can be managed in such a way that the factors leading to the animal's decline or extinction no longer operate, and if a range of other requirements has been met.[54] But it must not be forgotten that, in the case of animals like primates, which rely heavily on learning as a means of coping with their environment, reintroduction is particularly difficult and expensive and has a good chance of failing.

So, if there is any possibility that a wild population of a species exists, priority should always be given to assessing the status of this population and the cost, and likely effectiveness, of measures to conserve it in its natural habitat. Major resources should be devoted to a captive-breeding project only if it is clear from this assessment that a wild population has no reasonable probability of survival; for once captive projects are launched, they almost inevitably distract attention from the need for conservation measures in the wild.

Are there species in the West African forests I have been discussing that should be considered for captive-breeding programs? Because conservation has been so ineffective over much of the West African forest zone, some of the most vulnerable species living in these forests, including several primates, might seem like good candidates for captive propagation. In Sierra Leone the breakdown of an organized state made conservation efforts impossible, and it is not out of the question that political instability will be more widespread in Africa in the future. Despite the difficulties associated with captive breeding and reintroduction, it might be foolish not to establish captive colonies of vulnerable species (or at least those that do well in captivity) so that these colonies can serve as insurance policies against disaster; such an approach lies at the heart of the original "zoo ark" concept. But many kinds of animal have proved very difficult to maintain in captivity, let alone to breed, and in these cases the highest priority should always be the protection of wild populations; in West Africa, for instance, red colobus monkeys fall into this category—they have never survived for long in captivity.

A balanced approach is surely necessary, so that disproportionate resources are not devoted to captive breeding when viable wild populations still exist that could be better managed. An example in West Africa is the "Pandrillus" project in Calabar, Nigeria, which has been gathering together captive drills, treating them for injuries and diseases, integrating them into social groups, and breeding them, with the aim of eventually reintroducing one or more groups to the wild.[55] This project, founded in 1991, the same year as the Cross River National Park, has received considerable international attention, including many grants and gifts both to feed and house the animals (which include a collection of chimpanzees), and to support the work of a dedicated volunteer staff and visits by a consultant veterinarian from overseas. The Pandrillus project is helping to establish a wildlife sanctuary in the mountains of the Afi River Forest Reserve in the north of Cross River State, and, like zoos in other countries, the project is playing a valuable role in public education—many children have visited the drill colony ("Drill Ranch") and been fascinated by the animals. But, as noted in chapter 6, foreign support for the Oban section of the Cross River National Park has been withdrawn, and little is being done to stop the poaching of wild drills that still live there, just twenty miles from Pandrillus's Calabar head-quarters. This suggests an imbalanced use of resources, especially since the drill is acknowledged to be one of the most endangered primates in the world.

Events in West Africa also suggest that we should not be too hasty in assuming that war and political instability make conservation in the wild a hopeless cause, leaving captive breeding in a safer environment the only option. In Liberia, for instance, the Sapo National Park, proba-bly the most important conservation area for rain forest primates in that country, was abandoned in 1991 as a terrible civil war spread. Park staff fled into the bush and foreign advisers left the country. Following the gradual return of peace and security to the Liberian countryside, a joint team of American and Dutch biologists and Liberian park administra-tors was able to visit Sapo in early 1997. They found evidence that wildlife populations in and around the park had increased during the civil war because so many people had left the area and hunting pressure had consequently eased. Efforts are now under way to rehabilitate Sapo.[56]

Twenty years previously, a scenario similar to that in Liberia had un-folded on Bioko Island in Equatorial Guinea. In primate surveys in 1986, Thomas Butynski and Stanley Koster found evidence that during the eleven brutal years of Francisco Macias Nguema's dictatorship, which had ended in 1979, forest cover and wildlife populations on the island had greatly increased, so that in 1986 there may have been more wildlife and wildlife habitat on the island than there had been at the turn of the century. During Nguema's rule, Bioko was estimated to have lost at least a third of its human population; indeed, many parts of the island were left with no settlements and farms, and plantations began reverting to forest. At the same time, guns were removed from the civilian population, so that hunting declined significantly.[57] Since Nguema's ouster, threats to the wildlife from logging and hunting have begun to increase, and it appears that primate populations are now declining.[58]

In contrast to the recovery of forest wildlife populations during periods when human societies in Liberia and Equatorial Guinea were disordered, forest wildlife in Ghana has continued to decline in the face of many years of relative peace and prosperity in the country. This suggests that civil disorder does not inevitably threaten wild animal populations, and so the threat of such disorder is not a strong argument in favor of captive breeding as a conservation strategy.

WHAT ABOUT TRANSLOCATION?

I have suggested that the most effective role that zoos can play in tropical conservation is not in the captive breeding of endangered species but in raising people's interest in wildlife and their concern for its conservation. However, the knowledge that zoos have of wild animal husbandry, together with their financial resources, have proved to be valuable assets in the management technique of translocation. This technique is especially appropriate where a population of animals has been greatly reduced or eliminated from an area of suitable habitat, but where the factors that led to population decline no longer operate; in this case, animals may be translocated from a similar area nearby with a healthy population. Alternatively, animals may be moved from an area where they are under severe threat to an area of lower threat. In either case the animals are not held for an extended period in captivity, and unlike animals bred in a zoo or other long-term holding facility, they are fully adapted to a wild environment. Translocation has long been used in the conservation and management of wild mammal populations. In North America, for instance, pronghorn antelopes were successfully reintroduced to California by translocation in 1947, and, in a much publicized project, wolves were reintroduced to Yellowstone National Park in 1985 by translocation from Alberta.[59] Evidence that wild primates can be successfully translocated was provided in the 1980s by the movement of three groups of savanna baboons in Kenya, and of a subgroup of rhesus macaques in India.[60]

A good example of how translocation can be applied successfully to a tropical-forest primate comes from Belize in Central America; a zoo-based scientist was closely involved in this project. Black howler monkeys became extinct in the forest of Belize's Cockscomb Basin in 1978 from the cumulative effects of a yellow-fever epidemic, a hurricane, and overhunting. But in 1986 Cockscomb Basin became a wildlife sanctuary, and, under the management of the Belize Audubon Society, its protection improved and hunting declined. In 1990 the sanctuary was increased in size from less than 6 square miles to almost 160 square miles. These developments made feasible the reintroduction of howlers to Cockscomb, and sixty-two howlers were moved there from 1992 to 1994 from another Belizean protected area, the Community Baboon Sanctuary near Bermudian Landing (see plate 29). The howler monkey population in the Baboon Sanctuary had been increasing as a result of a conservation program that began in 1986. Two key individuals in this translocation project were Robert Horwich, who had played a major role in the establishment of the Baboon Sanctuary, and Fred Koontz of the Bronx Zoo and the Wildlife Conservation Society. The experience of Koontz and his colleagues in the management of zoo animals helped to ensure that the capture, temporary holding, transportation, and release of the monkeys took place with a minimum of stress. In January 1997, more than four years after the initial release of fourteen monkeys, the Cockscomb howler population was estimated at eighty to a hundred monkeys. Koontz has estimated the reintroduction cost per monkey at $1,597, which includes postrelease monitoring and local staff salaries.[61]

Although I do not see a strong case for using captive-breeding programs to conserve the West African forest primates mentioned in this book, translocation could be a useful conservation technique in West Africa, especially if it is combined with the strategy most urgently needed in the forest zone: the rigorous protection of some of the most important remaining fragments of natural habitat. The most appropriate areas of remaining forest to protect are those that have a good chance of persisting well into the future because they are relatively large and ecologically still reasonably intact.

In Ghana, the original rain forest is now fragmented across dozens of reserves and parks, many of which are quite small. It is unlikely that in the foreseeable future resources will be available to provide relatively strong protection for more than a very small number of these forest patches. Because of habitat change and hunting, red colobus monkeys are probably already extinct in Ghana's forests, and Diana monkeys and white-naped mangabeys have become very rare, as noted in the previous chapter. If Diana monkeys and mangabeys are found still surviving in reserves where they have little chance of being effectively protected, their translocation to one or more well-protected areas (where they were once present but are now rare or absent) might be a sensible conservation option, provided measures are taken to minimize disturbance to existing primate populations and to prevent the transmission of diseases to them.

CONCLUSIONS

Zoos can and do play an important part in tropical conservation efforts. Their exhibits can help to stimulate an interest in wildlife and in conservation issues, both in developed and developing countries. Some zoos already play significant roles in conservation by directly supporting field research and protection efforts, a leading example being the international program of New York's Wildlife Conservation Society, based at the Bronx Zoo, which has supported much of my own fieldwork. Such field activities should be more widely adopted; they can readily be incorporated into zoos' role in public enlightenment through the display of information on these activities alongside live-animal exhibits. And the expertise of zoo staff in animal husbandry can be usefully applied both in the management of wild animal populations and in translocation projects.

I accept the idea that captive breeding of endangered species in zoos can play *some* role in conservation; it is probably wise to ensure that small breeding colonies of at least the most threatened animal species are held in captivity as a safeguard against the failure of conservation in the natural habitat. But captive breeding in zoos should not be regarded as the primary means by which endangered animals may be conserved, and the maintenance of captive-breeding colonies must not be allowed to distract attention from the highest conservation priority: the protection of wild animals in their original habitats.

NINE

Conservation at the Close
of the Twentieth Century

For Love of Nature or Love of Money?

I began my studies in Africa with feelings of excitement and enthusiasm at experiencing tropical nature firsthand. Although I soon became aware of the political and economic problems that made nature conservation difficult in developing countries, I also saw that traditional parks and reserves could work to protect wildlife, especially if these protected areas had the backing of dedicated individuals. Thirty years later, as I look at the parts of West Africa with which I am most familiar, I often feel more gloomy than enthusiastic about the prospects for many wild animals and their habitats. Some of this gloominess has been brought on by witnessing the realities affecting human societies in Africa. Africa's population is estimated to have grown from 224 million in 1950 to 728 million in 1995,[1] and in many areas this huge increase has outpaced the growth of agricultural and industrial production; as a result shrinking wilderness areas are being pressured by more and more poor people who depend on subsistence farming and hunting. Meanwhile, at a political level several countries, including Sierra Leone, have sunk into chaos, and many others have been plagued by corrupt and brutal governments. These political realities have been poignantly described by the *Washington Post* journalist Keith Richburg, who traveled to Africa in 1991 full of hope and excitement (in part at the prospect of experiencing his African "roots") and left three years later feeling depressed and disillusioned.[2]

As an academic based in New York, with a special interest in the ecology of forest primates, I can have virtually no influence on the course of societal and political trends in Africa. But, as described in earlier chapters, while involved in efforts to conserve a few special areas of forest and their wildlife I have often advised, and sometimes worked for, international conservation organizations and the forestry or wildlife departments of African governments. My experiences tell me that, despite the huge problems facing conservation in Africa, these foreign and local organizations have the potential to make a difference in at least limited areas; but this potential is not being effectively realized.

In this book I have given examples of how the fashionable strategy of integrating conservation with economic development has failed to protect wildlife in the forests of West Africa. Here, I emphasize the point that this strategy has tended to lead the people and organizations involved in its implementation to place more emphasis on the short-term pursuit of money than on the long-term protection of nature. I argue that organizations that describe themselves as primarily concerned with wildlife conservation must refocus their efforts to give more attention to the basic protection of nature. I use the example of India to show that it is possible for a country with great problems of human poverty to pursue, with some success, conservation policies that emphasize the protection of nature for its own sake. And I argue that some of the attitudes toward wildlife displayed by the Indian public can be inculcated among young people in Africa. I suggest that protection-orientated conservation does not have to be very costly, and that, where financial assistance is needed for the long-term recurrent costs of protection, trust funds are a promising mechanism for channeling assistance to protected areas. Such funds can also help sustain key organizations or individuals through periods of political turmoil.

THE CORRUPTING EFFECTS OF BIG MONEY

Although the present for both people and wildlife is bleak in many parts of Africa, the long-term future is not necessarily so, and therefore I do not believe that the cause of conservation in Africa is a hopeless one. But as I have attempted to show in this book, in parts of Africa some conservationists are making the prospects for wild nature worse by the apparently unthinking pursuit of flawed policies. These policies regard conservation as one aspect of a process of economic development in which human material needs are given priority. In addition, conservationists now frequently propose that wildlife and forests be directly managed by the members of rural communities rather than by agencies of national governments. Not only have such approaches failed to protect nature in West Africa, but the international development strategies of which they are a part have also been remarkably ineffective. To quote R. W. Stevenson's September 1997 article in the *New York Times* about the World Bank's president: "The entire development field . . . is under scrutiny as never before. . . . Critics say the many hundreds of billions of dollars in development aid have failed abysmally in efforts to build foundations for sustainable economic growth in many regions."[3] A large number of foreign-sponsored development efforts have failed in Africa because so many of the resources devoted to them have been absorbed by government departments (and often by corrupt leaders and officials) and by contracts given to consultants and corporations from the aid-giving countries. Little of the development aid has led to fundamental changes in practices and attitudes, or to enduring improvements in education and infrastructure. Bringing wildlife conservation under this very leaky umbrella has meant that conservation has entered an arena in which people who are already relatively rich and powerful compete for access to aid money. This approach has therefore encouraged the involvement in conservation of those pursuing personal gain, while marginalizing those who seek to protect nature for its own sake.

Once the emphasis on human needs and economic development became a central feature of international conservation policy following the publication of the World Conservation Strategy in 1980, the continued move toward community-based approaches was inevitable because development organizations themselves were becoming increasingly enamored of "community development." Ironically, community development has still required large sums of money to be spent both in the headquarters of the international development-aid and conservation organizations that administer the programs and in the developing countries, where the programs themselves are not only subsidized but often also employ highly paid foreign community-development specialists.

Examples of the high cost and flawed design of community-based conservation in Africa are provided by Zimbabwe's famous Communal Areas Management Programme for Indigenous Resources (CAMPFIRE) project and Zambia's Administrative Management Design for Game Management Areas (ADMADE) project, each of which has had WWF and USAID as major sponsors. In each project, fees from safari hunters and development agencies go into funds used to pay both for development projects and for wildlife management efforts such as the employment of villagers as game guards.

The CAMPFIRE program consumed $7 million of USAID funding between 1989 and 1996, with other major revenue coming from the sale of trophy-hunting licenses, whose fees range from seventy-five dollars for an impala to ten thousand dollars for an elephant. But it is reported that some district councils, which are the project implementors, have ignored program directives, failed to invest revenue in village projects, and taught people little about wildlife management. Senior officials in the richest CAMPFIRE district are said to have misappropriated funds and accepted kickbacks for granting illegal hunting rights;[4] and although Zimbabwe's elephant population has increased, there has also been an increase in elephant poaching on communal lands.[5] Because CAMPFIRE has relied on large infusions of aid money it is unclear whether it can be truly self-sustaining in the long run as a means of managing wildlife; however, it is now said to have become as much a forum for rural governance as a wildlife conservation mechanism.[6]

In an insightful review of the ADMADE project, Clark Gibson and Stuart Marks describe similar problems. Chiefs, designated by the project as links between outside interests (government and the sponsoring agencies) and rural communities, are said to have used their positions to monopolize development projects and obtain positions for their relatives. The ADMADE revenues have been too small to make much impact on local communities, who have had little say in the design of hunting regulations. Village scouts have been unpopular in many communities— their appointment to government jobs produced social tensions, and some guards colluded with hunters. The amount of meat taken by local hunters in the project area did not decline; instead, hunters switched to killing smaller animals and using less-detectable hunting methods. Gibson and Marks note that development assistance is available to residents whether or not they contribute to the conservation program, so that there is little incentive to combat hunting, and they point out that although money and projects have flowed into an impoverished area, the program is not truly self-supporting and requires continuing support from outside donors.[7]

In another study of ADMADE, focused on the Malama chiefdom where the project began, Dale Lewis and Andrew Phiri found that, seven years after the project's formal commencement in 1988, wildlife snaring was occurring at a high intensity. Lewis and Phiri also noted that safari hunters were finding less game near villages, that development aid funding for the area (from the Norwegian Agency for Development) far exceeded revenues from safari licenses, and that the small portion of safari revenues that had reached the Malama villages had not been used for any community facilities.[8]

Ironically, while projects such as CAMPFIRE and ADMADE (like development-orientated conservation projects elsewhere in Africa) have tended to breed corruption and foster the attitude that conservation is a business, the outsiders who have been the prime instigators of these projects have often proceeded as if they were leading a political crusade. For instance, two recent major reports prepared in part to guide international conservation planners stress the need to "empower" local people.[9] This form of paternalism seems to be an entrenched feature of Third World development and humanitarian aid projects, which are typically planned and implemented by highly educated middle-class Westerners. The project planners and managers generally maintain (or improve) their own lifestyles, while displaying attitudes that seem to be colored both by colonial-style paternalism toward people they regard as the benighted peasants of the Third World, and by guilt for the perceived wrongdoing of their colonial antecedents. This pursuit of a mixture of material and sociopolitical aims has become endemic in Third World conservation projects initiated by Westerners and, as I have argued, has its roots in the liaison that developed in the 1970s between international conservation and development organizations.

STRAINS IN THE CONSERVATION
AND DEVELOPMENT RELATIONSHIP

At high levels, however, the compromise between conservation and development is unraveling. The second United Nations "Earth Summit," held in New York in June 1997, received far less attention than the first conference (the UN Conference on Environment and Development), held in Rio de Janeiro in 1992, and was widely regarded as a failure. As I read in a local newspaper while traveling through rural Ghana in June 1997 in quest of populations of vanishing forest primates, "since Rio, forests, farmlands and coral reefs have dwindled, pollution is increasing, oceans are overfished and people are so poor they threaten to use any resource available just to stay alive."[10] Reporting on the 1997 meeting in New York, the paper said that Third World nations "told the UN Earth Summit this week that they cannot protect the environment because of deep cuts in foreign aid and broken pledges by rich countries."

The Rio summit had been planned as a successor to the 1972 Stockholm conference, which had led to the founding of UNEP and at which the historic political and financial compromise between rich and poor countries had been forged: rich countries would pay for the economic development of poorer countries in return for commitments by poor countries to undertake environmental conservation measures. At the time of the Rio conference, for instance, official development assistance to Africa was still rising faster than the rate of population growth. Excluding a few countries with incomplete data, "official" aid to sub-Saharan African countries rose from an annual average of $8.27 billion during 1984–86 to $15.6 billion during 1991–93.[11] Annual population growth in sub-Saharan Africa over this period was about 3 percent. But global political changes and the mismanagement of many development projects have caused rich countries to cut back on their foreign aid budgets. In *Agenda 21*, the action plan signed by world leaders in Rio, rich countries agreed to raise their annual foreign-aid contributions to .70 percent of their gross national product. Instead, their average contributions fell from .33 percent of GNP in 1992 to .24 percent in 1996, the lowest level since 1973; the country showing the greatest decline in official aid was the United States, whose official aid in 1996 was only .12 percent of GNP.[12] Of fifty countries in sub-Saharan Africa, twenty-three therefore suffered a cut in their foreign aid in 1994.[13]

Meanwhile, the cost to some Third World countries of servicing the debt on accumulated foreign loans has come to equal or exceed the value of new loans. In 1994 the total external debt of sub-Saharan African countries was estimated at 79 percent of their combined annual GNP, but for several countries (including Côte d'Ivoire, Tanzania, and Zambia) debt was more than 200 percent greater than GNP.[14] Given population increases, this means that the net inflow of foreign-aid money on a per capita basis has been declining steeply, and that debt repayments take a huge bite out of governments' limited budgets. Having argued that wildlife should be conserved as a component of economic development rather than for more aesthetic or ethical reasons, international conservation organizations now find that their argument has been widely accepted at high levels of government—conservation may occur in poor countries if rich countries pay for it with development aid, but few government resources will be devoted to conservation in the absence of more aid money. "If financial resources were forthcoming," my Ghanaian newspaper quoted Zimbabwean President Robert Mugabe as saying to the New York meeting, "Africa would refrain from killing wild animals for food, cutting down trees for fuel or polluting water resources for lack of appropriate technologies."

While the amount of resources devoted by many African governments to conservation has not kept pace with the destructive pressures acting on wildlife and its habitats, there has been no obvious diminution in the amount of money flowing to international conservation organizations and to foreign consultants. Conservation organizations have increased their staffs and often expanded their office space. Much of the funding to allow this expansion has come from development-aid agencies, which have come to be widely referred to as "the donor community" (the real donors in most cases are, of course, taxpayers in rich countries). It is not surprising, therefore, that a substantial part of the energy of large conservation organizations is now devoted to raising and managing funds from the development agencies. For example, a 1997 advertisement by WWF International for a new regional director for its Africa and Madagascar Programme specified that one of the key requirements for the position was "a proven track record in managing and fund raising for large, multi-donor programmes."[15]

The number of consultants employed on conservation projects has also increased, as has the rate at which consultants expect to be reimbursed. Consultants in conservation, like consultants in many fields, are typically employed on short-term contracts for periods ranging from a few weeks to a few years. The relatively high pay that such consultants receive is justified on the grounds of the uncertain nature of their employment. The short-term nature of most consultancy contracts means that the consultants rarely have a long-term commitment to a given project, and they often seem well aware that their final reports will accumulate along with many others on the shelves and in the filing cabinets of government departments and development or conservation organizations. As I have said already, much of international conservation has come to operate as a business, just as envisaged in the mid-1980s by the founder of Earthlife. In this context, it is not strange that Maurice Strong, the man who played a major role in running both the 1972 Stockholm conference and the 1992 Earth Summit, is a wealthy Canadian business-man who began his career as a fur trader with the Hudson's Bay Company.[16]

My perception, then, is that much of the activity in the name of conservation that I have observed in recent years in West Africa has been motivated as much, or more, by a love of money than by a love of nature. As noted in chapter 6, I was struck by the fact that few consultants working on the Cross River National Park project in Nigeria showed much interest in making extended visits to the forest simply to enjoy nature for its own sake, and I noticed the same phenomenon among consultants employed to advise on the development of Ghana's forest parks. This lack of eagerness on the part of a new generation of conservation professionals to experience wilderness is in marked contrast to the attitude both of the leaders of the wilderness movement who played such an important role in the establishment of America's national parks, and of the founders of the national parks in eastern and southern Africa. I believe that the transformation of conservation to an economic activity has been deeply corrupting, and is the primary reason why so many conservation projects have failed in what should be their chief mission: safeguarding the long-term future of threatened communities of plants and animals. I believe that many conservation organizations have lost sight of their original aim of trying to save threatened wildlife and habitat, and that this aim must be brought back into central focus.

IS NATURE-FOCUSED CONSERVATION A REALISTIC OPTION?

But, many people say, giving priority to wildlife protection is not a realistic option in much of Africa and other parts of the Third World, given the rising numbers of people who are attempting just to maintain current living standards. In the face of the needs of the poor, this argument goes, how can it be justifiable to set aside areas of land where wild nature comes first? And, realistically, even if such a goal can be justified, can it be achieved?

At a national level, the argument that it is immoral to put nature first in certain areas can be countered by a consideration of the relatively small size of these areas. In Ghana, India, Nigeria, and Sierra Leone, for instance, less than 5 percent of the land area is currently set aside in areas where protection of nature is supposed to have priority. Extending existing economic activities over these nominally protected areas, which are mostly land of marginal agricultural value, would not bring substantial long-term national benefits to human populations growing at 2–3 percent each year.[17] Increases in human well-being on a national scale are much more likely to be promoted by political, social, and economic reform.

But even if the greater utilization of nature in limited areas will not have much impact on national economies, what of effects at more local levels? Can strong nature-protection policies be justified if they deprive even a few people of access to resources that contribute to a local economy? This is a question lying at the heart of the conservation policies I have been reviewing in this book. I answer it with several points. First, many key areas for wildlife conservation in the tropics, including most of the forests I have described in this book, are located in hinterlands quite far from regions with dense human populations; in the recent past, relatively small numbers of people lived in most of these areas. Second, most of these areas have had some level of protection for many decades (for instance, as forest reserves) and this status was generally accepted at a local level. Third, where pressures to exploit a protected area have recently increased, this has often been the result of the migration of people into the vicinity from a considerable distance away; these newcomers rarely have any long-standing connection to, or dependence on, the land of the protected area.

The establishment of a national park, therefore, in the location of an existing forest reserve in the Cross River State of Nigeria or the Western Region of Ghana deprived few of the original human inhabitants of the area of economic opportunities. Beyond relatively small local subsistence needs, the exploitation of these forests has usually been in the hands of people who are not native to the area and who have sold the timber, bushmeat, and other products they have harvested from the forest in distant markets (and even in foreign countries). The exploitation has not, therefore, had a large impact on the local economy, and depriving local people of the opportunity to exploit the forests has often been a relatively minor interference in the lives of a small number of people. It is also a relatively small disruption compared with the major upheavals inflicted on many people throughout the world in the course of building dams, industrial plants, highways, and airports. Everyone now lives in a world of nation-states, in which it is widely accepted that resources of national and international importance are most appropriately managed (or their management overseen) by national governments, which are supposed to act in the long-term best interests of the people as a whole, even where this causes some disadvantage to a small segment of the population. I do not think, therefore, that the park or reserve concept should be rejected because of possible difficulties such a protected area may cause for a few people, and although it must be right to help remedy the losses some people may suffer as a result of establishment of a park, these remedies should not be allowed to overwhelm the original purpose of the park.

HOW CAN PROTECTED AREAS BE PROTECTED?

That said, it remains a fact that human populations in Africa and many other parts of the tropics are growing rapidly, and that migration to agricultural frontiers is increasing. In the face of these pressures, how can protected areas be made to work? I have argued that buying people off with development projects close to conservation areas is not a viable strategy to ensure protection of those areas. Such projects can breed corruption and attract people into fragile areas, and if outside financial support for the projects is not maintained in the long term (or never materializes in the quantities expected), resentment will build against the conservation program that was the rationale for the development efforts. A case can be made, perhaps, for siting development projects at some distance from protected areas, to draw people away from their boundaries and reduce pressure on their resources,[18] and it may make conservation sense to provide incentives for people living near a park to participate in such projects. It can be worthwhile, therefore, for governments to engage in the regional, cross-sectoral planning recommended long ago by Max Nicholson and encouraged by *Caring for the Earth* in 1991. But the need for such planning should not distract those government departments and nongovernmental organizations whose primary concern is nature conservation from giving the major part of their attention to the protection of wildlife and its habitats. Conservation organizations may encourage national or foreign agencies to plan development projects away from protected areas, but they should not themselves play a major role in the projects; rather, they should return to their roots and dedicate themselves to the safeguarding of the protected areas.

Protected areas are best safeguarded by combining strong policing with the raising of public concern for the value of the area. All modern societies use some kind of police to enforce laws so that antisocial behavior does not undermine collective efforts directed toward a perceived common good. Even in developed countries where nature reserves and national parks have broad public support, these areas have to be patrolled and inevitable lawbreakers prosecuted. In developing countries, where there may be less local support and where some resources inside a park (such as the wood of even a single tree, or the meat of a single antelope) are relatively very valuable compared to average incomes, strong policing is even more necessary. Such policing may not always be fully effective, but it can act as a brake on exploitation and so ensure that the poaching of animals or plants does not occur at a rate faster than that at which populations can replenish themselves. If national governmental or nongovernmental agencies cannot afford to pay for this protection, but a protected area is regarded as internationally significant, then it is appropriate for foreigners to subsidize policing costs, perhaps through the trust-fund mechanisms I will discuss below.

It is also true that no conservation programs or protected areas will work unless they have some significant measure of public support. This support has to exist at several levels: local, national, and international. Local support will not be forthcoming if people feel that they suffer only costs and no benefits from the presence of a protected area. Apart from making efforts to discuss with local residents the potential benefits of protected areas (for instance, in maintaining water supplies), conservation agencies should, therefore, try to give local people employment opportunities in activities directly related to the maintenance of the protected area, such as those related to protection, tourism, and ecological research. Beyond this, local and national efforts to raise appreciation of nature for its own sake should be strongly encouraged. This is another issue I will return to toward the end of this chapter.

THE INDIAN EXAMPLE

My experiences in India have shown me that an approach to conservation that emphasizes the protection of nature for its intrinsic value, rather than for the economic benefits it may bring, can work even in poor, developing countries with large social and economic problems. India has the world's second-largest population (an estimated 936 million people in 1995) living in an area that is less than one-third the size of the United States (about 1.1 million square miles). The whole of Africa was estimated to have only 728 million people in 1995, living in almost 11.4 million square miles. In other words, India's population density in 1995 was 122 people/square mile, compared with 10 for Africa and 11 for the United States.[19] Although the Indian middle class has made great strides in recent years, there are still vast numbers of poor people in rural India, and in 1995 India's annual gross domestic product per capita (even at "purchasing power parity") was estimated at only $1,422, compared with $1,533 for all of sub-Saharan Africa and $26,977 for the United States.[20] In addition to very high human population densities and great poverty, Indian government has also been criticized for inefficiencies and corruption, especially at the state level. Despite all these factors weighing against it, conservation in India has worked, and much of this conservation involves "conventional" national parks, reserves, and sanctuaries.

Returning to India in 1995, after an absence of more than seventeen years, I was struck by the gains that conservation had made. During this time, the population had grown by more than 250 million people (in other words, India's population increment alone was similar to the entire population of the United States). India's cities, I found, had expanded greatly and were even more densely packed with people and vehicles and their air considerably more polluted than when I had last experienced them. Driving on roads most of which had not been widened, but which carried many more trucks and buses, was a terrifying experience. Yet many of the hill areas I visited in South India seemed to have more trees, and wildlife appeared to be more abundant. My former study area at Kakachi in the Kalakkadu Sanctuary was undisturbed and appeared virtually unchanged (see plates 30 and 31). As I described in chapter 2, this area had even stricter protection than when I had first worked there; it was now part of a national Tiger Reserve that included some rain forest areas that I had urged be given better protection back in 1976.

These improvements in nature conservation in India, in spite of the vast human pressures, were especially striking to me in comparison with what I had experienced over seventeen years of frequent visits to West Africa, where I had witnessed a steady erosion of forests and wildlife populations. The differences between India and West Africa have several causes. Perhaps most important, Indian governments have taken a strong line in defense of nature in recent years. Logging was stopped in government forests in the state of Tamil Nadu in 1978, and in the adjacent states of Kerala in 1982 and Karnataka in 1985; the governments had apparently recognized that the remaining small areas of forest were precious resources and that further felling would provide a negligible economic benefit to the people of their states. A complete ban on hunting had been in force in India since 1992. The poaching of trees and wildlife has, of course, continued, but with a few exceptions this poaching is not excessive and is kept under reasonable control by the authorities. Tiger poaching, largely fueled by a demand for tiger parts in China, is a recognized problem, however.[21]

When I visited Mundanthurai in 1995 I discussed the relative success of government-sponsored conservation in India with my colleague Rauf Ali and with Neil Pelkey, a graduate student from the University of California at Davis, who was studying conservation policy. Although they agreed that underlying cultural attitudes were important, they argued that one of the most important factors in India's success was the strength and continuity of the Indian civil service (which includes forest departments). Civil servants are not badly paid relative to the population as a whole, and corruption, although it occurs, is not so prevalent as to seriously undermine the existence of relatively fair and effective government. I think it is very likely that government and its conservation actions are given a measure of respect in India because the country has managed to maintain a lively, participatory democracy—something that has been sadly lacking in most of Africa. The separation of powers between government and the judiciary has also been much more effective in postcolonial India than in Africa, with the result that courts have successfully blocked many environmental abuses.[22] On December 12, 1996, for instance, the Indian Supreme Court banned any tree felling on both public and private land in India that did not conform to plans approved as part of the 1988 National Forest Policy, which recommends that 66 percent of hill areas and 33 percent of the plains be covered with forest.[23]

In 1995 I also visited the tea estates of the Anaimalai Hills, where I met M. C. Muthanna, who had been the general manager of the Bombay Burmah Trading Company's Singampatti group of estates at the time when I was living there in 1975–76. It was Muthanna who in 1976 had been given the task of informing me of his company's aggravation with our conservation work, after Indira Gandhi's actions halted the company's forest clearance. Muthanna was now Director of all BBTC's plantations, not only in India but also in Tanzania and Indonesia. He greeted me warmly, and rather than expressing resentment at the central government's actions of twenty years previously, he said that he felt many people in India now appreciated Indira Gandhi's actions on behalf of wildlife, and he told me with pride of one of the Singampatti estates that had been converted to the organic growing of tea—without the use of pesticides and chemical fertilizers.

Muthanna's attitudes are a reflection of an important facet of Indian culture that has led to better prospects for the small remaining protected areas. Appreciation of nature and respect for other living things is widespread, and because of Hindu abstinence from meat-eating, hunting is not a strong tradition for a majority of the population. I witnessed another clear sign of the widespread Indian appreciation for wildlife during my 1995 visit when primatologist Mewa Singh took me on a tour of the Indira Gandhi Wildlife Sanctuary in the Anaimalais. We met many ordinary Indians using public transport to visit the sanctuary; they were not the poorest of peasants, perhaps, but they were certainly not wealthy people. Mewa Singh tells me that that there is growing concern for wildlife conservation among the Indian middle class.

Although there are major underlying cultural differences between the people of India and West Africa (for instance, widespread vegetarianism in India), it is not obvious that these are largely responsible for the differences in conservation practice. Most of India's forests and wildlife were destroyed long ago, in spite of Hinduism, and they were still in retreat when I arrived in India in 1975. Their comeback is a recent phenomenon.

Not only was I impressed to see that "conventional" conservation, sponsored by government, was working tolerably well despite great rural poverty, I was also struck by the lack of foreign-aid projects in India. I should not have been surprised, I suppose, because when I had lived in India twenty years before I had become aware of Indian nationalism and the desire to be independent of foreign powers (an attitude cultivated by Nehru after independence); and I had lived in an area where I rarely saw non-Indians. Even so, the contrast with what I had become used to in Africa was striking. Published statistics support this contrast; official development assistance to India in 1995 was $1.7 billion (spread across 936 million people), compared with $18.3 billion for sub-Saharan Africa (728 million people).[24] The low level of development aid to India has inevitably meant that rather little money has been available for foreign-sponsored conservation and development projects, and this seems to have benefited rather than harmed wildlife conservation.

THE IMPORTANCE OF CHANGING ATTITUDES

If wildlife conservation can be made to work in the forests of India, then it is surely possible in Africa. I acknowledge that the Indian example is most relevant to those parts of Africa in which areas identified for nature conservation make up only a small percentage of the land area. In these situations, the setting aside of land for conservation has only a marginal impact on a national economy, and the fact that many wildlife species and relatively undisturbed habitat are restricted to limited areas makes it easier for people to appreciate their special value. While the Indian example is therefore relevant to West Africa, it may be less useful as a detailed model in parts of East and central Africa (for instance, 18.0 percent of Botswana is in protected areas, 15.0 percent of Tanzania, and 8.5 percent of Zambia).[25] However, several general principles from India would seem to have general applicability:

1. In Third World countries, government can act effectively to conserve wildlife in conventional protected areas; such conservation is most likely to work where government has the support of the people being governed.
2. Even in the face of great poverty, conservation can work without strong linkages to economic development projects.
3. Conservation is much easier where a large number of people appreciate the intrinsic value of nature.

In light of these principles, to what extent can individuals and conservation organizations inside and outside Africa contribute to making conservation work better on that continent?

Foreign conservationists and conservation organizations cannot themselves bring more representative government to Africa. Ultimately, this is a change that must come from within Africa. But whenever it is appropriate, outsiders can add their voices in favor of democracy and more open government, and they can acknowledge how important these things are for conservation and resource management generally. At least one well-known conservationist in Africa, Richard Leakey, has argued that there are direct links between conservation and fair government. He has expressed the view that the protection of wildlife is ultimately a matter of human values rather than economics, and something that government must support for the public good. Leakey dismisses the idea that conservation should be considered a matter of economics; species, he argues, "are priceless, as are human dignity and freedom. Government and intergovernment policies and actions should be based firmly on this premise, which is not negotiable."[26]

In terms of the second principle, I have already made clear my view that the close linkage between conservation and economic development is not wise and has led to many conservation decisions being made on the basis of how they will enrich project participants, rather than how they will protect nature. Richard Leakey is evidently arguing the same thing. Conservation organizations should look for ways to make nature conservation work in Africa outside the now pervasive framework of integrated conservation and development projects.

The third principle suggests that it is vital to change public attitudes in favor of nature. Outside organizations should continue to support African groups working in their own countries to increase an understanding of wild nature and promote an appreciation of its value, especially among young people. For instance, the Ghana Wildlife Society is already doing an excellent job of encouraging the formation of wildlife clubs among schools. Cultivating an appreciation of wild nature is surely the second major role, after protecting nature, to which international conservation organizations can sensibly apply themselves. It is rare to find young people anywhere in the world who cannot become fascinated by animals, and nurturing this innate interest is bound to yield benefits for conservation. Rennie Bere, one of the prime movers in the establishment of Uganda's National Parks, recognized this in the 1950s when he argued that a basic duty of the national park authorities was to encourage the local appreciation of wildlife, and that one way of doing this was to bring groups of schoolchildren to visit the parks.[27] Our program at Tiwai encouraged such visits to the wildlife sanctuary, and in Calabar, Nigeria, I have seen the fascination of schoolchildren with the primates at the Drill Ranch.

I pointed out in chapter 8 that zoos have played an important role in nurturing an interest in wildlife in many developed countries. Most large African cities have zoos, but these are often poorly run and are therefore much less effective at promoting an interest in wildlife than they might be. I have suggested that zoos in wealthier countries could do more to help improve the management of African zoos, and that in this way they would likely make a more significant long-term contribution to species conservation than they can by breeding threatened animals in captivity.

I think it is important to emphasize that even though there are evident cultural differences between places like West Africa and India, attitudes can change and there are no fundamental factors to prevent the spread in Africa of greater appreciation for wildlife. Many people in Lagos, Nigeria, for instance, demonstrate an inherent interest in animals by keeping pets, including tropical fish. And in many villages in Nigeria, as in Ghana and other parts of West Africa, certain species are regarded as sacred and are not harmed even if they cause significant economic hardship. Small populations of sacred monkeys in the eastern Nigerian villages of Akpugoeze and Lagwa, and in the Ghanaian villages of Boabeng and Fiema, steal food and damage crops, but they are tolerated.[28] Rural Africans do not, therefore, always view animals from a strictly nutritional or economic viewpoint. Edward Wilson, George Schaller, and Richard Leakey, experienced scientists who have each been strongly involved with conservation, have all independently made the same point, that people everywhere have an inherent appreciation of nature; Schaller has endorsed the idea that this appreciation can be increased by an exposure to animals as pets or in zoos, and to wildlife and wild places on television.[29]

However, even if increased efforts are made to encourage among young Africans an appreciation of the value and beauty of nature, it will be some time before such efforts have a strong effect on conservation policies. Political changes that would be beneficial for conservation in Africa are also likely to be slow in coming to many countries. It is therefore vitally important to arrange better protection now for the relatively small remaining fragments of nature in regions like West Africa, so that these areas are still there when attitudes and political contexts change. These are hardly novel ideas. Back in 1959, for instance, Nigeria's Chief Conservator of Forests, D. R. Rosevear (whose visits to Oban I described in chapter 6) argued that it is important to raise awareness among young people of the value of wildlife, but also stressed the importance of immediate protection by the "actual prevention of harmful acts and the effective legal discouragement of mere destroyers."[30]

Even if only fragments of nature can be protected, the wildlife within them will be given some chance for the future. That future cannot be reliably predicted, but we can reasonably hope that in time the growth of human populations in Africa will slow, and that education, prosperity, and good governance will put down deeper and wider roots. At that point, plants and animals that have found refuge in reserves may be able not only to flourish within protected areas, where their value will have become more widely appreciated, but also to recolonize some of their former habitats in the same way that several species have recently done in parts of North America and Europe.

PAYING FOR BETTER CONSERVATION

But how is nature conservation to be paid for, if not as a component of economic development and if African governments are presently unable or unwilling to adequately fund their departments of wildlife and forestry? The first point to stress is that efforts to give better protection to parks and reserves and to raise appreciation of nature's intrinsic value are not necessarily expensive tasks. Neither the costly infrastructure of "development" nor large teams of highly paid expatriate consultants are needed for such work. Most of the necessary work in protection and education can be done by national staff, perhaps occasionally advised by visiting technical experts. The policing of reserves and the teaching of natural history do not require expensive equipment or buildings, but obviously some level of recurrent expenditure on salaries, books, vehicles, and physical plant is necessary.

Such expenditures are much more likely to be indefinitely sustainable—as they must be for effective conservation—if they are as low as possible, commensurate with needs. Individuals or organizations helping to plan for conservation in developing countries should therefore consider the *least* expensive ways to meet management goals. This is the opposite of the way in which many such conservation projects are currently planned. Planners I have dealt with both in Africa and elsewhere often seem to be under pressure to make their budgets as large as possible; large budgets bring in larger "administrative charges" for the organizations involved, and personal and organizational kudos are closely related to the size of a budget being proposed or administered. Added to this pressure is the fact that development-aid agencies will generally not consider proposals for spending small sums of money, apparently because the costs of processing the paperwork and holding meetings over small amounts of money are felt to be too high.

Not only does the present system therefore encourage the pursuit of expensive conservation solutions, and especially the expenditure of a great deal of money at the headquarters of conservation organizations and on expatriate consultants, it also encourages short-term rather than long-term spending. Aid agencies and conservation organizations like to make plans and commitments for periods of only a few years—commonly three to five. Yet what is needed for effective conservation is the expenditure of small amounts of money for prolonged periods.

How best could long-term, moderate expenditure for the maintenance of conservation areas be guaranteed in places like West Africa? We can hope that in the future the national governments of Third World countries will provide budgets sufficient to fully manage their natural resources, but at the present time these governments are often either unwilling or unable to commit adequate revenue to conservation. The most promising alternative to government support lies in the establishment of trust funds or endowments. This conservation-support mechanism has been described in World Bank and WWF-US working papers and discussed in recent publications by Randall Kramer and Narendra Sharma and by Tom Struhsaker.[31] It is an option I discussed earlier in this book, in my accounts of the national park projects in Nigeria's Cross River State and in western Ghana. Trust funds or similar charities have already been established, or formally proposed, to support conservation or research activities at protected areas in several parts of the world, including three sites described in this book: Kakum in Ghana, Kibale in Uganda, and Kalakkad-Mundanthurai in India.

Trust funds are typically controlled by boards of trustees who are appointed for periods of a few years. World Bank guidelines suggest that the board include representatives of government, of a conservation nongovernmental organization, of the scientific community, and of any donor agency involved in establishing the trust.[32] While it may be sensible or even inevitable that these groups be represented on a board, it seems unwise to establish boards dominated by the representatives of institutions likely to have commitments in many other areas and that may be under strong political constraints. I think it best if a majority of trustees are not institutional representatives but independent individuals, selected on the basis of their experience, their proven integrity, and their evident commitment to conservation of the protected areas concerned; at the same time, they should not have personal financial interests in the management of the protected area. Difficult issues that must be resolved when a trust is established include the assignment of voting powers on the board and the question of who has ultimate responsibility for appointing and removing trustees.

A board of trustees can be responsible not only for administering funds but also for raising them, perhaps acting in concert with existing conservation organizations. Typically, the board will select an existing financial institution to manage the trust's money; most sensibly this institution will be based in a country with a stable financial system and freely convertible currency, and will make investments in similar countries. The institution will be expected to make investments yielding an annual return sufficient to underwrite the direct management of the protected area, as well as other activities that may aid conservation, such as education, research, and where this is necessary, compensation to local residents whose lives are disrupted by conservation activities. Part of the annual income should be added to the trust fund, which will thereby increase. Trustees should have authority only to disburse interest from the trust and not to touch its principal.

Where is the money to come from for conservation trusts? At this time, most will probably have to come from people in rich countries. Adequate money is obviously available. Millions of dollars of European taxpayers' money has, for instance, already been spent in the name of conservation on the Cross River National Park project, and Struhsaker has pointed out that between 1990 and 1997 USAID spent nearly $7 million on a project to develop a research station in the Kibale Forest; much of the Kibale money was used to pay for the salaries of expatriates and for vehicles, and at the end of this period no funds remained for the future operation of the research station. Struhsaker noted that if the same money had been put into a trust fund, the annual return on the investment could have supported the basic operating costs of four or five African forest parks and research stations in perpetuity.[33] In the first instance, then, money for conservation trusts can be sought from the sources that have been funding the kinds of projects I have described: American, European, and other governmental development agencies, and multilateral donors such as the World Bank. The Global Environment Facility, administered by the World Bank, has already helped to establish several trust funds, including one supporting a broad range of conservation activities in Bhutan and one supporting the conservation of Uganda's Bwindi Impenetrable National Park.[34]

But development-aid organizations are only one of several potential sources of income for trusts. Where there is a significant level of tourism to a protected area, income derived from tourism can be deposited in the trust fund. Individuals and businesses can also be approached for donations, just as they are currently solicited by organizations such as WWF. Oil companies, for instance, have been persuaded to sponsor several of the field projects of the Nigerian Conservation Foundation. Debt-for-nature swaps, where an organization purchases a part of a developing country's foreign debt at a discounted value, is another source of money that has already been used to establish conservation trust funds in several countries, including the Philippines and Bolivia.[35] Finally, the emerging mechanism of carbon-emissions trading may turn out to be an important source of money for tropical forest conservation; for instance, two large American utility companies, American Electric Power and Pacificorp, along with British Petroleum, are currently experimenting with offsetting some of their emissions by paying for the preservation of 5 million acres (7,800 square miles) of Bolivian forest that is otherwise threatened by logging.[36]

I do not wish to suggest that these funding mechanisms are panaceas for all the problems I have described in this book. They are possible solutions to the problem of paying for conservation, but they will not solve many day-to-day management problems or effectively counteract the large-scale economic, political, and cultural factors that have put the forests and wildlife of West Africa under such severe threat. Even where trusts can be established, a lengthy process of negotiation will likely follow in order to determine their functions in conjunction with park managers and local landholders. In the meantime, strong protection of parks and reserves must be instituted and maintained by whatever means possible.

BUT WHAT ABOUT CHAOS?

I have argued that conservation programs in parts of the world like West Africa must put much greater emphasis on the protection of nature in parks and reserves and less emphasis on community development projects. And I have suggested that trust funds may be one way of paying for such protection over the long term. But such an approach may be impractical in places like Sierra Leone, where the state fell apart and it became impossible for nationals or foreigners to even reach a supposedly protected area like Tiwai Island, let alone run a conservation program there. What is to be done to promote conservation in situations like this, situations that, some people have argued, may become more rather than less common in Africa's future?[37]

Two American couples working for New York's Wildlife Conservation Society have recently written about this problem following the political chaos that has engulfed conservation projects they were involved with in central Africa. Both John and Terese Hart (working in eastern Zaire—now renamed the Democratic Republic of Congo) and Cheryl and Robert Fimbel (working in Rwanda) have observed that trained local staff maintained a presence in conservation areas and did what they could to protect these areas.[38] In both cases, large-scale financial assistance from associated development projects was withdrawn at an early stage for political reasons (in Zaire, for instance, because of dissatisfaction with the corrupt regime of Mobutu). But moderate assistance from an outside conservation group (in this case WCS), whose personnel were able to visit intermittently, allowed committed local staff to keep working. Similar outside assistance also allowed some protection to be maintained for the mountain gorillas and their habitat in the Rwandan part of the Virunga Volcanoes.[39]

In light of these experiences, the Harts argue for establishment of a fund that would continue to provide support and professional development for internationally significant protected areas during crisis periods.[40] If externally based trust funds along the lines I have discussed above already existed for protected areas, then they could presumably fulfill this function. But in extreme cases even local staff and outside funds can do little for conservation; Tiwai Island is one example, where anarchy has prevented any recent conservation activities, and another is Rwanda, where the Dian Fossey Gorilla Fund's efforts to protect the Virunga mountain gorillas had to be suspended in 1997 because of the activities of Interhamwe insurgents.[41] However, even in cases like these a dedicated fund can support key individuals through a crisis and expedite the almost immediate launching of an effort to rehabilitate a protected area when conditions of insecurity and disorder ameliorate. An example is provided by the Dutch and American biologists who established the Society for the Renewal of Nature Conservation in Liberia in 1992. This group helped Alex Peal, the head of Liberia's national parks department, find a safe haven in the United States during the height of the Liberian civil war, and now that some measure of peace and security is returning to Liberia, the group is planning to help rehabilitate Sapo National Park.[42]

CONCLUSION

Wildlife conservation in Africa, and particularly in the rain forest zone of West Africa, faces many obstacles. But these obstacles are not insurmountable. While effective conservation over the long term requires that significant changes occur within Africa, in the immediate future people and organizations based outside Africa can help make wildlife conservation work better. But I believe that at present some of the policies being pursued by large international conservation organizations hinder rather than advance protection of threatened nature. These organizations should reconsider their policies and move back to a position closer to that which they originally occupied. It was, after all, Peter Scott, the World Wildlife Fund's first Chairman, who wrote soon after WWF's founding that ethical and aesthetic considerations, not economic motivations, should be the chief reasons for conserving wildlife. There are now numerous organizations in the world that have as their chief mandated goal the improvement of human material well-being; not least among these are national governments. The first priority for nature conservation organizations, therefore, should not be fulfillment of human material needs but rather protection of threatened nature from the destructive effects of human materialism.

Our societies have become increasingly materialistic, and, in George Schaller's words, they strongly encourage people in the "single-minded and self-indulgent pursuit of wealth."[43] The policies of governmental and nongovernmental conservation agencies tend inevitably to reflect the attitudes prevalent in the societies in which the individuals live who are responsible for formulating these policies. If humanistic materialism remains a dominant force in the decision-making of people who have an influence on the future of forests such as those in West Africa that have been the focus of this book, the long-term survival of such forests and their wildlife is unlikely.

In May 1985, Arne Naess gave a keynote address to the Second International Conference on Conservation Biology at the University of Michigan entitled "Intrinsic Value: Will the Defenders of Nature Please Rise?"[44] Prospects for the long-term survival of some of the forests and wildlife I have been talking about will be greatly increased if biologists, naturalists, and other experienced people who value nature for more than its ability to increase human material well-being will rise and express themselves more publicly. They can help conservation organizations rediscover the ethical principles that directed many of their founders, and these organizations could then lead public opinion in a fight on behalf of disappearing wildlife and wilderness. In so doing they would enrich the lives of future generations of humanity much more than they will do by following the materialistic philosophy that has come to influence their present policy so strongly.

Notes

Full publication details for books, journal articles, and printed reports cited here are provided in the bibliography. Complete citations to information published in newspapers, magazines, and newsletters are included in these notes, as these sources are not referenced in the bibliography. I have often used information from unbound, duplicated, or photocopied reports produced for or by conservation organizations. Such reports are a common way for information to be distributed in the conservation world and are usually widely circulated. Although I refer to these as "unpublished reports," the fact that they have been distributed means that technically they are publications.

PREFACE

1.   Adams and McShane (1992).
2.   International Union for the Conservation of Nature and Natural Resources, United Nations Environment Programme, and World Wildlife Fund (1980).

3.   International Union for the Conservation of Nature and Natural Resources, United Nations Environment Programme, and World Wildlife Fund (1991).

4.   Struhsaker and Oates (1995).

ONE. A PILGRIMAGE TO ESHOBI

1.   Durrell (1953).

2.   "The Lost Childhood," in Greene (1969).

3.   R. Naoroji, "African Diary," *Hornbill* no. 3 (1984): 3–6.

4.   As Paul Fussell and others have said, Greene made "seediness" his trademark (Fussell [1980]); Greene himself recalled that a significant motivation for his first visit to Africa in 1935 (which involved a trek through Liberia after crossing Sierra Leone by rail), was to experience real seediness and to reach back to and better understand the conditions from which "civilised man" had come (Sherry [1989]).

5.   Durrell told one of his biographers, David Hughes, that in writing *The Overloaded Ark* he learned to tell a story through "suitable exaggeration" and by editing events and changing their actual sequence (Hughes [1997]).

6.   World Resources Institute (1996).

7.   Durrell (1953), p. 32.

8.   After Durrell's first visit to Eshobi in 1947–48, the village continued to play an important part in the development of his career. As he describes in *The Bafut Beagles* (Durrell [1954]), he returned there in 1949, to collect pygmy scaly-tailed flying squirrels. And in 1957 he was back in Eshobi again, trying to get hold of gray-headed rock-fowls (*Picathartes oreas*); on this third visit, when he again ventured into the forests with Elias, Durrell was collecting animals that could form the nucleus of his own zoo, which was eventually to become the Jersey Wildlife Preservation Trust (Durrell [1960]). Durrell was apparently drawn to Eshobi by reading the account of a 1932–33 zoological expedition to the Cameroons serialized in *Wide World* magazine, to which his brother Leslie subscribed (Hughes [1997]). The leader of that expedition, Ivan T. Sanderson, collected many of his specimens at Eshobi (Sanderson [1940]). In his popular book *Animal Treasure*, Sanderson (1937) describes how his own course to the Cameroons was set after learning about the tropics at school in the "grey, cold and damp of Edinburgh."

9.   Elias is described as "short and stocky, with a receding ape-like forehead and protruding teeth" and with "fat lower regions"; Andreas was said to be "very tall, and extremely thin" (Durrell [1953]). In 1996 I found each man, in old age, to be of rather average Cameroonian build, with Andreas just a little taller and paler-skinned than Elias. A photograph in Elias's house showed that he had had rather protuberant teeth, but now some of his front teeth were missing.

10.   World Resources Institute (1996).

11.   Ibid.

12.   Bell (1987); Tutin and Oslisly (1995); Fairhead and Leach (1996).

13.   Embroidering the scene in *The Overloaded Ark,* Durrell describes his line of carriers being swallowed up by the multicolored undergrowth of a dense forest as soon as they crossed the bridge, but there is in fact a large grassy area with exposed rocks immediately adjacent to the bridge on the north bank of the Cross. An Eshobi man assured me that the vegetation had been like that since he was a small boy in the 1940s.

14.   Durrell (1953), p. 23.

15.   Wilkie et al. (1992); Oates (1996).

16.   Durrell (1953), chapter 12; Webb (1953).

17.   D. Gunston, "Zoos through the Ages," *Zoo Life* 3 (1948): 21–23.

18.   Introduction to Attenborough (1980).

19.   David Attenborough's later TV productions apparently had an even greater influence on young zoologists. According to Charles Arthur and Fiona Sturges, demand in Britain for university places in zoology increased as a direct result of Attenborough's *Life on Earth* series (1979), leading a new generation of zoologists to be called "Attenborough's children" ("TV Wildlife Fans Queue Up to Be Zoologists," *Independent on Sunday* [London], 23 March 1997).

20.   D. Attenborough, "Expedition to Sierra Leone," *Zoo Life* 10 (1955): 11–20.

21.   Durrell (1976).

22.   Attenborough (1956).

23.   "Fernando Po: Spain in Africa," *Geographical Magazine* 36 (1964): 540–46.

24.   J. Oates, "Expedition to Fernando Po," *Animals* 7 (1965): 86–91.

25.   Kingsley (1897).

26.   Charles-Dominique (1977).

TWO. FROM COLLECTING TO CONSERVATION

1.   In 1965 Bioko had the highest per capita GNP in tropical Africa. In 1979, after eleven years of bloody dictatorial rule by Francisco Macias Nguema, a third of the population had left the country and the economy of Bioko had collapsed; Macias Nguema was executed in a coup in 1979 (Fegley [1991]).

2.   J. Hemingway quotes William Drury Jr.'s comments on attempts to collect an African cattle egret seen in the United States in 1952: "Before the environmental movement, if you wanted to convince people that you had found a rare bird, you shot it." Hemingway, "An African Bird Makes Its Move around the World," *Smithsonian* 18 (1987): 60–68.

3.   Moorehead (1959).

4.   In a postscript to *A Zoo in My Luggage,* Durrell (1960) talks of his new Jersey Zoo as a place that can interest people in animal life and conservation; Carson (1962).

5.   Fitter and Scott (1978); "History of WWF," document on WWF's World Wide Web site, 1997.

6.   Fitter and Scott (1978).

7.   It was later to become the Fauna and Flora Preservation Society and then, in 1995, Fauna and Flora International.

8.   Worthington (1950).

9.   Fitter and Scott (1978).

10.   Yates (1935); Cowie (1961).

11.   Schaller (1963).

12.   Goodall (1963).

13.   Beadle (1974); Eltringham (1969).

14.   See Lamprey (1969); among some of the notable projects conducted in the early days of SRI were those of H. Kruuk on spotted hyenas, G. Schaller on lions, P. Jarman on impala, A. R. E. Sinclair on buffalo, and R. H. V. Bell on grassland utilization by ungulates.

15.   Jewell (1963).

16.   *Euoticus* (or *Galago) inustus;* now called *G. matschiei* (L. Nash et al. [1989]).

17.   Listowel (1973); Sathamurthy (1986).

18.   In older accounts, *Igbo* is often spelled *Ibo.*

19.   Schwarz (1968).

20.   Oates and Jewell (1967).

21.   Even in 1963, most of Igboland had a density of more than 388 people per square mile, and some parts supported 1,036 people per square mile (Afolayan and Barbour [1982]); in 1950, Rwanda had 33 people per square mile (World Resources Institute [1994]).

22.   R. L. Bryant, "The Rise and Fall of *Taungya* Forestry: Social Forestry in Defence of the Empire," *Ecologist* 24 (1994): 21–26.

23.   Grove (1992).

24.   Adeyoju (1975); P. R. O. Kio, J. E. Abu, and R. G. Lowe, "High Forest Management in Nigeria" (paper presented to the International Union of Forest Research Organizations, Eberswalde, Germany, 1992).

25.   J. F. Oates, "Wildlife of Biafra," *Animals* 11 (1968): 266–68; J. F. Oates, "The Lower Primates of Eastern Nigeria," *African Wild Life* 23 (1969): 321–32.

26.   Even in 1997, debate continued about the extent to which people as a whole in Eastern Nigeria supported secession or were coerced by Ojukwu and his associates. Chief Mokwugo Okoye was quoted in the national press as saying that dissidents to secession were not encouraged: "If you were called a saboteur, anything could happen to you" (S. Igboanugo, "Controversy Thick-

ens over Ojukwu's Role in Declaration of Secession," *Guardian* [Lagos], 13 January 1997).

27.   Reader's Digest Association (1970).

28.   T. J. Synnott, "Working Plan for the Mt. Elgon Central Forest Reserve" (Uganda Forest Department, Entebbe, 1968, unpublished).

29.   Struhsaker (1975); Oates (1977).

30.   Struhsaker (1972).

31.   Taï became a national park in 1972, Korup became a national park in 1986, and Kibale became a national park in 1994. Plans for a national park at Douala-Edéa were shelved after the start of oil exploration there in 1979.

32.   H. D. Thoreau, quoted in R. Nash (1973).

33.   R. Nash (1973).

34.   Ibid., chapter 13.

35.   Naess (1985); Naess (1986); Nations (1988).

36.   Quoted by R. Nash (1973), p. 49; Kramer and van Schaik (1997) make a similar point about the historical roots of differences in conservation approaches in the United States and Europe.

37.   Fethersonhaugh (1951).

38.   Regarding the forests on Mount Nimba, see Coe and Curry-Lindahl (1965); regarding the Taï Forest, see H. H. Roth, "We All Want Trees—Case History of the Taï National Park in Ivory Coast" (World Conservation Monitoring Centre, Cambridge (circa 1982), unpublished).

39.   Yates (1935).

40.   Cowie (1961). Cowie died in 1996 at the age of eighty-eight; in an obituary, Richard Fitter described him as "the father of East African wildlife conservation," and said that "without his energy and persistence most of Kenya's national parks might well not have been declared in time, and so now be submerged under farmland and even industrial development" (*Oryx* 30 [1996]: 235).

41.   J. L. Mason and J. F. Oates, "Blue Mountains of the Moon," *Geographical Magazine* 49 (1977): 648–53. A Rwenzori Mountains National Park was declared in 1991.

42.   Sathyamurthy (1986).

43.   K. G. van Orsdol, "The Extent of Poaching by Tanzanian Soldiers and Ugandan Civilians in Ugandan National Parks" (5 August 1979, unpublished report); see also Struhsaker (1997).

44.   Edroma (1980).

45.   Struhsaker (1997).

46.   Adams and McShane (1992).

47.   Terzian (1985); Ghanem (1986).

48.   From a report of the Secretary-General of the United Nations, reprinted in *Population and Development Review* 17 (1991): 749–51. Such trends have caused

the 1980s to be called Africa's "lost decade" (J. Darnton, "In Poor, Decolonized Africa, Bankers Are New Overlords," *New York Times*, 20 June 1994; McNeely et al. [1994]).

49.   World Resources Institute (1996).

50.   Davies and Oates (1994).

51.   Green and Minkowski (1977).

52.   S. Green, personal communication to the author, March 1998.

53.   In 1997, Haidar was India's Foreign Affairs Minister.

54.   Malhotra (1989).

55.   On Gandhi's interest in wildlife conservation, see Malhotra (1989). In a foreword to Gee (1964), Nehru had written, "Life would become very dull and colourless if we did not have these magnificent animals and birds to look at and to play with. We should, therefore, encourage as many sanctuaries as possible for the preservation of what yet remains of our wild life. Our forests are essential for us from many points of view. Let us preserve them. As it is, we have de-stroyed them far too much." Gandhi's concern about lion-tailed macaque pro-tection is stated in a letter from S. Haidar to S. Green (5 November 1975).

56.   *Hindu* (Madras), 1 February 1976.

57.   At the height of the cold war, and especially after 1971, American scholars were frequently denied visas for research in India or, if they were admitted to the country, often suspected of being secret agents (B. Crossette, "From Guru to Rogue: America Re-examines India," *New York Times*, 17 May 1998). My 1975–76 studies received only provisional clearance from the Indian government, which never issued full permission despite many meetings and correspondence with officials; I could therefore have been asked to leave at any time. In 1980, Harvard graduate student James Moore had to abandon his planned studies of langurs in northwest India when the state government similarly failed to follow through with a formal research permit after giving him provisional clearance (J. Moore, personal communication to the author, 1997).

58.   Peter Scott, in introduction to Scott and Scott (1962).

THREE. CONSERVATION FALLS IN LOVE
WITH ECONOMIC DEVELOPMENT

1.   "Ecology in Development Programmes: An IUCN Action Project," *IUCN Bulletin*, n.s., 2 (1970): 141.

2.   Nicholson (1970).

3.   Cramp et al. (1977); *The Birds of the Western Palearctic* was completed with the publication of volume 9 in 1994, a volume for which Nicholson wrote the

foreword. Nicholson summarizes the history of his work in ornithology and conservation in a chapter entitled "Ecology and Conservation: Our Pilgrim's Progress," Goldsmith and Warren (1993), pp. 3–14.

4.   Grzimek and Grzimek (1960); Cowie (1961).

5.   Writing in 1969, Fisher, Simon, and Vincent said that the ultimate protection of nature demanded, among other things "an enlightened exploitation of its wild resources based on scientific research and measurement" (Fisher et al. [1969]). In 1972 Michael Crawford wrote, "With present population pressures on land in Europe and Africa, the only hope for the remaining large mammals is conservation through utilisation" (Crawford [1972]).

6.   For instance, the number of articles in the *New York Times* on the environment climbed from about 150 in 1960 to about 1,700 in 1970 (W. Sachs, "Environment and Development: The Story of a Dangerous Liaison," *The Ecologist* 21 [1991]: 252–57).

7.   Provisional International Union for the Protection of Nature (1947).

8.   Fitter and Scott (1978); "Turning Points Interview: Max Nicholson," *Earthlife News* no. 5 (1986): 57–58; "History of WWF," document on WWF's World Wide Web site, 1997.

9.   Sachs (1991), see note 6.

10.   Ward and Dubos (1972).

11.   *IUCN Bulletin*, n.s., 3 (1972).

12.   *IUCN Bulletin*, n.s., 6 (1975): 23.

13.   From 1975 to 1978, IUCN received $2.8 million from UNEP (*IUCN Bulletin*, n.s., 10 [1979]: 58).

14.   *IUCN Bulletin*, n.s., 8 (1977): 30.

15.   Ibid., 35.

16.   *IUCN Bulletin*, n.s., 10 (1979): 58.

17.   *IUCN Bulletin*, n.s., 6 (1975): 13.

18.   R. Allen (1973).

19.   *Second Draft of a World Conservation Strategy* (Morges, Switzerland: IUCN, UNEP, and WWF, 1978).

20.   IUCN, UNEP, and WWF (1980).

21.   *IUCN Bulletin*, n.s., 11 (1980): 33–34.

22.   In preface to R. Allen (1980).

23.   Sachs (1991), see note 6.

24.   IUCN, *An Introduction to the World Conservation Strategy* (IUCN, Gland, Switzerland, 1984).

25.   Meier (1995).

26.   Rich (1994).

27.   World Commission on Environment and Development (1987).

28. From the explanatory publication *Global Environment Facility* (World Bank, Washington, D.C., December 1991).

29. Mittermeier and Bowles (1994).

30. IUCN, UNEP, and WWF (1991).

31. Gibson and Marks (1995).

32. Midgley (1986).

33. G. Allen (1981).

34. Midgley (1986).

35. Arensberg (1961).

36. Redfield (1955) says that a human community is defined by four qualities: "distinctiveness, smallness, homogeneity, and all-providing self-sufficiency."

37. Midgley (1986).

38. Gibson and Marks (1995); Midgley (1986).

39. Hill (1986).

40. Turnbull (1972).

41. Kideckel (1993); ironically, socialist Romania was cited by Ward and Dubos (1972) as a good example of effective urban and land use planning by a central government in a partially industrialized society.

42. IUCN, UNEP, and WWF (1991), p. 57.

43. See, for instance, International Institute for Environment and Development (1994); and Wells (1995).

44. Biodiversity Support Program (1993).

45. Lewis and Carter (1993). The short span of the colonial era is rarely mentioned in such accounts. Colonial control did not extend to much of Africa's interior until after the Berlin West Africa Conference of 1884–85, and the era began to close with Ghana's independence in 1957.

46. Ludwig et al. (1993).

47. Spinage (1996).

48. Redford (1991).

49. Robinson (1993).

50. Brandon and Wells (1992).

51. Noss (1997).

52. E. M. Pires, "The Rhetoric and Reality of Decentralized Natural Resource Management in Senegal" (paper presented at the 91st Annual Meeting of the Association of American Geographers, Chicago, Ill., March 1995).

53. The political compromise embedded within *Caring for the Earth* has been openly acknowledged by David Munro and Martin Holdgate (Holdgate succeeded Munro as Director General of IUCN). Responding to Robinson's critique, they stress that *Caring for the Earth* was written for a political purpose, namely to win the support of "the governments in the species-rich tropical countries who

are trying to improve the desperate conditions of hundreds of millions of their citizens" (Holdgate and Munro [1993]).

FOUR. TIWAI

1. Fyfe (1962).
2. Holsoe (1977).
3. Grace (1977).
4. Ibid.
5. Pa Luseni Koroma was the town chief when I first visited Kambama in 1979. When I interviewed him in 1983 about the history of Kambama and Tiwai, I estimated that he was more than ninety years old.
6. The meeting described by Pa Luseni sounds remarkably similar to the meeting of chiefs called by T. J. Alldridge in Bandasuma, south of Kambama, in March 1890; at Bandasuma, Alldridge met "the Queen, Niarro, of that country." To quote Alldridge (1901), "I told [the people] that for many generations tribal wars had been going on; but that now the British Government would no longer permit these wars. It was therefore proposed that the chiefs should be invited to enter into a friendly treaty with the Government, pledging themselves to cease from war, and also to permit British subjects to come into their countries for the purpose of trading." Alternatively, Pa Luseni may have been recalling a meeting in Bandasuma in March 1893, again arranged by Alldridge, at which one hundred chiefs from the region were called to meet the Governor of Sierra Leone, Sir Francis Fleming; a major purpose of this meeting was to bring chiefs into friendly communication with each other (Alldridge [1901], p. 169).
7. David Attenborough also had to wade through a rice swamp on his first trek in Sierra Leone in search of *Picathartes* (D. Attenborough, "Expedition to Sierra Leone," *Zoo Life* 10 [1955]: 11–20).
8. About half a mile below Kambama, the river runs into rock formations and breaks up into a series of small channels with tumbling rapids. We were later to learn to our cost that these rapids were a prime breeding site for onchocerciasis-transmitting blackflies. Several other Tiwai researchers and I became infected with onchocerciasis (river blindness) during our stay on the island.
9. Struhsaker and Oates (1975).
10. Primate taxonomists usually group the different African colobus species into three main sets, or subgenera: the black-and-white (*Colobus*), the red (*Piliocolobus*), and the olive colobus (*Procolobus*). Apart from the coat-color features that have given these monkeys their different common names, the three types of colobus have a range of anatomical and behavioral differences. In some respects

the olive colobus more closely resembles the red colobus (for instance, females have a swelling of their perineal tissue around the time of ovulation), but it has several unique attributes; among other things, the olive colobus is only about half the body weight of the red colobus (making it the smallest of all colobine monkeys), and it is the only monkey in which the infant, instead of clinging to the mother's coat, is carried in her mouth (Oates et al. [1994]).

11.   Booth (1957).

12.   Booth (1954, 1958).

13.   Grubb (1978).

14.   Hill (1952).

15.   The circumstances of Booth's death are mysterious. For many years I heard rumors that he had died from a virus infection acquired from a monkey, but his wife, Cynthia P. Booth, informs me that his doctor did not know what his illness was; his death certificate recorded "encephalitis," but there are suggestions that he might have been poisoned (C. P. Booth, in letter to the author, 11 April 1991).

16.   In 1982, Jacques Verschuren reported that there was one gun for every twelve inhabitants of Liberia, and that more than thirteen thousand guns were sold *officially* in 1977; he said that no game survived within four miles of main highways and that monkeys were seen only in remote areas (Verschuren [1982]).

17.   This information is from Theo Jones, who had worked at Njala from 1945 until 1960 and had once lived in the fine colonial-era house overlooking the Taia River, occupied in 1979 by Peter White. Jones was involved in efforts to control crop damage by animals, including monkeys. Because monkeys were not hunted in those days, they were abundant and caused serious damage to crops such as maize, coffee, and cocoa. This led to a series of "monkey drives," in which more than ten thousand monkeys were killed each year in the late 1940s and early 1950s (T. S. Jones, personal communication to the author, 1985; see also Mackenzie [1952]). It was during these drives that the olive colobus was first discovered in Sierra Leone. Jones helped Jack Lester on his postwar collecting trips to Sierra Leone for London Zoo and organized the logistics for Jack Lester and David Attenborough on the first *Zoo Quest* expedition in 1954; Njala was the expedition's base (T. S. Jones, personal communication to the author; Attenborough [1955], cited in note 7). From Sierra Leone, Jones moved to Uganda, where he became Permanent Secretary in the Agriculture Department and assisted Steve Gartlan during his Ph.D. studies in the early 1960s. His next posting was to Cameroon, where as a manager with the Cameroon Development Corporation he met Struhsaker and Gartlan during their primate surveys described in chapter 6. Jones died in 1996, soon after my last meeting with him.

18.   Even sixty years ago, F. J. Martin wrote, "rain forest . . . probably does not exceed 5% of the whole country" (1938).

19. Durrell (1972).

20. Norman Myers has estimated that in the years 1966–74, Ivory Coast lost 39.9 percent of its closed forest as a result of logging and subsequent cultivation (1980).

21. Subsequently, both Anh and Gérard Galat wrote doctoral dissertations based on their observations in Taï, and they published one major paper on the community ecology of the Taï monkeys (Galat and Galat-Luong [1985]).

22. J. F. Oates, "Report on a Pilot Study of *Colobus verus* and Other Forest Monkeys in Southern Sierra Leone with Comments on Conservation Problems" (report to Sierra Leone Forestry Division, 1980, unpublished). This report was sent to the Chief Conservator of Forests in Sierra Leone; through its Wildlife Conservation Branch, the government's Forestry Division has responsibility for administering wildlife policies.

23. J. Phillipson, "Wildlife Conservation and Management in Sierra Leone" (report to Ministry of Agriculture and Natural Resources, Freetown, and the British Council, 1978, unpublished).

24. White left Njala in 1986 and was succeeded by Abu Sesay; the master's program never commenced. Because of a lack of agreement with local people over the terms of compensation for their land and other problems, the Outamba-Kilimi National Park was not gazetted until 1995.

25. See, for example, Oates (1988); Whitesides (1991); Dasilva (1994); Fimbel (1994); C. M. Hill (1994).

26. Oates et al. (1990).

27. Moller and Brown (1990); Bakarr et al. (1991); Hartley (1992).

28. The documentary film *Tiwai: Island of the Apes* was first broadcast on "Survival Special" in the United Kingdom on August 16, 1991, and on WNET's "Nature" in the U.S. on January 13, 1992. The chimpanzee nut-cracking behavior at Tiwai is described in Whitesides (1985).

29. *Sierra Leone Gazette* (Freetown), 29 October 1987.

30. Alieu (1995).

31. A typical Mende chiefdom is subdivided into sections, under section chiefs; each section is subdivided into towns, with town chiefs; and each town is divided into households, or extended families, each of which has a head. A chiefdom is ruled by a council, usually made up of the heads of extended families, and these councilors elect the Paramount Chief, or Mahei. The right to use land is also divided among sections, towns, and families. Families with use-rights to a parcel of land continue to have the right to use it, and while the Paramount Chief is the trustee of the land, he cannot expropriate the right of a family to use their land. However, the chiefdom council can make a law that governs how land is to be used, if this is agreed to be for the general good (Kelfala Kallon, personal communication to the author, 1996).

32.   J. I. Clarke has noted that many chiefdom boundaries are ill-defined "and are causes of dispute, especially in alluvial diamond mining areas where river boundaries are common" (1969).

33.   Alldridge (1901).

34.   Abraham (1978).

35.   Alldridge (1901) describes concluding a treaty with Paramount Chief Joseh of Koya at "Borbabu" on April 20, 1890.

36.   In the mid-1980s, several of us working in Sierra Leone came to the view that there was a need for a nongovernmental organization in which a variety of people concerned with conservation issues could actively participate. There was already one conservation nongovernmental organization, the Sierra Leone Environment and Nature Conservation Association (SLENCA), but members could join SLENCA only by invitation. Glyn Davies and I tried to persuade Daphne Toboku-Metzger, the Secretary of SLENCA, to open the association to general membership and to sponsor a public seminar on conservation problems in the country. Toboku-Metzger declined, citing suspicion of forestry personnel, whom she said might join the organization and undermine it. We therefore encouraged the formation of a new organization, and this was founded in 1986 as the Conservation Society of Sierra Leone, initially supported by a grant from the Macarthur Foundation administered by WWF-US. We proposed Sama S. Banya, a former government minister, as the first president, for he was a respected man who had shown a great deal of interest in the Tiwai project and other conservation matters.

37.   Eichenlaub laid out a zoning arrangement in his management plan, which appeared the following year ("Tiwai Island Wildlife Sanctuary: General Management Plan," [Tiwai Island Administrative Committee, Freetown, 1989]); although this plan appeared under the name of the Tiwai Island Administrative Committee, it was written by Eichenlaub.

38.   The CCF alone gave permission for the Anglia documentary film crew to operate at Tiwai. The Anglia crew took over part of the field station, erected metal towers in the primate study area, and encouraged local people to bring them animals that could be filmed (thereby inevitably encouraging hunting and trapping in areas near Tiwai); my understanding is that in return the film crew promised to provide the Forestry Division with a film projector. The researchers at Tiwai were not consulted about how the filmmakers would operate, and although the filmmaking was a commercial undertaking, no payment was made to the chiefdoms or to the research or conservation projects.

39.   Luke and Riley (1989).

40.   For population figures, see Clarke (1969); World Bank (1984).

41.   Luke and Riley (1989).

42.   United Nations Development Programme (1991).

43. A very similar situation arose through the misrule and corruption of Mobutu's regime in Zaire (now the Democratic Republic of Congo), which was eventually overthrown by a rebel insurgency. "The pauperization . . . meant that Government officials take bribes, doctors ignore patients who do not offer gifts, factory workers steal parts from assembly lines, and soldiers wave guns to get 'donations'" (N. D. Kristof, "In Congo, a New Era with Old Burdens," *New York Times*, 20 May 1997). In his book *The Ends of the Earth*, Robert Kaplan uses Sierra Leone as a paradigm for the collapse of the nation-state in the Third World (Kaplan, 1996).

44. K. R. Noble, "Liberian President Leads the Good Life While His Country Grows Poorer," *New York Times*, 26 March 1990.

45. K. R. Noble, "Liberian Conflict Engulfs Neighbor," *New York Times*, 16 April 1991.

46. Our Freetown Correspondent, "The Dust Settles," *West Africa*, 18–24 May 1992, pp. 840–41.

47. Reuters news agency report, 28 February 1995.

48. Richards (1996); Reuters News Agency Report, 23 October 1998.

49. In May 1996, David Orr reported on gross atrocities in rural areas, which an Amnesty International representative said could have no reason "apart from inspiring terror in the civilian population" ("A Nation Sinks into Savagery," *Independent on Sunday* [London], 5 May 1996). The idea that access to diamonds was the main concern of the rebels is supported by the observation that most violence occurred in the diamond-producing areas of the country (report by G. Aligiarh, *BBC Television News*, 30 January 1996); it is probably not coincidental that, unlike gold and several other commodities whose prices have increased little or declined in recent years, average diamond prices rose 50 percent between 1986 and 1996 ("Glass with Attitude," *Economist* [20 December 1997]: 113–15). An alternative view is offered by anthropologist Paul Richards, who has argued that the rebels' aims were essentially political, to replace a patrimonial system with a grassroots democracy, and that much looting was done by bandits imitating the rebels (Richards, 1996).

50. E. Rubin, "An Army of One's Own," *Harper's Magazine* (February 1997): 44–55; D. G. McNeil, "Pocketing the Wages of War," *New York Times, Week in Review*, 16 February 1997; Reuters news agency report, online, 7 March 1998.

51. H. W. French, "African Rebel with Room Service," *New York Times*, 23 June 1996; H. W. French, "Sierra Leone a Triumph of Peacemaking by Africans," *New York Times*, 2 December 1996.

52. Situation report from Momoh Magona, 13 January 1998.

53. "Fighting in Sierra Leone with Hunters Kills 80," Reuters news agency report in the *New York Times*, 7 May 1997; Reuters news agency report, online, 10 May 1997.

54.   This summary of events surrounding the May 1997 coup is based on information I gathered from newspapers and radio broadcasts while traveling in England, Nigeria, and Ghana in May–July 1997.

55.   H. W. French, "Nigerians Take Capital of Sierra Leone as Junta Flees," *New York Times*, 14 February 1998; R. Bonner, "U.S. Reportedly Backed British Mercenary Group in Africa," *New York Times*, 13 May 1998. In an echo of the reported arrangements between Executive Outcomes and the Strasser government, the mercenary group Sandline International is said by Bonner to have been awarded diamond concessions in Sierra Leone.

56.   While I was making final revisions to my manuscript, I received from the Chief Conservator of Forests in Freetown another report from Magona, dated April 30, 1998. Magona described a visit to Tiwai in August 1997, during which he found evidence of continued hunting and mining and saw that the field station building was badly damaged. As of April 1998, Kamajor militia were said to be in control of the area and people were returning to their villages, but all the houses in Kambama had been burned down and people were living in temporary thatched structures.

57.   D. Orr, "Boy Soldiers Get Lesson in Peace," *Independent* (London), 1 May 1996.

58.   Oates (1986a).

59.   Hardiman (1986).

FIVE. OKOMU

1.   In a review of the status of all the world's primates published in 1983, Jaclyn Wolfheim noted that there was no evidence on the species' present existence, and she cited a 1974 personal communication from Stephen Gartlan to the effect that it might be extinct (Wolfheim [1983]).

2.   Menzies (1970).

3.   World Resources Institute (1988).

4.   A. Cowell, "Oil: Nigeria's Mixed Blessing," *New York Times*, 23 July 1981.

5.   Oates (1982).

6.   In the coming years I was to see many individuals of *C. erythrogaster* in the wild in Nigeria; all had gray bellies. It was not until 1994 that I discovered a population with rust bellies living in the Lama Forest in the south of the Bénin Republic, west of Nigeria.

7.   Rosevear (1953).

8.   Lowe (1996).

9.   Personal communication from the Deputy Chief Conservator of Forests, Bendel State, June 1982.

10. Chief Conservator of Forests, "Working Plan for the Benin Division African Timber and Plywood Forests" (Western Region Department of Forestry, Ibadan, 1950, unpublished).

11. Nicholas Harman, "The Most African Country," *Economist* (23 January 1982).

12. A valuable perspective on political, economic, and social changes in Nigeria since 1947 is provided in the memoir by J. L. Brandler (1993). Brandler developed a major timber business that operated in Western Nigeria, Cross River, Cameroon, and Liberia.

13. "Chief S. L. Edu—Profile of the Chairman," *Nigerian Conservation Foundation Newsletter* (December 1984): 5.

14. P. A. Anadu and J. F. Oates, "The Status of Wildlife in Bendel State, Nigeria, with Recommendations for Its Conservation" (report to Bendel State Ministry of Agriculture and Natural Resources, Benin City; the Nigerian Federal Ministry of Agriculture, Lagos; and the Nigerian Conservation Foundation, Lagos, 1982, unpublished).

15. "Drowning in Unsold Oil," *Time* (12 April 1982): 48. By the end of November 1998, North Sea Brent crude oil (similar to Nigeria's crude) had fallen in price to less than eleven dollars per barrel.

16. World Bank (1984); World Resources Institute (1988).

17. *Bendel State of Nigeria Gazette*, notice no. 198, vol. 22, no. 52 (11 December 1986): 305.

18. "Working Plan for the Benin Division African Timber and Plywood Forests" (1950), see note 10.

19. P. J. Darling, "Masterplan for Okomu Forest Reserve, Edo State, Nigeria" (draft report to the Nigerian Conservation Foundation, Lagos; WWF, Godalming, Surrey; and ODA, London, February 1995).

20. Ibid.

21. L. J. T. White, personal communication to the author, 1989.

22. Press release from D. I. Aimufia, Director of Forestry, Bendel State, 1 November 1988.

23. Letter from P. A. Anadu to Professor Agnes Uduebor, Commissioner for Agriculture and Natural Resources, Bendel State, 20 March 1990.

24. Letter from P. A. Anadu to Col. Tunde Ogbeha, Military Governor of Bendel State, 2 May 1990.

25. Holland et al. (1989).

26. L. J. T. White, letter to the author, 9 November 1988.

27. D. M. Edwards, "Wildlife Consultancy Report to the Forestry Assistance Project, Okomu Forest Reserve, Bendel State, Nigeria, 12 February–9 March 1990" (draft report to ODA, London, March 1990).

28. J. Hudson, ODA Forestry Projects Manager, letter to the author, 23 September 1992.

29. "Okomu Benin Native Authority Forest Reserve (Amendment) Order, 1950," Benin Division Native Authority, Native Authority Public Notice no. 86 of 1950.

30. F. I. Omorodion, "Socio-Economic Survey of Okomu Forest Reserve, Final Report" (Nigerian Conservation Foundation, Lagos, December 1991, unpublished).

31. R. Okunlola, "Okomu Forest Reserve Support Zone Income Generation Activities Report" (Nigerian Conservation Foundation, Lagos, 22 February 1993, unpublished).

32. D. I. Aimufia, Director of Forestry, Edo State, personal communication to the author.

33. B. Coates, "Cost Benefit Analysis of Land Use Alternatives, Okomu Forest Reserve" (advisory paper submitted on behalf of WWF/NCF to Governor of Edo State, June 1993).

34. Darling (1975).

35. R. Barnwell, letter to the author, 16 September 1996.

36. See note 19.

37. In 1997, reports reached NCF headquarters in Lagos that logging had been taking place within the wildlife sanctuary since 1992. An investigatory team visited Okomu in February 1998 and confirmed these reports. Several NCF employees were implicated in this illegal activity, and they were dismissed or reprimanded (personal communication from Philip Hall, June 1998).

38. White and Oates (in press).

39. J. F. Oates and L. J. T. White, "Advisory Paper on the Conservation of the Okomu Forest Reserve, Edo State, Nigeria" (report to Nigerian Conservation Foundation, Lagos, April 1996, unpublished).

40. Philip Hall, personal communication to the author, 23 June 1997.

41. T. B. Larsen, "Report on the Butterflies of the Okomu Nature Reserve (25–29 November 1996)" (Nigerian Conservation Foundation, Lagos, 1996, unpublished).

42. World Resources Institute (1996).

SIX. PEOPLE FIRST: THE CROSS RIVER NATIONAL PARK

1. Collier (1934).

2. Petrides (1965).

3. Hall (1981).

4. Talbot (1912).

5. Rosevear (1979).

6. For example, C. M. Wicks in "Okwangwo and Korup Coastal Rainforest Conservation Projects," a proposal to the Commission of the European Communities (WWF-UK, Godalming, 1992).

7.   Brandler (1993).

8.   Talbot (1912) described walking in 1909 from Oban to Aking along "a forest path, 8 to 10 feet wide, clear of trees, fern-fringed and carpeted ankle-deep with a thousand little flowers."

9.   J. F. Oates, "Wildlife of Biafra," *Animals* II, (1968): 266–68.

10.   According to J. L. Brandler, whose company had initiated the Calvenply operation, U.S. Plywood sold its interest in the mill soon after the end of the civil war to the South-Eastern State government, huge losses were incurred, and the mill never made a profit (Brandler [1993]).

11.   Ash and Sharland (1986).

12.   J. S. Ash, "Nigeria: Surveys of Selected Bird Conservation Areas (Wetlands and Forests)" (International Council for Bird Preservation, Cambridge; and the Nigerian Conservation Foundation, Lagos, March 1987, site reports).

13.   L. J. T. White and J. C. Reid, "Survey of Nigerian Forest Areas to the East of the Cross River Adjacent to the Korup National Park in the Camerouns" (Nigerian Conservation Foundation, Lagos, 1988, unpublished).

14.   Struhsaker (1975); T. Struhsaker, personal communication to the author, October 1996.

15.   T. T. Struhsaker, "Preliminary Report on a Survey of the Korup Reserve, West Cameroon" (report to New York Zoological Society, Bronx, N.Y., 24 April 1970, unpublished).

16.   Letter from R. G. Goelet, President of New York Zoological Society, to the President of Cameroon, 29 March 1971.

17.   J. S. Gartlan and T. T. Struhsaker, "A Second Reconnaissance of the Douala-Edéa Reserve" (1972, unpublished report).

18.   Balinga (1986); J. S. Gartlan, personal communication to the author, March 1997.

19.   J. S. Gartlan, personal communication to the author, October 1996.

20.   J. S. Gartlan, "The Korup National Park: A Strategy for Rainforest Conservation" (report in the files of World Conservation Monitoring Centre, Cambridge, U.K., 1987, unpublished).

21.   J. S. Gartlan and P. C. Agland, "A Proposal for a Program of Rain-Forest Conservation and National Park Development in Cameroon, West-Central Africa" (World Wildlife Fund, Gland, Switzerland, 1981, unpublished).

22.   "A Charity for the Eighties," *Earthlife News* no. 5 (1986): 7.

23.   B. Johnson, ed. *Paradise Lost?* (London: Earthlife Foundation, 1986).

24.   In 1987 the Overseas Development Administration was renamed the Department for International Development.

25.   Wicks (1986).

26.   Gartlan and Macleod (1986).

27.   Julian Caldecott, personal communication to the author, June 1996.

28.   Appendix 6 to Caldecott, Oates, and Ruitenbeek (1990).

29.   M. Infield, "No Small Measures in Korup National Park," *WWF Reports* (December 1988– January 1989): 12–15.

30.   J. A. Powell, "Korup Forest Research Project: Status Report, January-June 1991" (WCI and USAID, 1991); "New Poaching Threat to Forest Elephants," *WCI Bulletin* (March– April 1991): W1, W4. In January 1991, WCI held a workshop at the Ikenge station for the scientists of its central African forests program; some of the participants in this workshop later told me how few large mammals they had seen in the park, presumably because of the high and continuing hunting pressure.

31.   J. Powell, personal communication to the author, October 1996.

32.   J. S. Gartlan, personal communication to the author, October 1996.

33.   K. Horta, "The Last Big Rush for the Green Gold: The Plundering of Cameroon's Rainforests," *Ecologist* 21 (1991): 142–47.

34.   World Wide Fund for Nature, United Kingdom, "Proposal for the Creation of the Oban National Park and Supporting Integrated Rural Development Programme" (WWF-UK, Godalming, England, 1988).

35.   Caldecott (1986).

36.   Caldecott (1988).

37.   Caldecott (1996).

38.   Ibid.

39.   Holland et al. (1989).

40.   Caldecott et al. (1989).

41.   The Chief Conservator of Forests of Cross River State, Dr. G. E. Ogar, wrote to the Permanent Secretary in the State Ministry of Agriculture and Natural Resources on January 14, 1987, noting that there was a long-standing proposal to convert the Boshi and Boshi Extension as well as the Okwangwo Forest Reserves into sanctuaries or game reserves, but that the plans had been impeded by a lack of funds.

42.   Obudu Cattle Ranching Company, Limited, *Information Leaflet* (Obudu Cattle Ranching Company, Obudu, Nigeria, n.d.).

43.   The ornithologist John Elgood visited the Obudu Plateau in 1960, 1961, and 1962 and added six new bird species to the Nigerian list, but he also noted the changing conditions brought by the establishment of the cattle ranch and hoped that those responsible for future developments would be aware "of the need to conserve this unique habitat" (Elgood [1965]).

44.   J. Allen (1931).

45.   Sanderson (1937, 1940). The Cameroonian forests to the southeast of the Obudu Plateau have a limited degree of protection as the Takamanda Forest Reserve.

46.   March (1957). Until the formation of the Federal National Parks Authority in 1991, all wildlife protection in Nigeria was the responsibility of state and federal Forestry Departments.

47.   P. O. Nwoga, "Eastern Regional Notice no. 529, Eastern Region Forest Law, 1955 (E.R. no. 41 of 1955), Boshi Extension Forest Reserve," *Eastern Region of Nigeria Gazette* 7, no. 36 (12 June 1958): 328.

48.   T. T. Struhsaker, "Preliminary Report on a Survey of High Forest Primates in West Cameroon" (report to New York Zoological Society, Bronx, N.Y., 17 January 1967, unpublished report).

49.   Cousins (1978).

50.   Ebin (1983).

51.   From the transcript of a 1983 speech by the Cross River State Commissioner of Natural Resources, Okon J. Ndok, in the files of the Forestry Department, Obudu.

52.   Ebin (1983).

53.   Ash and Sharland (1986).

54.   Collier (1934).

55.   Ash (1987), cited in note 12; J. S. Ash, "Surveys of *Picathartes oreas, Malimbus ibadanensis* and Other Species in Nigeria" (International Council for Bird Preservation and the Nigerian Conservation Foundation, Lagos, November 1987, unpublished); Ash (1991).

56.   Fossey and Harcourt (1977); Harcourt and Groom (1972); Harcourt (1981).

57.   J. H. Mshelbwala, "Kanyang Mountain Gorilla Report" (Nigerian Conservation Foundation, Lagos, 27 July 1987, unpublished); I. M. Inaharo, "Kanyang Gorilla Project" (Nigerian Conservation Foundation, Lagos, 24 August 1987, unpublished).

58.   In December 1986, before the survey by Harcourt et al., evidence for the continuing presence of gorillas on the edge of the Obudu Plateau was found by David Harris of the Ahmadu Bello University at Zaria in northern Nigeria when he visited the cattle ranch with two companions and saw gorilla nests and dung in the nearby forest; these observations were reported to the IUCN/SSC Primate Specialist Group (see Harris et al. [1987]), but apparently not to the NCF (I. M. Inaharo, personal communication to the author, March 1990).

59.   Harcourt et al. (1989).

60.   J. Brooke, "Nigerians Discover Gorillas Thought Extinct," *New York Times*, 1 August 1988.

61.   J. F. Oates, D. White, E. L. Gadsby, and P. O. Bisong, "Conservation of Gorillas and Other Species," unpublished appendix to Caldecott et al. (1990).

62.   Elgood (1965); Hall (1981).

63.   Ash and Sharland (1986).

64. Caldecott et al. (1990).

65. One ECU was worth $1.21 in January 1990 and $1.34 in January 1991.

66. An example of how real the risk is from armed poachers is provided by an article in the *Guardian* newspaper in Lagos dated January 22, 1997. The article reports how a former Commissioner of Agriculture in Ogun State (Mrs. Iyabo Anisulowo) had encountered log thieves during a tour of inspection of a state forest reserve: "As the Commissioner's entourage chased them, the robbers opened fire on the officials, who beat a retreat."

67. Caldecott (1996).

68. Adams and McShane (1992).

69. Minutes of a meeting at the Directorate-General for Development, Commission of the European Communities, Brussels, 16 March 1992.

70. Directorate-General for Development, Commission of the European Communities, "Terms of Reference and Objectives, T.A. Contracts Nos. 1 & 2, Programme Oban Hills, Nigeria" (Commission of the European Communities, Brussels, February 1992); C. M. Wicks in "Okwangwo and Korup Coastal Rainforest Conservation Projects" (proposal to the Commission of the European Communities, WWF-UK, Godalming, England, 1992).

71. From conversations during 1996 with the Director of National Parks, Federal Republic of Nigeria, the General Manager of Cross River National Park, and Elizabeth Gadsby.

72. K. Schmitt, "Zoological Survey in the Oban Division, Cross River National Park" (Oban Hills Programme, Calabar, January 1996, unpublished); B. Dickinson, "A Reconnaissance Survey of the Elephant Population in the Oban Division of Cross River National Park, Nigeria; March & August 1995" (Oban Hills Programme, Calabar, 1995, unpublished).

73. T. B. Larsen, "Butterfly Research in the Oban Hills, Cross River National Park," (Oban Hills Programme, Calabar, December 1995, second interim unpublished report).

74. Keith Kinross, Acting Manager, WWF Cross River National Park Project, personal communication to the author, July 1992.

75. Talbot (1912).

76. Letter from E. L. Gadsby to General Manager of Cross River National Park, 8 September 1994.

77. Memorandum from K. Schmitt to Oban Hills Programme Project Manager, 14 November 1994.

78. K. Drasler, personal communication to the author, 16 January 1997.

79. F. Hurst and H. Thompson, "A Review of the Okwangwo Division of the Cross River National Park" (WWF-UK, Godalming, July 1994, unpublished).

80. Ibid.

81. Oates et al. (1990), cited in note 61.

82.   G. Armstrong, T. Fawcett, J. White, and D. Okali, "Cross River State Forestry Project, Nigeria; Report on a Project Preparation Visit; 17 January–8 February 1990" (draft report to ODA, London, 1990, unpublished).

83.   This information is based on an unpublished review by a World Bank consultant; personal communications from E. L. Gadsby, P. D. Jenkins and others in Calabar; U. Egbuche, "The WEMPCO Tussle," *Nature Watch* (NCF newsletter), (April–September 1996): 2; and Y. Sheba, "WEMPCO Produces EIA for Ikom Project," *Guardian on Sunday* (Lagos), 7 July 1996.

84.   Caldecott (1996).

85.   Brandon and Wells (1992).

86.   A survey of the gorilla population in the Boshi Extension forests was at last begun by the research branch of the park program in December 1997. I joined the survey team in the forest for five days in January 1998, and we found a few old gorilla nest sites.

87.   After my January 1999 visit to the Okwangwo Division of Cross River National Park, park officials took me and my student Richard Bergl to the police and charged us with "illegal entry to a national park," even though we had been escorted into the park by a uniformed ranger. Another ranger told us that a local hunter had killed a gorilla in the park shortly before our visit; the hunter had not been arrested because, we were told, he was armed and the rangers were not. The charge against us was eventually dropped after discussions with park management and the park's lawyer.

88.   In the January–March 1997 issue of *Newsflash,* the newsletter of the Okwangwo Programme, it was reported that villagers in the support zone had been barricading roads, seizing park vehicles, and harassing park officials.

SEVEN. THE EMPTY FORESTS OF GHANA

1.   Redford (1992).

2.   Asibey (1978); Asibey and Owusu (1982).

3.   Posnansky (1987).

4.   Edgerton (1995); see also Fage (1966); and Maier (1987).

5.   Hawthorne and Abu-Juam (1995); C. Martin (1991).

6.   Moloney (1887).

7.   From a 1927 Forest Ordinance quoted by Hawthorne and Abu-Juam (1993).

8.   C. Martin, "Management Plan for the Bia Wildlife Conservation Areas" (WWF/IUCN, Gland, Switzerland, 1982).

9.   Collins (1958).

10.   Ibid.

11.   C. Martin (1991).

12.   Curry-Lindahl (1969).

13.   Booth (1956).

14.   Curry-Lindahl (1969).

15.   Jeffrey (1970).

16.   M. G. Rucks, "A Study of Faunal Dispersion in the Proposed Krokosua Hills National Park and Proposed Tawya Game Production Area" (Department of Game and Wildlife, Accra, n.d. [probably written in 1973], unpublished).

17.   J. Bishop and S. Cobb, "Protected Area Development in South-west Ghana, Final Report" (Environment and Development Group, Oxford, 1992, unpublished); Hawthorne (1993).

18.   J. S. Gartlan, "The Forests and Primates of Ghana: Prospects for Protection and Proposals for Assistance," *Laboratory Primate Newsletter* 21 (1982): 1–14.

19.   Olson (1986); M. Rucks, "Monkey Miscellany Means Safety in Numbers," *Wildlife* 20 (1978): 268–70.

20.   C. Martin, "Report on a Survey of the Ankasa River Forest Reserve" (Department of Game and Wildlife, Accra, Ghana, 1976, unpublished).

21.   Gartlan (1982), see note 18.

22.   Nini-Suhien/Ankasa file, GW/A.274/SF.1. Ghana Wildlife Department, Accra.

23.   Gartlan (1982), see note 18.

24.   Dutson and Branscombe (1990).

25.   C. Martin (1976), see note 20.

26.   Bishop and Cobb (1992), see note 17.

27.   J. Grainger, personal communication to the author, August 1993.

28.   European Commission, "Financing Proposal for Protected Areas Development Programme, Ghana" (paper no. VIII/406/94-EN, European Commission, Brussels, 1994); letter from J. Zeller (European Commission) to S. Flack (World Bank), 14 September 1995. In September 1995, one ECU was equivalent to $1.27.

29.   "Natural Resource Conservation and Historic Preservation, a Technical Assistance Funding Proposal for the Central Region Integrated Development Project, Cape Coast, Ghana" (U.S. Agency for International Development from MUCIA, Columbus, Ohio, 1991).

30.   T. T. Struhsaker and J. F. Oates, "Kakum National Park, Ghana, Field Trip Report for March-April 1993" (report to Conservation International, Washington, D.C.; and the Ghana Department of Game and Wildlife, Accra, April 1993, unpublished).

31.   J. F. Oates, "Kakum National Park, Ghana, Wildlife Specialist's Report on Visit of 9–29 August 1993" (report to Conservation International, Washington, D.C.; and the Ghana Department of Game and Wildlife, Accra, September 1993, unpublished); T. T. Struhsaker, "Ghana's Forests and Primates, Report of Field Trip to Bia and Kakum National Parks and Boabeng-Fiema Monkey Sanctuary

in November 1993" (report to Conservation International, Washington, D.C.; and the Ghana Department of Game and Wildlife, Accra, December 1993, unpublished).

32.   G. H. Whitesides and J. F. Oates, "Wildlife Surveys in the Rain-Forest Zone of Ghana" (report to Ghana Department of Wildlife, Accra; Primate Conservation Incorporated, East Hampton, N.Y.; and the World Bank, Washington, D.C., December 1995, unpublished).

33.   Hawthorne and Abu-Juam (1995); Wagner and Cobbinah (1993); J. Wong, Forest Resources Management Project, Kumasi, personal communication to the author, 1995.

34.   Hawthorne and Abu-Juam (1995).

35.   J. F. Oates, "The Status of Ghana's Forest Primates, with Special Reference to the Nini-Suhien National Park" (report to Ghana Wildlife Department, Accra; Conservation International, Washington, D.C.; and the Wildlife Conservation Society, Bronx, N.Y., January 1996, unpublished).

36.   C. Martin (1976), see note 20.

37.   Twum-Baah et al. (1995).

38.   K. Mbir, "Nini-Suhien National Park and Ankasa Resource Reserve: A Rapid Assessment Survey of Human Activities" (report from the Ghana Program of Conservation International to the Ghana Wildlife Department, 1996, unpublished).

39.   Y. Ntiamoa-Baidu, "Local Perceptions and Value of Wildlife Reserves to Communities in the Vicinity of Forest National Parks," Appendix 1 to Bishop and Cobb (1992), cited in note 17.

40.   Whitesides and Oates (1995), see note 32; Oates (1996), see note 35.

41.   M. Abedi-Lartey, personal communication to the author, September 1996.

42.   European Union Service Contract SVC 01/97/EDF as described in letter from the Delegate of the European Commission in Ghana, 4 June 1997 (in files of Ghana Wildlife Department).

43.   A. Rabinowitz, "Killed for a Cure," *Natural History* 107 (1998): 22–24.

44.   Ntiamoa-Baidu (1992), see note 39.

45.   Noss (1997).

EIGHT. CAN ZOOS BE THE ARK?

1.   Foose et al. (1987).

2.   According to the *Oxford English Dictionary*, the original meaning of the English word *park* is "an enclosed tract of land held by royal grant or prescription for keeping beasts of the chase."

3.   Street (1961); Fitter and Scott (1978). In 1869, Père David was to bring the attention of the outside world to another very unusual animal, the giant panda.

4.   Beck and Wemmer (1983); Whitehead (1993); Yunhua Liu, personal communication to the author, December 1997.

5.   Durrell (1976).

6.   Hughes (1997).

7.   Durrell (1960).

8.   Jersey Wildlife Preservation Trust, *Jersey Wildlife Preservation Trust, First Annual Report* (Trinity, Jersey: Jersey Wildlife Preservation Trust, 1964); see also Durrell (1960, 1976).

9.   G. Durrell, in Jarvis (1966), p. 293.

10.   Zuckerman (1960).

11.   J. C. Mallinson, "Conference on the Breeding of Endangered Species as an Aid to Their Survival," in Jersey Wildlife Preservation Trust, *Jersey Wildlife Preservation Trust, Ninth Annual Report, 1972* (Trinity, Jersey: Jersey Wildlife Preservation Trust, 1973).

12.   Scott (1966). The Wildfowl Trust is now called the Wildfowl and Wetlands Trust.

13.   G. Durrell, "Plans for the Future," in Jersey Wildlife Preservation Trust, *Jersey Wildlife Preservation Trust, Fourth Annual Report* (Trinity, Jersey: Jersey Wildlife Preservation Trust, 1967).

14.   Kear and Berger (1980); May (1991).

15.   Until 1984, the golden lion tamarin was usually regarded as a subspecies, *Leontopithecus rosalia rosalia*. In that year, an analysis of variation in the skull and dental anatomy of lion tamarins was published that suggested that the three commonly recognized subspecies of *L. rosalia* were best regarded as separate species (see Rosenberger and Coimbra-Filho [1984]). Today, four species of lion tamarin are generally recognized.

16.   Coimbra-Filho (1969).

17.   Coimbra-Filho and Mittermeier (1977); Kierulff and de Oliveira (1996).

18.   Coimbra-Filho and Mittermeier (1977).

19.   Ibid.

20.   Kleiman et al. (1991).

21.   Coimbra-Filho and Mittermeier (1977).

22.   Kleiman et al. (1986, 1991); Kleiman and Mallinson (1998).

23.   B. D. Beck and A. F. Martins, "Golden Lion Tamarin Reintroduction, Annual Report, 1996" (1997, unpublished report).

24.   Kleiman et al. (1991).

25.   D. Pessamilio, cited in Balmford et al. (1995); J. D. Ballou, "Their Current Status," *Tamarin Tales, Newsletter of the* Leontopithecus *International Recovery and Management Committees* 1 (1997): 2–3.

26. Coimbra-Filho and Mittermeier (1977).

27. Kierulff and de Oliveira (1994, 1996).

28. D. G. Kleiman, "Update on Golden Lion Tamarin Conservation Activities," *Tamarin Tales, Newsletter of the* Leontopithecus *International Recovery and Management Committees* 1 (1997): 6–8; Kierulff and de Oliveira (1998).

29. Pope (1996); Caughley (1994).

30. Seal (1986).

31. Soulé (1980).

32. Foose (1991).

33. Oates (1986b).

34. M. Stevenson, T. J. Foose, and A. Baker, "Global Captive Action Plan for Primates" (IUCN/SSC Captive Breeding Specialist Group, Apple Valley, Minn., 1991, discussion edition).

35. Stevenson et al. (1992).

36. S. Ellis, "Conservation Breeding Specialist Group," *Species* 26/27 (1996): 139–40; CBSG page on the World Wide Web, http://www.cbsg.org/about.htm (1997).

37. Sankhala (1977).

38. Schaller (1993).

39. Rabinowitz (1995).

40. A plan for conserving the Sumatran rhinoceros based on mathematical modeling is summarized in Maguire et al. (1987).

41. Caughley (1994).

42. Balmford et al. (1995).

43. Snyder et al. (1996).

44. Conway (1980).

45. Conway (1986).

46. Baillie and Groombridge (1996).

47. Hutchins and Conway (1995).

48. S. A. Toth, "Eye to Eye with Gibbon and Snake," *New York Times,* 13 April 1997, sec. 5, p. 31.

49. E. Wenman, "Mauritius Expedition 1995," *Zoological Society of London Members' Newsletter* (January 1996).

50. Similar points have been made by Ardith Eudey (1995). Not unexpectedly, Seal (1991) has argued strongly that zoos are not solely motivated by the desire to acquire exhibit specimens.

51. S. Ormrod, "Showboat as Ark," *BBC Wildlife* (July 1994): 40–44.

52. The Jersey Wildlife Preservation Trust has a training program specifically tailored to zoo personnel from developing countries. Gerald Durrell saw such training, as well as the promotion of conservation education in habitat countries, as important components of Jersey Zoo's activities (Durrell [1991]).

53.   Toth (1997), see note 48.

54.   Conditions under which reintroduction may be a sensible option have been summarized by the IUCN/SSC Re-introduction Specialist Group in their "Guidelines for Re-introductions" (Gland, Switzerland: IUCN, 1998); see also Stuart (1991); and Kleiman et al. (1994).

55.   "Meet the Drill," *International Primate Protection League News* 21 (1994): 3–6.

56.   Appleton and Morris (1997).

57.   T. M. Butynski and S. H. Koster, "The Status and Conservation of Forests and Primates on Bioko Island (Fernando Poo [*sic*]), Equatorial Guinea" (1990, unpublished photocopy); Butynski and Koster (1994).

58.   Schaaf (1994); J. Fa, personal communication to the author, July 1998.

59.   Nielsen and Brown (1988); McNamee (1997).

60.   Strum and Southwick (1986).

61.   F. W. Koontz, personal communication to the author, 1997; Koontz (1997).

NINE. CONSERVATION AT THE
CLOSE OF THE TWENTIETH CENTURY

1.   World Resources Institute (1996).

2.   Richburg (1997).

3.   R. W. Stevenson, "The Chief Banker for the Nations at the Bottom of the Heap," *New York Times,* 14 September 1997.

4.   G. Gugliotta, "Hunting the Elephant in AID's Budget," *Washington Post,* 18 February 1997; "Why Are American Taxpayers' Dollars Being Used to Promote Trophy Hunting of African Elephants?" press release from the Humane Society of the United States, February 1997; M. Scully, "Kill an Elephant, Save an Elephant," *New York Times,* 2 August 1997.

5.   Afterword, in Adams and McShane (1996), pp. 249–63.

6.   Ibid.

7.   Gibson and Marks (1995).

8.   Lewis and Phiri (1998).

9.   International Institute for Environment and Development (1994); Wells (1995).

10.   "3rd World Nations Express Concern," *Daily Graphic* (Accra, Ghana), 28 June 1997.

11.   World Resources Institute (1996).

12.   Flavin (1997); Randel and German (1996).

13.   Randel and German (1996); United Nations Development Programme (1998).

14.   United Nations Development Programme (1997).

15.   "Job Opportunities," on WWF's World Wide Web site, 1997.

16. G. Lean, "$ a Year for UN's Number Two," *Independent on Sunday* (London), 27 April 1997.

17. World Resources Institute (1996).

18. Brandon and Wells (1992); van Schaik and Kramer (1997).

19. World Resources Institute (1996).

20. United Nations Development Programme (1998).

21. Currey (1997).

22. M. Singh, personal communication to the author, 21 November 1997.

23. "Judiciary Saving India's Forests," *Tigerlink News* 3 (1997): 1.

24. World Resources Institute (1996).

25. Ibid.

26. R. Leakey, extracts from a speech at the 1997 CITES conference in Harare, Zimbabwe, 12 June 1997, reprinted in *International Primate Protection League News* 24, no. 2 (1997): 11-14.

27. Bere (1957).

28. Oates et al. (1992).

29. Wilson (1984); Schaller (1997); Leakey (1997), cited in note 26.

30. Rosevear (1959).

31. M. Wells, "Trust Funds and Endowments as a Biodiversity Conservation Tool" (Divisional Working Paper no. 1991-26, Environmental Policy and Research Division, World Bank, Washington, D.C., 1991); J. Resor, and B. Spergel, "Conservation Trust Funds: Examples from Guatemala, Bhutan, and the Philippines" (Working Paper, World Wildlife Fund-US, Washington, D.C., 1992); Kramer and Sharma (1997); Struhsaker (1997).

32. M. Wells (1991), cited in note 31.

33. Struhsaker (1997).

34. M. Wells (1991), cited in note 31; T. Butynski, personal communication to the author, December 1997.

35. Kramer and Sharma (1997).

36. P. Passell, "Trading on the Pollution Exchange," *New York Times,* 24 October 1997.

37. R. D. Kaplan, "The Coming Anarchy," *Atlantic Monthly* 273 (1994): 44-76; Kaplan (1996).

38. Hart and Hart (1997); Fimbel and Fimbel (1997).

39. D. Steklis, "Karisoke Research Center—1994," *Gorilla Conservation News* 9 (1995): 15-16.

40. Hart and Hart (1997).

41. E. Williamson, "Update from the Karisoke Research Centre, Rwanda: January 1998," *Primate Eye* no. 64 (1998): 16-17.

42. Appleton and Morris (1997).

43. Schaller (1997).

44. Naess (1986).

Bibliography

Abraham, A. 1978. *Mende Government and Politics under Colonial Rule.* Freetown: Sierra Leone University Press.

Adams, J. S., and T. O. McShane. 1992. *The Myth of Wild Africa.* New York: W. W. Norton.

———. 1996. *The Myth of Wild Africa.* Paperback edition. Berkeley and Los Angeles: University of California Press.

Adeyoju, S. K. 1975. *Forestry and the Nigerian Economy.* Ibadan: Ibadan University Press.

Afolayan, A., and K. M. Barbour. 1982. "Population Density and Distribution." In *Nigeria in Maps,* edited by K. M. Barbour, J. S. Oguntoyinbo, J. O. C. Onyemelukwe, and J. C. Nwafor, pp. 58–59. London: Hodder and Stoughton.

Alieu, E. K. 1995. "People's Participation in the Development and Management of Tiwai—Sierra Leone's First Game Sanctuary." *Nature et Faune* 11:11–21.

Alldridge, T. J. 1901. *The Sherbro and Its Hinterland.* London: Macmillan.

Allen, G. 1981. "Community Development up to Date." *Nigerian Field* 46:3–9.

Allen, J. G. C. 1931. "Gorilla Hunting in Southern Nigeria." *Nigerian Field* 1:4–9.

Allen, R. 1973. *Natural Man.* London: Aldus Books.

―――. 1980. *How to Save the World: Strategy for World Conservation.* London: Kogan Page.

Appleton, M., and J. Morris. 1997. "Conservation in a Conflict Area." *Oryx* 31:153–55.

Arensberg, C. M. 1961. "The Community as Object and as Sample." *American Anthropologist* 63: 241–64.

Ash, J. S. 1991. "The Grey-Necked Picathartes *Picathartes oreas* and Ibadan Malimbe *Malimbus ibadanensis* in Nigeria." *Bird Conservation International* 1:93–106.

Ash, J. S., and R. E. Sharland. 1986. *Nigeria: Assessment of Bird Conservation Priorities,* ICBP Study Report no. 11. Cambridge, England: International Council for Bird Preservation.

Asibey, E. O. A. 1978. "Primate Conservation in Ghana." In *Recent Advances in Primatology, Volume 2, Conservation,* edited by D. J. Chivers and W. Lane-Petter, pp. 55–74. London: Academic Press.

Asibey, E. O. A., and J. G. K. Owusu. 1982. "The Case for High-Forest National Parks in Ghana." *Environmental Conservation* 9:293–304.

Attenborough, D. 1956. *Zoo Quest to Guiana.* London: Lutterworth Press.

―――. 1980. *The Zoo Quest Expeditions.* Guildford, England: Lutterworth Press.

Baillie, J., and B. Groombridge. 1996. *1996 IUCN Red List of Threatened Animals.* Gland, Switzerland: IUCN.

Bakarr, M. I., A. A. Gbakima, and Z. Bah. 1991. "Intestinal Helminth Parasites in Free-Living Monkeys from a West African Rainforest." *African Journal of Ecology* 29:170–72.

Balinga, V. S. 1986. "The Importance of Wildlife Research for Forest Conservation." In *Proceedings of the Workshop on Korup National Park, Mundemba, Ndian Division, South-West Province, Republic of Cameroon,* edited by S. Gartlan, and H. Macleod. Gland, Switzerland: WWF/IUCN.

Balmford, A., N. Leader-Williams, and M. J. B. Green. 1995. "Parks or Arks: Where to Conserve Threatened Mammals?" *Biodiversity and Conservation* 4:595–607.

Beadle, L. C. 1974. "The Nuffield Unit of Tropical Animal Ecology (1961–1971)." *Journal of Zoology, London* 173:539–48.

Beck, B. B., and C. Wemmer, eds. 1983. *The Biology and Management of An Extinct Species: Père David's Deer.* Park Ridge, N.J.: Noyes Publishing.

Bell, R. H. V. 1987. "Conservation with a Human Face: Conflict and Reconciliation in African Land Use Planning." In *Conservation in Africa: People, Policies and Practice,* edited by D. Anderson, and R. Grove, pp. 79–101. Cambridge: Cambridge University Press.

Bere, R. M. 1957. "The National Park Idea: How to Interest the African Public." *Oryx* 4:21–27.

Biodiversity Support Program. 1993. *African Biodiversity: Foundation for the Future.* Washington, D.C.: Biodiversity Support Program, World Wildlife Fund.

Booth, A. H. 1954. "The Dahomey Gap and the Mammalian Fauna of the West African Forests." *Rev. Zool. Bot. Afr.* 50:305–14.

———. 1956. "The Distribution of Primates in the Gold Coast." *Journal of the West African Science Association* 2:122–33.

———. 1957. "Observations on the Natural History of the Olive Colobus Monkey, *Procolobus verus* (van Beneden)." *Proceedings of the Zoological Society of London* 129:421–30.

———. 1958. "The Zoogeography of West African Primates: A Review." *Bulletin de l'Institut français de l'Afrique noire,* serié A, 20:587–622.

Brandler, J. L. 1993. *Out of Nigeria: Witness to a Giant's Toils.* London: Radcliffe Press.

Brandon, K. E., and M. Wells. 1992. "Planning for People and Parks: Design Dilemmas." *World Development* 20:557–70.

Butynski, T. M., and S. H. Koster. 1994. "Distribution and Conservation Status of Primates in Bioko Island, Equatorial Guinea." *Biodiversity and Conservation* 3:893–909.

Caldecott, J. O. 1986. "An Ecological and Behavioral Study of the Pig-Tailed Macaque." *Contributions to Primatology* no. 21. Basel, Switzerland: S. Karger.

———. 1988. *Hunting and Wildlife Management in Sarawak.* Gland, Switzerland: International Union for the Conservation of Nature and Natural Resources.

———. 1996. *Designing Conservation Projects.* Cambridge: Cambridge University Press.

Caldecott, J. O., J. G. Bennett, and H. J. Ruitenbeek. 1989. *Cross River National Park (Oban Division): Plan for Developing the Park and Its Support Zone.* Godalming, England: World Wide Fund for Nature UK.

Caldecott, J. O., J. F. Oates, and H. J. Ruitenbeek. 1990. *Cross River National Park (Okwangwo Division): Plan for Developing the Park and Its Support Zone.* Godalming, England: World Wide Fund for Nature UK.

Carson, R. 1962. *Silent Spring.* Boston: Houghton Mifflin.

Caughley, G. 1994. "Directions in Conservation Biology." *Journal of Animal Ecology* 63:215–44.

Charles-Dominique, P. 1977. *Ecology and Behaviour of Nocturnal Primates.* London: Duckworth.

Clarke, J. I. 1969. "Chiefdoms." In *Sierra Leone in Maps,* edited by J. I. Clarke, pp. 32–33. 2d ed. London: Hodder and Stoughton.

Coe, M., and K. Curry-Lindahl. 1965. "Ecology of a Mountain: First Report on Liberian Nimba." *Oryx* 8:177–84.

Coimbra-Filho, A. F. 1969. "Mico-leão, *Leontideus rosalia* (Linnaeus, 1766), situação atual da espécie no Brasil (Callithricidae, Primates)." *An. Acad. Brasil. Ciênc.* 41 (suppl.): 29–52.

Coimbra-Filho, A. F., and R. A. Mittermeier. 1977. "Conservation of the Brazilian Lion Tamarins (*Leontopithecus rosalia*)." In *Primate Conservation*, edited by H. S. H. Prince Rainier and G. H. Bourne, pp. 59–94. New York: Academic Press.

Collier, F. S. 1934. "Notes on Gorilla." *Nigerian Field* 3:92–102.

Collins, W. B. 1958. *The Perpetual Forest*. London: Staples Press.

Conway, W. G. 1980. "An Overview of Captive Propagation." In *Conservation Biology: An Evolutionary-Ecological Perspective*, edited by M. E. Soulé and B. A. Wilcox, pp. 199–208. Sunderland, Mass.: Sinauer Associates.

———. 1986. "The Practical Difficulties and Financial Implications of Endangered Species Breeding Programmes." In *International Zoo Yearbook*, pp. 210–19. Vol. 24/25. London: Zoological Society of London.

Cousins, D. 1978. "Gorillas—a Survey." *Oryx* 14:254–58.

Cowie, M. 1961. *Fly, Vulture*. London: George C. Harrap.

Cramp, S., K. E. L. Simmons, I. J. Ferguson-Lees, R. Gillmor, P. A. D. Hollom, R. Hudson, E. M. Nicholson, M. A. Ogilvie, P. J. S. Olney, K. H. Voous, and J. Wattel. 1977. *The Birds of the Western Palearctic*. Vol. 1. Oxford: Oxford University Press.

Crawford, M. 1972. "Conservation by Utilisation." *Oryx* 11:427–32.

Currey, D. 1997. *The Political Wilderness—India's Tiger Crisis*. London: Environmental Investigation Agency.

Curry-Lindahl, K. 1969. "Report to the Government of Ghana on Conservation, Management, and Utilization of Ghana's Wildlife Resources." Supplementary paper no. 18, *IUCN Publications, New Series*. Morges, Switzerland: IUCN.

Darling, P. J. 1975. "The Earthworks of Benin: Some Cross-profiles." *Nigerian Field* 40:159–68.

Dasilva, G. L. 1994. "Diet of *Colobus polykomos* on Tiwai Island: Selection of Food in Relation to Its Seasonal Abundance and Nutritional Quality." *International Journal of Primatology* 15:1–26.

Davies, A. G., and J. F. Oates, eds. 1994. *Colobine Monkeys: Their Ecology, Behaviour and Evolution*. Cambridge: Cambridge University Press.

Durrell, G. 1953. *The Overloaded Ark*. London: Faber and Faber.

———. 1954. *The Bafut Beagles*. London: Rupert Hart-Davis.

———. 1960. *A Zoo in My Luggage*. London: Rupert Hart-Davis.

———. 1972. *Catch Me a Colobus*. London: William Collins.

———. 1976. *The Stationary Ark*. London: Collins.

———. 1991. *The Ark's Anniversary*. New York: Arcade Publishing.

Dutson, G., and J. Branscombe. 1990. "Rainforest Birds in South-West Ghana: The Results of the Ornithological Work of the Cambridge Ghana Rainforest Project 1988 and the Ghana Rainforest Expedition 1989." *ICBP Study Report*, no. 46. Cambridge, England: International Council for Bird Preservation.

Ebin, C. O. 1983. *An Appraisal of the Biotic and Material Resources of Some Game Reserves and Wildlife Management in Nigeria.* Lagos: Nigerian Conservation Foundation.

Edgerton, R. B. 1995. *The Fall of the Asante Empire.* New York: Free Press.

Edroma, E. L. 1980. "Road to Extermination in Uganda." *Oryx* 15:451–52.

Elgood, J. H. 1965. "The Birds of the Obudu Plateau, Eastern Region of Nigeria." *Nigerian Field* 30:60–69.

Eltringham, S. K. 1969. "The Work of the Nuffield Unit of Tropical Animal Ecology in the Uganda National Parks." *Journal of Reproduction and Fertility, Supplement* 6, 483–86.

Eudey, A. E. 1995. "To Procure or Not to Procure." In *Ethics on the Ark: Zoos, Animal Welfare and Wildlife Conservation,* edited by B. G. Norton, M. Hutchins, E. F. Stevens, and T. L. Maple, pp. 146–52. Washington, D.C.: Smithsonian Institution Press.

Fage, J. D. 1966. *Ghana: A Historical Interpretation.* Madison: University of Wisconsin Press.

Fairhead, J., and M. Leach. 1996. *Misreading the African Landscape: Society and Ecology in a Forest-Savanna Mosaic.* Cambridge: Cambridge University Press.

Fegley, R. 1991. "Equatorial Guinea." *World Bibliographical Series.* Vol. 136. Oxford: Clio Press.

Fethersonhaugh, A. H. 1951. "Malaya's National Park." *Oryx* 1:198–203.

Fimbel, C. 1994. "The Relative Use of Abandoned Farm Clearings and Old Forest Habitats by Primates and a Forest Antelope at Tiwai, Sierra Leone, West Africa." *Biological Conservation* 70:277–86.

Fimbel, C., and R. Fimbel. 1997. "Rwanda: The Role of Local Participation." *Conservation Biology* 11:309–10.

Fisher, J., N. Simon, and J. Vincent. 1969. *The Red Book: Wildlife in Danger.* London: Collins.

Fitter, R., and P. Scott. 1978. *The Penitent Butchers.* London: Fauna Preservation Society.

Flavin, C. 1997. "The Legacy of Rio." In *State of the World 1997,* pp. 3–22. W. W. Norton: New York.

Foose, T. J. 1991. "Viable Population Strategies for Re-introduction Programmes." *Symposia of the Zoological Society of London* 62:165–72.

Foose, T. J., U. S. Seal, and N. R. Flesness. 1987. "Captive Propagation as a Component of Conservation Strategies for Endangered Primates." In *Primate Conservation in the Tropical Rain Forest,* edited by C. W. Marsh, and R. A. Mittermeier, pp. 263–99. New York: Alan R. Liss.

Fossey, D., and A. H. Harcourt. 1977. "Feeding Ecology of Free-Ranging Mountain Gorilla (*Gorilla gorilla beringei*)." In *Primate Ecology,* edited by T. H. Clutton-Brock, pp. 415–47. London: Academic Press.

Fussell, P. 1980. *Abroad: British Literary Traveling between the Wars*. New York: Oxford University Press.

Fyfe, C. 1962. *A History of Sierra Leone*. Oxford: Oxford University Press.

Galat, G., and A. Galat-Luong. 1985. "La communauté de primates diurnes de la forêt de Taï, Côte d'Ivoire." *Revue d'Ecologie* 40:3–32.

Gartlan, S., and H. Macleod, eds. 1986. *Proceedings of the Workshop on Korup National Park, Mundemba, Ndian Division, South-West Province, Republic of Cameroon*. Gland, Switzerland: WWF/IUCN.

Gee, E. P. 1964. *The Wild Life of India*. London: Collins.

Ghanem, S. 1986. *OPEC: The Rise and Fall of an Exclusive Club*. London: KPI.

Gibson, C. C., and S. A. Marks. 1995. "Transforming Rural Hunters into Conservationists: An Assessment of Community-Based Wildlife Management Programs in Africa." *World Development* 23:941–57.

Goldsmith, F. B., and A. Warren, eds. 1993. *Conservation in Progress*. Chichester, England: John Wiley.

Goodall, J. 1963. "Feeding Behaviour of Wild Chimpanzees: A Preliminary Report." *Symposia of the Zoological Society of London* 10:39–47.

Grace, J. J. 1977. "Slavery and Emancipation among the Mende in Sierra Leone, 1896–1928." In *Slavery in Africa: Historical and Anthropological Perspectives*, edited by S. Miers and I. Kopytoff, pp. 415–31. Madison: University of Wisconsin Press.

Green, S., and K. Minkowski. 1977. "The Lion-Tailed Monkey and Its South Indian Rain Forest Habitat." In *Primate Conservation*, edited by H. S. H. Prince Rainier, and G. H. Bourne, pp. 289–337. New York: Academic Press.

Greene, G. 1969. *Collected Essays*. London: Bodley Head.

Grove, R. H. 1992. "Origins of Western Environmentalism." *Scientific American* 267:42–47.

Grubb, P. 1978. "Patterns of Speciation in African Mammals." *Bulletin of the Carnegie Museum of Natural History* 6:152–67.

Grzimek, B., and M. Grzimek. 1960. *Serengeti Shall Not Die*. London: Hamish Hamilton.

Hall, J. B. 1981. "Ecological Islands in South-Eastern Nigeria." *African Journal of Ecology* 19:55–72.

Harcourt, A. H. 1981. "Can Uganda's Gorillas Survive? A Survey of the Bwindi Forest Reserve." *Biological Conservation* 19:269–82.

Harcourt, A. H., and A. F. G. Groom. 1972. "Gorilla Census." *Oryx* 11:355–36.

Harcourt, A. H., K. J. Stewart, and I. M. Inaharo. 1989. "Gorilla Quest in Nigeria." *Oryx* 23:7–13.

Hardiman, M. 1986. "People's Involvement in Health and Medical Care." In *Community Participation, Social Development and the State*, edited by J. Midgley, pp. 45–69. London: Methuen.

Harris, D., J. M. Fay, and N. Macdonald. 1987. "Report of Gorillas from Nigeria." *Primate Conservation* 8:40.

Hart, T., and J. Hart. 1997. "Zaire: New Models for an Emerging State." *Conservation Biology* 11:308–9.

Hartley, D. 1992. "Forest Resource Use and Subsistence in Sierra Leone." Ph.D. diss., University College London.

Hawthorne, W. D. 1993. "Forest Regeneration after Logging." *ODA Forestry Series*, no. 3. Chatham, England: Natural Resources Institute.

Hawthorne, W. D., and M. Abu-Juam. 1995. *Forest Protection in Ghana*. Cambridge, England: IUCN.

Hill, C. M. 1994. "The Role of Female Diana Monkeys, *Cercopithecus diana*, in Territorial Defence." *Animal Behaviour* 47:425–31.

Hill, P. 1986. *Development Economics on Trial*. Cambridge: Cambridge University Press.

Hill, W. C. O. 1952. "The External and Visceral Anatomy of the Olive Colobus Monkey (*Procolobus verus*)." *Proceedings of the Zoological Society of London* 122:127–86.

Holdgate M., and D. A. Munro, "Limits to Caring: A Response." *Conservation Biology* 7:938–42.

Holland, M. D., R. K. G. Allen, D. Barton, and S. T. Murphy. 1989. *Cross River National Park, Oban Division: Land Evaluation and Agricultural Recommendations*. Chatham, England: Overseas Development Natural Resources Institute.

Holsoe, S. E. 1977. "Slavery and Economic Response among the Vai." In *Slavery in Africa: Historical and Anthropological Perspectives*, edited by S. Miers and I. Kopytoff, pp. 287–303. Madison: University of Wisconsin Press.

Hughes, D. 1997. *Himself and Other Animals: A Portrait of Gerald Durrell*. London: Hutchinson.

Hutchins, M., and W. G. Conway. 1995. "Beyond Noah's Ark: The Evolving Role of Modern Zoological Parks and Aquariums in Field Conservation." In *International Zoo Yearbook*, pp. 117–30. Vol. 34. London: Zoological Society of London.

International Institute for Environment and Development. 1994. *Whose Eden? An Overview of Community Approaches to Wildlife Management*. London: IIED.

International Union for the Conservation of Nature and Natural Resources, United Nations Environment Programme, and World Wildlife Fund. 1980. *World Conservation Strategy: Living Resources for Sustainable Development*. Gland, Switzerland: IUCN, UNEP, and WWF.

———. 1991. *Caring for the Earth: A Strategy for Sustainable Living*. Gland, Switzerland: IUCN, UNEP, and WWF.

Jarvis, C., ed. 1966. *International Zoo Yearbook*. Vol. 6. London: Zoological Society of London.

Jeffrey, S. 1970. "Ghana's Forest Wildlife in Danger." *Oryx* 10:240–43.

Jewell, P. A. 1963. "Wild Life Research in East and Central Africa." *Oryx* 7: 77–87.

Kaplan, R. D. 1996. *The Ends of the Earth.* New York: Random House.

Kear, J., and A. J. Berger. 1980. *The Hawaiian Goose: An Experiment in Conservation.* Calton, England: T. and A. D. Poyser.

Kideckel, D. A. 1993. *The Solitude of Collectivism: Romanian Villagers to the Revolution and Beyond.* Ithaca: Cornell University Press.

Kierulff, M. C. M., and P. P. de Oliveira. 1994. "Habitat Preservation and the Translocation of Threatened Groups of Golden Lion Tamarins, *Leontopithecus rosalia.*" *Neotropical Primates* 2 (suppl.): 15–18.

———. 1996. "Re-assessing the Status and Conservation of the Golden Lion Tamarin *Leontopithecus rosalia* in the Wild." *Journal of the Wildlife Preservation Trust* 32:98–15.

———. 1998. "Reserva Biológica Fazenda União, Rio de Janeiro." *Neotropical Primates* 6:51.

Kingsley, M. H. 1897. *Travels in West Africa.* London: Macmillan.

Kleiman, D. G., B. B. Beck, J. M. Dietz, and L. A. Dietz. 1991. "Costs of a Reintroduction and Criteria for Success: Accounting and Accountability in the Golden Lion Tamarin Conservation Program." *Symposia of the Zoological Society of London* 62:125–42.

Kleiman, D. G., B. B. Beck, J. M. Dietz, L. A. Dietz, J. D. Ballou, and A. F. Coimbra-Filho. 1986. "Conservation Program for the Golden Lion Tamarin: Captive Research and Management, Ecological Studies, Educational Strategies, and Reintroduction." In *Primates: The Road to Self-Sustaining Populations,* edited by K. Benirschke, pp. 959–79. New York: Springer-Verlag.

Kleiman, D. G., and J. J. C. Mallinson. 1998. "Recovery and Management Committees for Lion Tamarins: Partnerships in Conservation Planning and Implementation." *Conservation Biology* 12:27–38.

Kleiman, D. G., M. R. Stanley-Price, and B. B. Beck. 1994. "Criteria for Reintroductions." In *Creative Conservation: Interactive Management of Wild and Captive Animals,* edited by P. J. S. Olney, G. M. Mace, and A. T. C. Feistner, pp. 287–303. London: Chapman and Hall.

Koontz, F. W. 1997. "Zoos and *in situ* Primate Conservation." In *Primate Conservation: The Role of Zoological Parks,* edited by J. Wallis, pp. 62–81. Norman, Oklahoma: American Society of Primatologists.

Kramer, R. A., and N. Sharma. 1997. "Tropical Forest Biodiversity Protection: Who Pays and Why." In *Last Stand: Protected Areas and the Defense of Tropical Biodiversity,* edited by R. A. Kramer, C. P. van Schaik, and J. Johnson, pp. 162–86. New York: Oxford University Press.

Kramer, R. A., and C. P. van Schaik. 1997. "Preservation Paradigms and Tropical Rain Forests." In *Last Stand: Protected Areas and the Defense of Tropical Biodiversity*, edited by R. A. Kramer, C. P. van Schaik, and J. Johnson, pp. 3–14.
New York: Oxford University Press.

Lamprey, H. F. 1969. "Ecological Research in the Serengeti National Park." *Journal of Reproduction and Fertility, Supplement* 6: 487–93.

Lewis, D. M., and N. Carter, eds. 1993. *Voices from Africa: Local Perspectives on
Conservation.* Washington, D.C.: World Wildlife Fund.

Lewis, D. M., and A. Phiri. 1998. "Wildlife Snaring—an Indicator of Community Response to a Community-Based Conservation Project." *Oryx* 32:
111–21.

Listowel, J. 1973. *Amin.* Dublin: IUP Books.

Lowe, R. G. 1996. "Review of Natural Resources Conservation Action Plan,
Final Report." *Nigerian Field* 61:78–80.

Ludwig, D., R. Hilborn, and C. Walters. 1993. "Uncertainty, Resource Exploitation, and Conservation: Lessons from History." *Science* 260:17, 36.

Luke, D. F., and S. P. Riley. 1989. "The Politics of Economic Decline in Sierra
Leone." *Journal of Modern African Studies* 27:133–41.

Mackenzie, A. F. 1952. *Proceedings of the Zoological Society of London* 122:541.

Maguire, L. A., U. S. Seal, and P. F. Brussard. 1987. "Managing Critically Endangered Species: The Sumatran Rhino as a Case Study." In *Viable Populations for Conservation*, edited by M. E. Soulé, pp. 141–58. Cambridge: Cambridge University Press.

Maier, D. J. E. 1987. "Asante War Aims in the 1869 Invasion of Ewe." In *The
Golden Stool: Studies of the Asante Center and Periphery; Anthropological Papers of
the American Museum of Natural History* edited by E. Schildkrout and C. Gelber, pp. 232–44. Vol. 65. New York: American Museum of Natural History.

Malhotra, I. 1989. *Indira Gandhi: A Personal and Political Biography.* London: Hodder and Stoughton.

March, E. W. 1957. "Gorillas of Eastern Nigeria." *Oryx* 4:30–34.

Martin, C. 1991. *The Rainforests of West Africa: Ecology—Threats—Conservation.*
Basel: Birkhäuser Verlag.

Martin, F. J. 1938. *A Preliminary Survey of the Vegetation of Sierra Leone.* Freetown:
Government Printer.

May, R. M. 1991. "The Role of Ecological Thinking in Planning Re-introduction
of Endangered Species." *Symposia of the Zoological Society of London*
62:145–163.

McNamee, T. 1997. *The Return of the Wolf to Yellowstone.* New York: Henry Holt.

McNeely, J. A., J. Harrison, and P. Dingwall, eds. 1994. *Protecting Nature: Regional Reviews of Protected Areas.* Gland, Switzerland: IUCN.

Meier, G. M. 1995. *Leading Issues in Economic Development.* 6th ed. New York: Oxford University Press.

Menzies, J. I. 1970. "An Eastward Extension to the Known Range of the Olive Colobus Monkey (*Colobus verus,* van Beneden)." *Journal of the West African Scientific Association* 15:83–84.

Midgley, J., ed. 1986. *Community Participation, Social Development and the State.* London: Methuen.

Mittermeier, R. A., and I. A. Bowles. 1994. "Reforming the Approach of the Global Environmental Facility to Biodiversity Conservation." *Oryx* 28:101–6.

Moller, P., and B. Brown. 1990. "Meristic Characters and Electric Organ Discharge of *Mormyrops curviceps* Roman (Teleostei: Mormyridae) from the Moa River, Sierra Leone, West Africa." *Copeia* 1990:1031–40.

Moloney, A. 1887. *Sketch of the Forestry of West Africa.* London: Sampson Low, Marston, Searle, and Rivington.

Moorehead, A. 1959. *No Room in the Ark.* London: Hamish Hamilton.

Myers, N. 1980. *Conversion of Tropical Moist Forests.* Washington, D.C.: National Academy of Sciences.

Naess, A. 1985. "Identification as a Source of Deep Ecological Attitudes." In *Deep Ecology,* edited by M. Tobias, pp. 256–70. San Diego: Avant Books.

———. 1986. "Intrinsic Value: Will the Defenders of Nature Please Rise?" In *Conservation Biology,* edited by M. E. Soulé, pp. 504–15. Sunderland, Mass.: Sinauer Associates.

Nash, L. T., S. K. Bearder, and T. R. Olson. 1989. "Synopsis of Galago Species Characteristics." *International Journal of Primatology* 10:57–80.

Nash, R. 1973. *Wilderness and the American Mind.* Rev. ed. New Haven: Yale University Press.

Nations, J. D. 1988. "Deep Ecology Meets the Developing World." In *Biodiversity,* edited by E. O. Wilson and F. M. Peter, pp. 79–82. Washington, D.C.: National Academy Press.

Nicholson, E. M. 1970. *The Environmental Revolution: A Guide for the New Masters of the World.* London: Hodder and Stoughton.

Nielsen, L., and R. D. Brown, eds. 1988. *Translocation of Wild Animals.* Milwaukee, Wisconsin: Wisconsin Humane Society.

Noss, A. J. 1997. "Challenges to Nature Conservation with Community Development in Central African Forests." *Oryx* 31:180–88.

Oates, J. F. 1977. "The Guereza and Man." In *Primate Conservation,* edited by H. S. H. Prince Rainier and G. H. Bourne, pp. 419–67. New York: Academic Press.

———. 1982. "In Search of Rare Forest Primates in Nigeria." *Oryx* 16:431–36.

———. 1986a. "African Primate Conservation: General Needs and Specific Priorities." In *Primates: The Road to Self-Sustaining Populations,* edited by K. Benirschke, pp. 21–29. New York: Springer-Verlag.

———. 1986b. *Action Plan for African Primate Conservation: 1986–90.* Stony Brook, N.Y.: IUCN/SSC Primate Specialist Group.

———. 1988. "The Diet of the Olive Colobus Monkey, *Procolobus verus*, in Sierra Leone." *International Journal of Primatology* 9:457–78.

———. 1996. "Habitat Alteration, Hunting and the Conservation of Folivorous Primates in African Forests." *Australian Journal of Ecology* 21:1–9.

Oates, J. F., P. A. Anadu, E. L. Gadsby, and J. L. Werre. 1992. "Sclater's Guenon—a Rare Nigerian Monkey Threatened by Deforestation." *National Geographic Research and Exploration* 8:476–91.

Oates, J. F., A. G. Davies, and E. Delson. 1994. "The Diversity of Living Colobines." In *Colobine Monkeys: Their Ecology, Behaviour and Evolution,* edited by A. G. Davies and J. F. Oates, pp. 45–73. Cambridge: Cambridge University Press.

Oates, J. F., and P. A. Jewell. 1967. "Westerly Extent of the Range of Three African Lorisoid Primates." *Nature* 215:778–79.

Oates, J. F., G. H. Whitesides, A. G. Davies, P. G. Waterman, S. M. Green, G. L. Dasilva, and S. Mole. 1990. "Determinants of Variation in Tropical Forest Primate Biomass: New Evidence from West Africa." *Ecology* 71:328–43.

Olson, D. K. 1986. "Determining Range Size for Arboreal Monkeys: Methods, Assumptions, and Accuracy." In *Current Perspectives in Primate Social Dynamics,* edited by D. M. Taub and F. A. King, pp. 212–27. New York: Van Nostrand Reinhold.

Petrides, G. A. 1965. *Advisory Report on Wildlife and National Parks in Nigeria, 1962.* Special publication no. 18. Bronx, N.Y.: American Committee for International Wild Life Protection.

Pope, T. R. 1996. "Socioecology, Population Fragmentation, and Patterns of Genetic Loss in Endangered Primates." In *Conservation Genetics: Case Histories from Nature,* edited by J. C. Avise and J. L. Hamrick, pp. 119–59. New York: Chapman and Hall.

Posnansky, M. 1987. "Prelude to Akan Civilization." In *The Golden Stool: Studies of the Asante Center and Periphery; Anthropological Papers of the American Museum of Natural History,* edited by E. Schildkrout and C. Gelber, pp. 14–22. Vol. 65. New York: American Museum of Natural History.

Provisional International Union for the Protection of Nature. 1947. *International Conference for the Protection of Nature: Proceedings, Resolutions and Reports. Brunnen, Switzerland, June 28th–July 3rd 1947.* Basel, Switzerland: Provisional International Union for the Protection of Nature.

Rabinowitz, A. 1995. "Helping a Species Go Extinct: The Sumatran Rhino in Borneo." *Conservation Biology* 9:482–88.

Randel, J., and T. German, eds. 1996. *The Reality of Aid 1996.* London: Earthscan Publications.

Reader's Digest Association. 1970. *The Living World of Animals*. London: Reader's Digest Association.

Redfield, R. 1955. *The Little Community: Viewpoints for the Study of a Human Whole*. Chicago: University of Chicago Press.

Redford, K. H. 1991. "The Ecologically Noble Savage." *Cultural Survival Quarterly* 15:46–48.

———. 1992. "The Empty Forest." *BioScience* 42:412–22.

Rich, B. 1994. *Mortgaging the Earth: The World Bank, Environmental Impoverishment, and the Crisis of Development*. Boston: Beacon Press.

Richards, P. 1996. *Fighting for the Rain Forest: War, Youth and Resources in Sierra Leone*. Portsmouth, N.H.: Heinemann.

Richburg, K. B. 1997. *Out of America: A Black Man Confronts Africa*. New York: Basic Books.

Robinson, J. G. 1993. "Limits to Caring: Sustainable Living and the Loss of Biodiversity." *Conservation Biology* 7:20–28.

Rosenberger, A. L., and A. F. Coimbra-Filho. 1984. "Morphology, Taxonomic Status, and Affinities of the Lion Tamarins, *Leontopithecus* (Callitrichinae, Cebidae)." *Folia Primatologica* 42:149–79.

Rosevear, D. R. 1953. *Checklist and Atlas of Nigerian Mammals*. Lagos: Government Printer.

———. 1959. "The Position of Wild Life Preservation in West Africa." *Oryx* 5:25–26.

———. 1979. "Oban Revisited." *Nigerian Field* 44:75–81.

Sanderson, I. T. 1937. *Animal Treasure*. London: Macmillan.

———. 1940. "The Mammals of the North Cameroons Forest Area." *Transactions of the Zoological Society of London* 24:623–725.

Sankhala, K. S. 1977. "Captive Breeding, Reintroduction and Nature Protection: The Indian Experience." In *International Zoo Yearbook*, pp. 98–101. Vol. 17. London: Zoological Society of London.

Sathamurthy, T. V. 1986. *The Political Development of Uganda: 1900–1986*. Aldershot, England: Gower Publishing.

Schaaf, C. D. 1994. "The Role of Zoological Parks in Biodiversity Conservation in the Gulf of Guinea Islands." *Biodiversity and Conservation* 3:962–68.

Schaller, G. 1963. *The Mountain Gorilla: Ecology and Behavior*. Chicago: University of Chicago Press.

———. 1993. *The Last Panda*. Chicago: University of Chicago Press.

———. 1997. "Behind the Scenes." *Wildlife Conservation* 100:2.

Schwarz, W. 1968. *Nigeria*. New York: Praeger.

Scott, P. 1966. *The Eye of the Wind*. Rev. ed. London: Hodder and Stoughton.

Scott, P., and P. Scott. 1962. *Animals in Africa*. London: Cassell.

Seal, U. S. 1986. "Goals of Captive Propagation Programmes for the Conservation of Endangered Species." In *International Zoo Yearbook*, pp. 174–79. Vol. 24/25. London: Zoological Society of London.

———. 1991. "Life after Extinction." *Symposia of the Zoological Society of London* 62:39–55.

Sherry, N. 1989. *The Life of Graham Greene, Volume I: 1904–1939*. New York: Viking.

Snyder, N. F. R., S. R. Derrickson, S. R. Beissinger, J. W. Wiley, T. B. Smith, W. D. Toone, and B. Miller. 1996. "Limitations of Captive Breeding in Endangered Species Recovery." *Conservation Biology* 10:338–48.

Soulé, M. E. 1980. "Thresholds for Survival: Maintaining Fitness and Evolutionary Potential." In *Conservation Biology: An Evolutionary-Ecological Perspective*, edited by M. E. Soulé and B. A. Wilcox, pp. 151–69. Sunderland, Mass.: Sinauer Associates.

Spinage, C. 1996. "The Rule of Law and African Game—a Review of Some Recent Trends and Concerns." *Oryx* 30:178–86.

Stevenson, M., A. Baker, and T. J. Foose. 1992. *Conservation Assessment and Management Plan for Primates*. 1st ed. Apple Valley, Minn.: IUCN/SSC Captive Breeding Specialist Group.

Street, P. 1961. *Vanishing Animals: Preserving Nature's Rarities*. London: Faber and Faber.

Struhsaker, T. T. 1972. "Rain-Forest Conservation in Africa." *Primates* 13:103–9.

———. 1975. *The Red Colobus Monkey*. Chicago: Chicago University Press.

———. 1997. *Ecology of an African Rain Forest: Logging in Kibale and the Conflict between Conservation and Exploitation*. Gainesville: University Press of Florida.

Struhsaker, T. T., and Oates, J. F. 1975. "Comparison of the Behavior and Ecology of Red Colobus and Black-and-White Colobus Monkeys in Uganda: A Summary." In *Socioecology and Psychology of Primates*, edited by R. H. Tuttle, pp. 103–23. The Hague: Mouton.

———. 1995. "The Biodiversity Crisis in South-Western Ghana." *African Primates* 1:5–6.

Strum, S. C., and C. H. Southwick. 1986. "Translocation of Primates." In *Primates: The Road to Self-Sustaining Populations*, edited by K. Benirschke, pp. 949–57. New York: Springer-Verlag.

Stuart, S. N. 1991. "Re-introductions: To What Extent Are They Needed?" *Symposia of the Zoological Society of London* 62:27–37.

Talbot, P. A. 1912. *In the Shadow of the Bush*. London: William Heinemann.

Terzian, P. 1985. *OPEC: The Inside Story*. London: Zed Books.

Turnbull, C. M. 1972. *The Mountain People*. New York: Simon and Schuster.

Tutin, C. E. G., and R. Oslisly. 1995. "*Homo, Pan,* and *Gorilla:* Co-Existence over 60,000 Years at Lopé in Central Gabon." *Journal of Human Evolution* 28:597–602.

Twum-Baah, K. A., T. K. Kumekpor, and K. E. de Graft-Johnson. 1995. *Analysis of Demographic Data, Volume 1, Preliminary Analysis Reports*. Accra: Ghana Statistical Service.

United Nations Development Programme. 1991. *Human Development Report 1991*. New York: Oxford University Press.

———. 1997. *Human Development Report 1997*. New York: Oxford University Press.

———. 1998. *Human Development Report 1998*. New York: Oxford University Press.

van Schaik, C. P., and R. A. Kramer. 1997. "Toward a New Protection Paradigm." In *Last Stand: Protected Areas and the Defense of Tropical Biodiversity*, edited by R. A. Kramer, C. P. van Schaik, and J. A. Johnson, pp. 212–30. New York: Oxford University Press.

Verschuren, J. 1982. "Hope for Liberia." *Oryx* 16:421–27.

Wagner, M. R., and J. R. Cobbinah. 1993. "Deforestation and Sustainability in Ghana." *Journal of Forestry* 91:35–39.

Ward, B., and R. Dubos. 1972. *Only One Earth: The Care and Maintenance of a Small Planet*. New York: W. W. Norton.

Webb, C. S. 1953. *A Wanderer in the Wind*. London: Hutchinson.

Wells, M. 1995. "Social-Economic Strategies to Sustainably Use, Conserve, and Share the Benefits of Biodiversity." In *Global Biodiversity Assessment*, edited by V. H. Heywood and R. T. Watson, pp. 1016–33. Cambridge: Cambridge University Press [for the United Nations Environment Programme].

White, L. J. T., and J. F. Oates. In press. "New Data on the History of the Plateau Forest of Okomu, Southern Nigeria: An Insight into How Human Disturbance Has Shaped the African Rain Forest." *Global Ecology and Biogeography Letters*.

Whitehead, G. K. 1993. *The Whitehead Encyclopedia of Deer*. Shrewsbury, England: Swan Hill Press.

Whitesides, G. H. 1985. "Nut Cracking by Wild Chimpanzees in Sierra Leone, West Africa." *Primates* 26:91–94.

———. 1991. "Patterns of Foraging, Ranging, and Interspecific Associations of Diana Monkeys (*Cercopithecus diana*) in Sierra Leone, West Africa." Ph.D. diss., University of Miami.

Wicks, C. M. 1986. "Prospects for Practical Assistance with Resettlement and Rural Development in the Ndian Division, Cameroon." In *Proceedings of the Workshop on Korup National Park, Mundemba, Ndian Division, South-West Province, Republic of Cameroon*, edited by S. Gartlan, and H. Macleod, pp. 71–76. Gland, Switzerland: WWF/IUCN.

Wilkie, D. S., J. G. Sidle, and G. C. Boundzanga. 1992. "Mechanized Logging, Market Hunting, and a Bank Loan in Congo." *Conservation Biology* 6:570–80.

Wilson, E. O. 1984. *Biophilia*. Cambridge: Harvard University Press.

Wolfheim, J. 1983. *Primates of the World: Distribution, Abundance, and Conservation*. Seattle: University of Washington Press.

World Bank. 1984. *World Development Report*. New York: Oxford University Press.

World Commission on Environment and Development. 1987. *Our Common Future*. Oxford: Oxford University Press.

World Resources Institute. 1988. *World Resources 1988–89*. New York: Basic Books.

———. 1994. *World Resources 1994–95*. New York: Oxford University Press.

———. 1996. *World Resources 1996–97*. New York: Oxford University Press.

Worthington, E. B. 1950. "The Future of the African Fauna." *Oryx* 1:44–50.

Yates, C. A. 1935. *The Kruger National Park: Tales of Life Within Its Borders*. London: George Allen and Unwin.

Zuckerman, S. 1960. Introduction to *International Zoo Yearbook*. Vol. 1. London: Zoological Society of London.

Index

Indexer:	Jean Mann
Compositor:	Impressions Book and Journal Services, Inc.
Text:	10/14 Palatino
Display:	Grotesque Black and Bauer Bodoni
Printer and binder:	Edwards Brothers, Inc.